Panorama of Buddhist Thought and Culture : 2

Glimpses of Buddhist Literature, Philosophy and Thought

(Collection of Articles from *The Indian Antiquary*)

Compiled by
P. Mittal
Geeta Dua

Re-arranged with an Introduction by
Prof. S R Bhatt

Originals
(an imprint of Low Price Publications)
Delhi-110052

First Published in (Indian Antiquary) 1872-1933
Compiled and Published 2008 (Q4)

ISBN 81-88629-49-9

Published by
Originals
(an imprint of Low Price Publications)
A-6, Nimri Commercial Centre,
Near Ashok Vihar Phase-IV,
Delhi-110052
Phones: 27302453
e-mail: info@Lppindia.com
visit us at: www.Lppindia.com

Printed at
D K Fine Art Press P Ltd.
Delhi-110052

PRINTED IN INDIA

CONTENTS

Introduction

The development of philosophical thought in India in ancient times can be classified under two traditions namely *Vaidika* and *Śramaṇika*. Both the traditions have interacted heavily and intermingled also. Their development has not been in mutual isolation. They have borrowed from and influenced each other. Within both these traditions again there have been diversions. Among the *Śramaṇika* viewpoints Buddhism occupies a very significant place. The other important *Śramaṇa* traditions pertain to Jainism and Ajivikas. We get good deal of information about Buddhism in Jaina literature and about Jainism in the Buddhist literature. Like-wise on Ajivikas also our major source of information has been Jaina and Buddhist literature. It is to be noted that no study of Vaidika, Buddhist, Jaina and Ajivikas views of reality and ways of living is possible without nothing their mutual influences. These different tendencies have developed by way of mutual give and take and also by way of mutual criticism. In so far as Buddhism is concerned it puts forth Anātmavāda in contrast to the Ātmavāda of the Vaidika tradition. Buddha was a radical thinker who outlined a new view of reality and a way of life. He was deeply concerned with the problems of mundane life and sought a way out of the sufferings in which mundane life is emmashed. He, therefore, propounded the Four Noble Truths and the Noble Eight-Fold Path as a part of that. He realised the Four Noble Truths in his intense meditative experiences and fomulated them after deep reflection. Buddha had a critical mind and rationalist approach and therefore even though, he himself experienced and realised the Four Noble Truths he wanted people to accept his statements only after critical enquiry and self-experience.

Buddha was highly benevolent and merciful. He wanted all suffering-beings to share his experiences and to strive to get freedom from the sufferings of mundane life. For this he wandered from one place to another disseminating his experiences. But he himself did not write anything. His disciples who accompanied him might have noted the details of his teachings. It seems that after his Mahāparinirvāṇa, his disciples codified his teachings in the form of Tripitakas. However, the teachings were understood and interpreted differently by different scholars who reflected on the teachings of the Buddha. So, different scholars of Buddhism came into existence. Not only Buddhism branched-off into several sects and sub-sects in India, such divisions took place in every country where Buddhism went. We have thus many sects and sub-sects of Buddhism in Tibet, China, Japan, Korea, Vietnam and other Buddhist countries. The differences are only in details and the basic Buddhistic principles and practices are common to all the divisions and sub-divisions. It is natural also that no two minds may think alike or express alike. The truth may be the same but descriptions may be many. This apart, there can be alternative approaches from different standpoints and objectives. Thus, Buddhism is varied and multi-hued. This multiplicity has provided richness to Buddhist thought and culture. Though the early history of Buddhism is shrouded in mystery and mythology we have accounts of Buddhism as it originated and developed in India and also outside India. Tārānatha's *History of Buddhism* is a classical work which gives valuable information about Buddhist literature, philosophy and thought. It presents very authentic account of Buddhist literature, Buddhist thinkers, Buddhist art, architecture and places of Buddhist pilgrimage. Tārānatha's account of Buddhism in Tibet is also very authentic, authoritative and significant.

So far as Theravada Buddhism is concerned, we have very authentic and detailed account in Dipavamsa and Mahavamsa written in Ceylon. The development of Buddhism in theravada tradition is largely based on these two texts. Many scholars went from India to Ceylon and many Ceylonese scholars came to India to study Buddhism. Their writings enriched Buddhist thought and culture. Apart from Tibet and Ceylon it was China which contributed tremendously in the development of Buddhist thought. The Indian scholars who went to China and trained the Chinese scholars or the Chinese scholars who came to India and went back to China, translated Buddhist works written in India. Most of the works are not available now in India but they are preserved in China, some in original and a large part in translations. Many of such works have also been transferred to India Office Library in London. The same situation prevails in Japan, Korea, Vietnam and other Buddhist countries. Buddhist literature is thus very vast and scattered in different countries and different language. It is a huge task to collect, collate and edit it. It is no doubt a team work but once it is done, it will reveal diverse facets of Buddhist thought and culture in their convergences and divergences.

Though Indian Buddhism provides the background and the starting point for all later Buddhistic developments in other countries. There have been innovating exposition in each country, which needs to be appreciated. The encounters with diverse cultures of different countries and the resultant transformations in Buddhist thought and culture have provided Buddhism varied faces. Buddhism is Oecumenical and Buddhist Oecumenism is due to its adaptability to newer times, places and circumstances.

The contribution of Indian Buddhist thinkers has been the guiding spirit for all Buddhist thinkers, all over the world. Thus, in the Theravāda traditions Pali texts provide the solid ground. In the Mahāyāna traditions, Nāgārjuna, Vasubandhu, Dinnāga, Āryadeva etc. may be mentioned. The Mahāyāna Sūtras and their expository commentaries written in India, were translated and explained in different ways in different Mahāyāna countries. This resulted in the rise of different Buddhistic schools in those countries. But the basic spirit of Buddhism has remained unchanged in spite of all these developments and differences.

S.R.Bhatt
Former Professor and Chair
Department of Philosophy, Delhi University
MP-23, Pitam Pura
Delhi-110088 (India).
20-7-2005

1

The Buddhist works in Chinese in the India Office Library*

Samuel Beal

There are 72 distinct Buddhist compilations in 112 volumes among the Chinese books in the Library of the India Office. Of these 47 are translation from the Sanskṛit.

1. There are two copies of a work styled the *Mo-ho-pan-nyi-pan-king* (*i.e.* the *Mahāparinibbana Sutta*). I was anxious to determine whether this work resembled the Sūtra known by the same name in the Southern School (Ceylon, Burmah, &c.); and, if not, to investigate, so far as possible, the degree and character of the divergence.

   The general outline is this; Buddha, on a certain occasion, proceeded to Kinsinagara, and entering a grove of *sāla* trees, there reposed. He received a gift of food from Chanda, an artizan of the neighbouring town. After partaking of the food he was seized with illness. He discoursed through the night with his disciples, and disputed with certain heretical teachers. At early dawn he turned on his right side, with his head to the north, and died. The *sāla* trees bent down to form a canopy over his head. The account then proceeds to relate the circumstance of his cremation, and the subsequent disputes, between the Mallas and others, for his ashes.

   In these main features the Northern sūtra is in agreement with the Southern,[1] but when considered in detail the divergence between the two is great. The whole of the first and some portion of the second books of the Chinese edition is occupied by the narrative of Chanda's offering; the details are most minute and wearisome, consisting of sections of a regularly recurring order. In the subsequent books the narrative is occupied with laboured proofs that Nirvāṇa is not the cessation of being, but the perfection of it, and that the four characteristics of Nirvāṇa are these : – Personality, Purity, Happiness, and Eternity. One chief peculiarity of this book is the particular stress it lays on the fact that it was the first made of all the Vāipuly a class of Buddhist works, and for that reason it sometimes gives expression to doubts whether or no it would be acknowledged as belonging to the canon. The history of Buddha's controversies with the heretical doctors Kaśyāpa, Basita, and others, is of an interesting nature, the point of the argument in every case being to prove that Nirvāṇa is the one true and universal condition of being, in opposition to all pre-existing theories respecting a future life in heaven, or that unintelligible state of existence supposed to be enjoyed in the Arupa worlds.

From the consideration of this *Sūtra* it seems likely that the plan adopted in the later (Northern) school of Buddhism, in the composition of their works (the *Mahāyana* and *Vāipulya Sūtras*), was to take the shorter and more ancient scriptures as a germ, and, by the interpolation of dialogues and discussions, and at the same time by tedious expansion of trivial events occurring in the course of the narrative, to produce a work under the same name of a totally different character. This method of development, I think, may be observed in nearly all the works of which we possess both Northern and Southern versions.

2. The above remarks apply with equal force to the *Fan-wang-king*. This is a Northern version of the *Brahmajāla Sūtra,* a work well known through the pages of the *Ceylon Friend,* in which Mr. Gogerly published a brief translation of it. The Chinese version was made by Kumārajīva about 420 A.D., but is has none of the characteristics of the Pāli work bearing the same name. As an instance of the dissimilarity, the Chinese version speaks of the origin of the name *Brahmajāla* as connected with the curtain (net, *jāla*) that surrounds the domain of Brahma or Indra,[2] and compares the gems that adorn that net to the countless worlds of space, over all which Vairojana

is supreme. Whereas the title is explained in the South as "a net in which Buddha caught the Brāhmaṇs."

The Chinese translation is only a portion of the entire work, and recounts the rules which bind the Bodhisatwa, in the same way as the *Pratimoksha* deals with the rules of the Bhikshus. All this is so foreign to the drift and object of the Southern Sūtra, that it is plain there is but little connection between the two, except in the name, which was borrowed probably to give popularity and authority to the expanded work.

3. The library possesses a Chinese copy of the *Abhinishkramana Sūtra,* under the name of *Fo-pen-hing-tsi-king*. The chief interest attaching to this book is the number of episodes (*Avadānas*) and *Jātakas* contained in it. Some of these will be found to explain the temple sculptures at Sānchi and Amravatī and Boro Bodor. I am inclined also to think that many of the newly discovered sculptures found by the Archæological Surveyor of India at Bharahut will be explained to some extent in this work. It seems probable that the book under review is only the expansion of the *Fo-pen-hing-king,* the earliest known translation of the life of Buddha. (This work was produced in China about 75 A.D.). My reason for this opinion is (1) the similarity of name; the addition of the symbol "*tsi*" to *Fo-pen-hing* would indicate that the new work was founded upon the more ancient one. (2) I find from the Buddhist Encyclopædia *Fa-yuen-chu-lin,* that passages quoted from the *Fo-pen-hing* really occur in the *Fo-pen-hing-tsi-king*. If my opinion is correct, it will tend to a settlement of the question of the date of the legends and stories, which are mixed up in such a remarkable manner, in the history of the founder of Buddhism.

4. Perhaps the most interesting result of the examination of these books is derived from a work entitled *King-tsang-yo-shwo*. In this book there are fifty Sūtras, translated at different dates and by various scholars, all of them from Sanskṛit or Pāli. The dates extend from A.D. 70 to A.D. 600. Among these Sūtras is one called the *Chen-tseu-king;* this I found to be a translation of the *Sāma Jātaka,* which is in fact a part of the story of Daśaratha and Rāma. This Jātaka has been briefly translated from the Singalese by Spence Hardy (*Eastern*

Monachism, p. 275), and I have identified it with the Sānchi sculpture found in Plate xxxii, fig. 1, of *Tree and Serpent Worship.* The Chinese version of this Jātaka is full and complete, and I hope soon to be able to publish it. A singular circumstance connected with the title of this Sūtra or Jātaka is this :—In the history of Fa-hian's travels (p. 157) it is stated that when in Ceylon, he witnessed on one occasion a religious festival during which pictures of Buddha's previous births were exhibited and hung up on each side of the road. Among others he speaks of the "birth as a flash of light" (the Chinese word is '*chen*'). Rémusat and his annotators having adopted this rendering in their version of Fa-hian, I was led to do the same in my own translation, although I had grave doubts at the time, and tried to explain the character of this birth by the history of the Fracolin given by Julien (II. 336). I now find that the Jātaka alluded to by Fa-hian was the *Sāma Jātaka,* of which the book under review gives an account. It is interesting to know that this Jātaka was so familiar to the Buddhists in Ceylon at the time of Fa-hian's visit (circa A.D. 410), as it was undoubtedly to the builders and sculptors at Sānchi, some centuries (perhaps) before.

A third Sūtra in this work deserving notice is the *Ta-shing-sse-fa-king,* which is the same as the *Arya Chatushka Nirahara Nama Mahāyana Sūtra,* a translation of which has been made by M. Léon Feer (*Etudes Buddhiques,* p. 131). On comparing the Chinese with this version, I find the two agree in the main. There are one or two passages, however, much more distinctly given in the Chinese translation. For example, at the opening of the Sūtra, as translated by M. Léon Feer, there is an obscure passage which he renders "n'ayant tous pour vêtement qu'un grand amulette" (Maha varma sannaddha); in the Chinese the passage runs thus—*'Kai-pi-kin-ku-ta-sze-shai-kwan,'* that is, "all of them completely armed with the helmet of their strong religious vows," a passage which, although somewhat obscure, is yet common enough in Buddhist books, denoting the power of the vow made by the Bodhisatwas not to give up their condition till they had accomplished the salvation of men (and others). Another passage, p. 134 (*op. cit.*), is thus given by

M. Feer—"Le fils d'un dieu reprit Manjucri en faveur de Brahma qui a les cheveux noués au sommet de la tête, et qui reside parmi les fils des dieux," etc., but in the Chinese version the rendering is "The Deva once more replied, Well said ! Ayushmat, the Bodhisatwa ought to be untiring in the work of his religious duties, as in old time was the Brahmarāja Sikhin and his associates," etc. The conduct of Sikhin is frequently alluded to in Buddhist books; he is generally indeed spoken of as one of the old Buddhas, but his exact religious conduct is the theme for constant laudation in the *Abhinishkramana Sūtra*. There are several discrepancies between the Chinese text and the translation from the Thibetan, which I cannot enter in to any length; the following will serve as examples :—iv. 1: "Meditation," *Chinese* "Faith." iv. 2: "Sagesse," *Chinese* "reliance on a virtuous friend." v.: "Production de pensée ā laquelle il serait dangereux pout les Bodhisatwas de se confier," *Chinese* "The Bodhisatwas ought to strive after a heart not capable of the four defilements." vi. 3: "La pensée qui consiste ā ne pas espérer en la maturité parfasite." *Chinese,* "A heart that does not anxiously look for the reward of good actions." ix. 2: "Production d'un pensée pour que ceux qui transgressent," etc., *Chinese* "Having been wronged by any one, not to remember the wrong done." ix. 3: "En quelquens contrées vastes et étendus," etc., *Chinese* "Not to remit any effort although dwelling in the midst of plenty (five desires)." x. 1: "Quand on est dans une maison,"*Chinese* "when leading a secular life x. 2: "Amoindrir les qualités de l'agitation," etc., *Chinese* "To practise the Dhūta rules." xi. 4: "Quand on a lié sa pensée ā la promulgation de la loī," etc., *Chinese* "Out of a glad heart ever to speak well of the conduct of a master of the law (spiritual master)," xvii. 2: "Le tresor caché de l'energie," *Chinese* "The treasure of dialectics, or of logical discussion." xvii. 4: "Le tresor caché de la bénédiction compléte en richesses inépuisables," *Chinese* "The treasure of worshipping or paying reverence to the highest riches, *i.e. the Three Gems,* Buddha, Dharma, Sangha. [I may observe here, throughout the translation from the Thibetan, the expression "bénédiction compléte" (vi. 4, xvi. 4, xvii. 4, xxxiii. 2) corresponds to *hwui-hiang* in the Chinese, which is a phrase employed to denote an act of *external worship,* or sometimes *mental adoration.*]

The Chinese version throws some light on the difficult passage xxii. 4: "Ne plus espérer en la transmigration, ā cause du désespoir de réussir dans la réalisation parfaite de toutes les qualités;" *Chinese* "Not to resent as a personal injury (with a view to retaliate) because a friend has not been invited with others to partake of charity or hospitality."

There is a Chinese version of the *"Chatur Dharmaka,"* according to the Great Vehicle. A translation of this also has been made by M. Léon Feer, from the Thibetan.[3] The Chinese version dates from the Tang dynasty, and was made by Devakara, a priest of mid-India. It agrees very closely with the Thibetan.

I now proceed to give a list of other Sūtras found in the work under review.

(a) *Fo-shwo-fan-pih-un-sing-king* (Buddha declares the causes which produce birth). This may be the same as the *Nidāna Sūtra.* The scene is laid by the banks of the Nairañjana river, under the *bodhi* tree; Buddha, lost in contemplation, dwells upon the falsity of all sources of joy and sorrow in the world. On this Mahā Brahma, lord of the *Sa-va* world, suddenly leaves the heavens and appears before Buddha. Buddha recounts to him the causes of existence (Nidānas); these are the same as those commonly found in Buddhist books, beginning with ignorance (*avidya*) and ending with old age, disease, and death. Whereupon Mahā Brahma worships at the feet of Buddha and departs.

(b) *Fo-shwo-ta-sing-i-king* (Buddha relates the great and secret principles [truth] of birth). The scene of this sermon is the village of Kuru Ananda having been troubled with thoughts respecting the origin of life, resolves to go to Buddha and request an explanation. Having arrived and saluted the All-Wise, he spake thus :—"World-adored, as I dwelt alone and revolved in my mind throughout the night the causes of life and death, I was greatly troubled. Would that you would deign to solve my doubts and explain my difficulties." On this Buddha proceeds to show how the perpetual recurrence of birth and death, and all the phenomena of life, result from ignorance of the causes of these things. Thus old age and death result from birth; destroy the seed of birth and there can be no old age or death (and so throughout the sermon).

(c) *Fo-shwo-u-kwo-king* (Buddha recites the history of U-Kwo) (*defend-country*). This Sūtra recounts how Buddha, when residing at Kuru, departed on a round of visits for the purpose of preaching. Having come to the village of *To-lo* (Tara ?) he was requested by a young Brāhmaṇ called *U-Kwo* to admit him into his society as a novice. Buddha inquired if he had his parents' permission. On being told he had not, Buddha declined to receive him. On this U-Kwo departs to his home, and after a great deal of entreaty he persuades his parents to permit him to become a Bhikshu. This having been accomplished, U-Kwo after a time returns to his native village, and whilst there, is the means of converting the king of Kuru by his teaching. On this the king becomes a Upasaka.

(d) *Fo-shwo-wou-shang-king* (Buddha preaches on impermanency—*anitya*). This sermon was delivered at Srāvasti, in the Jetavana; Buddha declares in it that there are three things in the world that are universally abhorred, viz.—old age, disease, and death. Had it not been for these, Buddha would not have come into the world. He then recites some verses to the same effect. After which, all the audience, filled with delight, worship him and depart.

(e) *Fo-shwo-tong-lai-pien-king* (Buddha declares the changes of the future). This Sūtra was delivered at Srāvasti, in the Jetavana, in the presence of 500 Bhikshus, and all the Bodhisatwas. Buddha describes the way in which religion (the law) will be destroyed by the neglect of first principles—morality, submission, self-discipline, and so on. He tells them that there will be jealousies and divisions amongst his followers after his own departure, and warns them against the ruin which will result.

(f) *Shi-shen-nieh-taou-king* (The Sūtra which relates to virtuous principles or a virtuous *Karma*). This Sūtra was delivered in the palace of Sāgara, a Nāgarāja, in the presence of 800 Great Bhikshus, and 23,000 Bodhisatwas Mahāsatwas; Buddha declares that all the differences which exist in life, and comparative conditions of happiness, result from the previous conduct of the persons concerned. He then lays down ten virtuous principles, by acting on which there must result consequent perfection and supreme wisdom (*bodhi*). The ten virtues are purely moral and personal, relating to benevolence, love of men, self-denial, energy, and watchfulness against error.

(g) *Fo-shwo-fa-yin-king* (Buddha declares what is the seal of the law). This sermon was delivered at Srāvasti, before all the Bhikshus. In it Buddha declares that the secret, or the seal, of the law, is to perceive the unreality of all phenomenal existence, and, by a conviction of this, to arrive at deliverance. [Deliverance is spoken of as threefold, and is thus denoted, ∴.]

(h) *Pu-sa-sing-ta-king* (The Sūtra of the ground of the birth of the Bodhisatwa). This Sūtra was delivered at Kapilavastu, under a *nyagrodha* tree, in the presence of 500 Bhikshus. A young nobleman, called Chamah, comes to Buddha, and begs him to explain the nature of a Bodhisatwa's conduct. On this Buddha lays it down that the fundamental principle of a Bodhisatwa's character is perfect patience and forbearance, and this patience exhibits itself under four aspects. (1) When reviled, the Bodhisatwa reviles not again. (2) When smitten, he receives the blow without resentment. (3) When treated with anger and passion, he returns love and good-will. (4) When threatened with death, he bears no malice. Buddha then recites some verses (*geyas*) to the same effect. Again, he says there are four things that distinguish every Bodhisatwa. (1) He loves the scriptures, and the way of salvation practised by the Bodhisatwas; with his utmost mind he defends the cause of religion, and desires to instruct men therein. (2) He removes himself from the company of all females, and will have no business with them. (3) He ever loves to bestow charity on Shaman and Brahmāchāri. (4) He avoids over-sleep, lest his heart should become indisposed to religion. Buddha then recites some verses to the same effect. On this, Chamah removes from his neck a beautiful string of pearls and precious stones, and offers them to Buddha. Buddha, by his spiritual power, causes them to ascend into the air, and form a canopy over his head. And now, from each precious stone, there appears as it were a man, to the number of 500, each wearing a similar necklace. On this, Chamah asks whence these persons came—to which Buddha replies, They come from nowhere; they are unreal and apparitional only, as a figure in a glass, or the reflection in a lake: and such is the nature of all phenomena, they are unreal, projected on the surface of the one reality, Supreme Wisdom (*Bodhi*). Such is the belief of the Son of Buddha, *i.e.* Bodhisatwa. On hearing this, Chamah, the four kings of disciples, and all the Nāgas, rejoice and accept it.

(i) *Fo-shwo-chuen-yeou-king* (Buddha delivers the Sūtra which relates to the revolution of existence). This Sūtra was delivered in the Kalandavenuvana near Rājagṛiha, in the presence of 1250 disciples and innumerable Bodhisatwas. Bimbasara Rāja having approached the place where Buddha was seated, saluted him and stood on one side. On this Buddha addressed him thus, "Mahārāja, suppose a man in a dream beheld a lovely maiden, bedecked with jewels; and suppose he dreamt of joys and pleasures partaken with her, would there be and solid truth in such fancied enjoyments ?" "No," answered the Rāja, "for it would be only a dream." "And if a man were, nevertheless, to hold the fancy that there was such a real maiden as he had seen in his sleep (or that the maiden were a real one), would this be a mark of wisdom ?" "No," answered the king, "for that dream-thought had no substance and was utterly vain." "Such," continued the Buddha, "is the nature of the teaching of the heretical doctors of religion. They use words to describe things which exist not. They receive certain impressions from without, and then they lay hold of these vain impressions and call them realities. They are thus bound by their own fictions, and, being bound, they become subject to all the evil consequences of their own inventions, viz.—covetous desire, anger, doubt (*raga, moha, trishna*), and perpetual cycles of birth and death. By giving up such imaginary names and laying hold of one reality, a man escapes these consequences and is set free."

(j) *Ta-fang-taug-sieou-to-lo-wang-king*. This is another translation of the previous work; the title is a singular one, and may be translated thus—The *Mahā-vāipulya-Sūtra-rāja-Sūtra*.

(k) *Shan-king-fa-siang-king* (The Sūtra which related to the thoughts present to those who practise Dhyāna). Delivered at Srāvasti, in the Jetavana; Buddha spoke thus to the Bhikshus: "If a man, in a snapping of a finger, can realize in his mind the thought of death, and remember perfectly that all which exists must die, this is no small progress to have made—this is not the hesitation of the foolish, or the charity of the Arab (*sih kwo yin*). How much more if he can grasp in a moment the thought of the sorrow, the impermanency, to vanity, the folly, etc., of earthly things—how much more has such a man advanced in the power of Dhyāna."

(l) *San-kwei-wu-kiai-sse-sin-im-li-kung-tih-king* (The Sūtrā that describes the great merit attaching to the three refuges—*tunsarāna,* the five moral rules, a loving heart, and rejecting the evil). Delivered at Srāvasti, in the Jetavana, for the sake of Aniruddha; Buddha speaks of a rich Brāhmaṇ, called Virama, and explains that, though he gave away all his wealth in charity, his merit would not be nearly so great as one who professed belief in Buddha, Dharma, and Sangha, and undertook to observe the five rules of a disciple.

(m) *Fo-shwo-hi-yeou-kan-liang-kung-tih-king* (Buddha delivers a discourse concerning the supreme source of merit). This sermon is directed to show the infinitely superior character of merit resulting from a profession of belief in the three gems to all others.

(n) *Li-hu-hwui-pu-sah-sho-man-li-fo-fa-king* (Questions asked by a Bodhisatwa, called *Li-hu-hwui,* as to the right way of paying worship to Buddha). This Sūtra was delivered at Srāvasti, in the Jetavana. The interlocutor is the Bodhistwa named in the title. He asks Buddha to explain the right method of worship. On this Buddha tells him that he should, with all his heart, pay adoration to all the Buddhas of the ten quarters, and afterwards prostrate himself on his knees, hands, and head to Buddha himself, beseeching him to bring about the salvation of all men, and cause an end to be put to all heretical teaching. He then proceeds to direct him to worship each of the Buddhas of the different regions of space, beginning with Akshobya of the eastern region, down to Vairojana, who is placed in the nadir.

(o) *Fo-shwo-ti-shing-pih-siang-king* (Buddha declares what are the hundred marks of merit belonging to the Great Vehicle). This Sūtra was delivered at Srāvasti, in palace called Po-Miu. The interlocutor is Manjuśrī. In it is given the names of the 80 inferior signs and the 32 greater signs on Buddha's person, also 80 symbols or figures found on the soles of his feet.

(p) *Man-chu-see-li-man-po-ti-king* (Manjuśri inquires as to the character of Bodhi). This Sūtra was delivered in Magadha, on Mount Gaya, in the presence of all the Bhikshus, and those Brāhmaṇs who had been converted by Buddha; the subject of it is the nature of that condition of mind called the "heart of Bodhi" (*esprit de Bodhi*).

(q) *Wou-tsun-hwui-pou-sah-king* (The Sūtra of Akchyamati Bodhisatwa). This Sūtra was delivered at Rājagṛiha, on Mount Gṛidrakuṭa, in the presence of 1250 Bhikshus. The interlocutor is Akchyamati, who inquires of Buddha the nature of the heart of Bodhi (as in the previous Sūtra).

(r) *Ta-shing-sze-fa-king* (The Sūtra of the four rules of the Great Vehicle). This is the same as the *Mahāyana-chaturdharmaka Sūtra*. It was delivered at Srāvasti, in the garden of Jeta (and has already been referred to).

(s) *Fo-shwo-ta-shing-sze-fa-king* (Buddha declares the four laws of the Great Vehicle). This Sūtra has already been referred to.

(t) *Fo-shwo-pou-sa-sheou-hing-sze-fa-king*. Another translation of the above.

(u) *Fo-shwo-tsing-nieh-chang-king* (Buddha narrates the obstacles in the way of a pure *karma*). This Sūtra was delivered when Buddha was dwelling at Vaisali, in the garden of the *amra* trees, in the presence of 500 Bhikshus and 32,000 Bodhisatwas Mahāsatwas. It relates to a conversation between a courtesan and a Bodhisatwa called Vimalanirbhāsa (*wou-hu-kwong*). The former, having used her magic arts, prevails over the Bodhisatwa. After this, being seized with intense remorse, he comes to Buddha; the latter comforts him by an assurance that all such things as a shadow and a dream on which the Bodhisatwa is reassured. Manjuśrī then enters into a discussion with Buddha relating to the character of the Great Vehicle.

(v) *Tching-u-ta-shing-kung-tih-king* (Buddha praises the superior excellency of the Great Vehicle). In this Sūtra Buddha describes the superiority of the Heart of Bodhi, and from that proceeds to define the infinite virtue of the Great Vehicle. (This Sūtra was translated from Sanskṛit by Hiwen Tsang.)

(w) *Ta-shing-fang-kwang-tsung-chi-king* (The Sūtra which describes the nature of the Dharani, used in the Yoga system of the Great Vehicle). This Sūtra was delivered at Rājagṛiha, on the Gṛidrakuṭa, mountain, in the presence of 62,000 Great Bhikshus. It contains certain Dharani.

(x) *Wou-shang-i-king* (The Sūtra of the highest reliance). This Sūtra, which is in two parts, contains an account of the relative merit of various actions. It was delivered in the Kalandavenuvana, before 1250 Bhikshus and various Bodhisatwas.

(y) *Fo-shwo-lo-niu-king* (The Sūtra in which Buddha describes the conduct of an aged woman). This Sūtra was delivered by Buddha at a place called *Lo-Yin* (musical sound), before 800 Bhikshus and 10,000 Bodhisatwas. He describes the conduct of an aged woman who desired to offer him a religious gift. Having only two small coins (mites) she purchased with them a little oil; taking this to a sacred place, she used it in a lamp, to burn for his honour. The lights of all the Brāhmaṇs were extinguished, and hers alone burnt incessantly.

(z) *Fo-shwo-chen-tseu-king* (Buddha relates the history of Sāma). This is the *Sāma Jātaka* referred to before.

(aa) *Tin-wong-tai-tseu-Pi-Lo-King* (The Sūtra of Pi-Lo, the eldest son of a heavenly king – (Devarāja). This Sūtra gives an account of Devarāja-kumara-Pi-Lo's visit to Buddha, during which he recites the history of the Great Brāhmaṇ, which is identical with the Avadāna translated by Stas. Julien, called "*Le roi et le grand tambour*" (*Les Avadānas,* tome I, No. 1).

(bb) *Fo-shwo-O-che-shai-wong-shau-ku-king* (The Sūtra of Ajatasatru's assurance). This Sūtra was delivered at Rājagṛiha, on the top of the mountain Gṛidrakuta, and contains an account of Ajatasatru's visit to Buddha, and the assistance that he would hereafter become a Chakravartti Rāja.

(cc) *Fo-shwo-tai-tseu-Muh-pih-king* (Buddha declares the history of Prince Muh-pih). This Sūtra was delivered at Srāvasti, in the Jetavana. Buddha recounts the history of the prince Muh-pih, the son of Varanirāja. He was a beautiful child, but unable to speak; having consulted the astrologers, they resolved to put him to death by burying him alive; when on the point of being thus sacrified, he opened his mouth and spake: he declared that, owing to rash words in the former birth, he had suffered punishment in hell. He had resolved, therefore, to remain silent, rather than risk a like punishment. (This Sūtra is one of the earliest translated into Chinese, A.D. 100.)

(dd) *Fo-shwo-'ng-wong-king* (Buddha declares the history of the five kings). There were once five kings, one of whom was wise, the other four were foolish. The wise king wishing to convert the others, asked them their several ideas of happiness. The first said, "Nothing would delight me more than during the spring-time to wander through gardens and parks, to see the flowers and watch the fountains. This would be pleasure." The second said, "Nothing would delight me more than as a king to mount my royal horses, to dwell in a lordly court, and ever to be surrounded by my faithful subjects paying me reverence." The third said, "Nothing would delight me more than the joys of wedded life surrounded by my children, beautiful and full of grace, ever desiring to give me happiness." The fourth said, "Nothing would delight me more than to dwell ever with my parents, in company with my brothers and sisters, with the daintiest food, clothed in the costliest raiment, and enjoying the indulgences of sense." The four having thus spoken, the wise king replied, "All these things are vain and perishable: for my part, I would desire nothing so much as a condition that admits of neither birth nor death, joy nor sorrow, nor any other extreme;" on which the others replied, "And where shall we find a teacher who will explain how this condition may be reached ?" Whereupon the wise king conducted them to the presence of Buddha, at the Jetavana Vihāra. Buddha then enters on a discourse in which he describes the eight kinds of sorrow which are incident to all conditions of life. In the end of four kings are converted.

(ee) *Fo-shwo-kin-che-'ng-fuh-ti-king* (Buddha declares the five conditions of happiness belonging to the virtuous man). This Sūtra was also delivered at Srāvasti, in the Jetavana Vihāra. Buddha declares that the virtuous man is in this life rewarded in five ways,—first, with long life; second, with great wealth; third, with graceful form; fourth, with honour and renown; fifth, with much wisdom. He then proceeds to explain the character of the truly virtuous man.

(ff) *Fo-shwo-U-lan-pwan-king* (Buddha declares the *Avalambana Sūtra*). This Sūtra was delivered at Srāvasti, in the Jetavana Vihāra. Mahā Mugalan, by the exercise of his spiritual power, beholds his mother suffering as a Preta from starvation; on proceeding to her side and offering her food, she was unable to receive is, as it was changed into burning ashes in her hand. On this he went, with many tears, to Buddha, and declared his great sorrow. Whereupon Buddha ordains a service to be held on the 15th day of the 7th month, for the purpose of providing food for all those suffering torments of hunger as Pretas. Mugalan, with great joy, performs this service, and so provides his mother with food.

(gg) *Ta-fong-kwang-fuh-hwa-yeh-king-sieou-sse-fun* (The charity section of the *Mahāvāi-pulyāvatamsaka Sūtra*). This Sūtra was delivered at Rājagṛiha, on the Vulture-peak mountain. It is a part of one of the most popular Sūtrās known in China, viz. *Fa-yen-king*.

(hh) *Fo-shwo-yin-un-sang-hu-king* (Buddha narrates the history of Sangharākshita). This indeed is a translation of the *Sangha Rākshita Avadāna,* know to us through the version given by Bourouf. (*Introd. to Ind. Bud.* p. 313, ff.) The Chinese translation agrees in the main with this version. It opens with an account of the Nāga, which assumed a human form and became a Bhikshu; having gone to sleep, accidently, his true nature was discovered; after having been instructed in the law, he was dismissed to his Dragon Palace by Buddha; here he was visited by Sangha Rākshita, and further instructed in the sacred books. The narrative then proceeds with the adventures of Sangha Rākshita after having been dismissed from the Dragon Palace. (The details are nearly the same as those given by Bournouf).

5. I shall now proceed to translate a short Sūtra called "Buddha's dying instruction" (*Fo-wei-kian-king*). The interest of this work is derived from the fact that it is generally bound up in China with the *Sūtra of Forty-Two Sections,* the first Buddhist work translated into Chinese. It will be seen that it is of the primitive type, and deals entirely with moral questions. It also speaks of the *Pratimoksha,* not as that work is known to us, but as certain rules of a simple prohibitive character, affecting the life of the disciple. It would appear from this that the bulky work now known as the *Pratimiksha* is a later compilation, drawn up in fact after the introduction of conventual life among the followers of Buddha.

"The Sūtra of Buddha's dying instruction," translated by Royal Command, by Kumārajiva, a Doctor of the Three Pitakas, in the reign of Yaou (Hing), Prince of T'sin[4] [397 to 415 A.D.].

"Śākyamuni Buddha, when he first began to preach, converted Ajanta Kāundinya (*O-jo-kiao-tchin-ju*); so, on the occasion of his last discourse, he converted Subhādra. Having thus done all that was appointed him to do, he reclined between two *sāla* trees, about to enter *nirvāṇa*. It was now in the middle of the night, perfectly quiet and still; on this occasion, for the sake of his disciples, he delivered a brief summary of his law.

"Bhikshus, after my death, regard, I pray you, with much reverence, the book of the *Pratimoksha* as a light shining in the darkness, or a precious pearl found by a poor man. Let this book be your teacher and guide, even as I should be, if I remained in the world. Keep the pure rules of discipline, viz. these—not to enter on any business engagements, whether buying or selling, or exchanging; to avoid all purchase of land or houses; all rearing of cattle, or dealing in servants or slaves, or any living thing; to put away all money, property, or jewels—as a man would avoid a burning pit. Not to cut down or destroy trees or shrubs; not to cultivate land, or dig the earth; not to engage in he decoction of medicines; not to practise divination, or casting lucky or unlucky days; not to study the stars or the movements of constellations; not to predict times of plenty or scarcity; not to enter on calculations of any sort; all these things are forbidden. Keep the body temperate in all things, and the vital functions in quiet subjection. Have nothing to do with worldly engagements, either in seeking places of authority, or pronouncing incantations, or courting the rich, or planning for the welfare of your worldly relatives. But, by self-control and right modes of thought, aim at emancipation; conceal none of your faults, but confess them before the congregation; be moderate and contended with the food, clothing, medicines, and bedding allowed you [*Jul*. I. 152], and be cautious against hoarding up that which is allowed. These are the rules of discipline, the observance of which is the true source of emancipation, and hence they are called 'The Rules of the Pratimoksha'. Keep then these precepts in their purity, O Bhikshus ! Let there be no careless negligence in this matter; the man who carefully observes them shall have power to fulfil all the duties of religion; the man who disregards them shall experience none of the rewards which a virtuous life is able to afford. And for this reason it is I bid you remember that the knowledge and practice of these rules is the first and chief necessity for attaining religious merit and final peace.

"If, Bhikshus, ye have attended to this point, and have observed the precepts religiously, then proceed to keep the five organs of sense in due check, not permitting them a loose rein, or to engage in the pursuit of pleasure (the five pleasures); just as a shepherd with his crook prevents the cattle from straying into the neighbouring pastures. But if you restrain not your senses, but permit them the indulgence of the five pleasures, and put to check upon them, then, as a vicious horse unchecked by the bridle hurries on and throws its rider into the ditch, so shall it be with you; your senses, getting the mastery of you, shall eventually hurry you on to the place of torment, where you shall endure untold misery for the period of an age (*sæculum*), without any mode of escape or deliverance. The wise man, therefore, restrains his senses and permits them not free indulgence – he keeps them fast bound, as robbers are held in bonds, and doing so he soon feels their power to hurt utterly destroyed. The heart (sin) is lord of these senses; govern, therefore, your heart well; watch well the heart, for it is like a noxious snake, a wild beast, a cruel robber, a great fire, and worse even than these. It may be compared to a man who is holding in his hand a vessel full of honey, and as he goes on his way his eyes are so bent in gazing on the sweet treasure in his dish, that he sees not the dreadful chasm in his way, down which he falls. It is like a mad elephant unchecked by the pointed crook – or like the ape which is allowed to escape into the tree, quickly it leaps from bough to bough, difficult to re-capture and chain up once more. Restrain, therefore, and keep in complete subjection your heart; let it not get the mastery; persevere in this, O Bhikshus, and all shall be well.

"With respect to food and drink, whether you have received common or dainty food, let it not excite in you either undue gratification or regret; and the same with clothing and medicinal preparations—take sufficient and be satisfied; even as the butterfly sips the honey of the flower and departs, so do ye, O Bhikshus, seek not more than is necessary: be satisfied with what is given to you, just as the wise man calculates the strength of the ox he uses, and gives it as much food as is necessary for it.

"Be careful, O Bhikshus, to waste no time, but earnestly to persevere in acquiring a knowledge of the true law. On the first and last nights of the month continue in the repetition of the sacred books without cessation. It is sloth and love of sleep that causes a whole life to be thrown away and lost. Think of the fire that shall consume the world, and early seek deliverance from it, and give not way to sleep. A man who indulges in immoderate sleep can have no inward satisfaction or self-respect; there is always a snake of dissatisfaction coiled up in his breast; whereas he who denies himself this indulgence is like the man who rises early, and, sweeping out his house, expels all that is hurtful, and so has continual safety and peace. Above all things, let modesty govern every thought and every word of your daily life a man without modesty is in no way different from the brute beast.

"Bhikshus, if a man should do you such injury as to chop your body in pieces limb by limb, yet you ought to keep your heart in perfect control; no anger or resentment should affect you, nor a word of reproach escape your lips; for if you once give way to a bitter thought, you have erred from the right way, and all religious merit is lost. Patience is a virtue (*this is the literal translation of the passage 'Jin che wei tih'*); to keep the rules of moral restraint without wavering, to exercise patience without tiring, this is the characteristic of the great man. If a man, because he does not enjoy everything as he would wish, loses patience, he is like a man who will not enter on the path of salvation because he cannot immediately quaff the sweet dew (*i.e.* attain immortality)."

The text then proceeds to speak of the advantage of moderation in all indulgences (pleasures), the happiness of a solitary life; "for they who live in mixed society are like the birds that congregate together in a tree, always afraid of a traps of the fowler; or like the old elephant in the mud unable to extricate himself. Continual perseverance is like a little fire that keeps on burning, but he who tires in the practice of religion is like a fire that goes out. Such is perseverance (*virya*).

"You ought, also, never to forget self-examination and reflection; if you neglect this, then all progress is at an end – in the practice of this you put on, as it were, a helmet of defence, so that no sword can hurt you, and no enemy get the advantage over you (*nim,* i.e. *śrāddha*). You ought to keep your mind fixed in contemplation (*dhyāna*) – by perseverance this power of fixed contemplation is always ready, even as water kept in the house is always for laying the dust out of doors. And so he who continues in the practice of *dhyāna* shall undoubtedly attain wisdom (*prajna*); and this is the Deliverance spoken of in my law. And true wisdom is this: to cross the sea of old age, disease, and death in a strong and trustworthy boat. It is a lamp shining in darkness, a medicine for all diseases, a hatchet to cut down the tree of sorrow, and for this reason you ought to aim above all things to attain this wisdom, and so bring to yourself lasting benefit. A man who has this wisdom is perfectly illuminated, and needs no other eyes.

"Again, Bhikshus, if you would obtain final release, you must put away from you all the foolish books (trifling discourses) met with in the world. Think only on the words I have given you, whether in the mountain pass or the depth of the valley, whether beneath the tree or in the solitary cell; think of the scriptures (law), and forget them not for a moment, persevere in studying them alone; I, as the good physician, knowing the disease which affects you, give this as a medicine fit for the case: without this you die. Or, like the guide who knows the way, I direct you where to go and what path to take: without a guide you perish. And now, if you have any doubts respecting the four great truths which lie at the bottom of my teaching, ask me, O Bhikshus, and explain your doubts; for while you doubt there can be no fixity."

This exhortation the world-honoured one repeated three times, but neither of the Bhikshus propounded any question, for so it was they had no doubts.

Then Aniruddha, reading the hearts of the congregation, addressed Buddha, and said: "World-honoured, the moon may scatter heat and the sun cause cold—but there can be no difference as to the truth and meaning of the four great doctrines which Buddha has placed at the bottom of his system. There is the great truth of 'sorrow' (*dukha*). Sorrow can never co-exist with joy, or produce it, 'Concourse' (the expression, 'concourse,' generally translated 'accumulation,' evidently refers to the 'rush' or 'concourse' of thoughts and events, experiences and anxieties, as the true cause of sorrow), this is the true cause (of sorrow); besides this there is no other. The 'destruction of sorrow' is just the destruction of cause, 'no cause, no fruit;' and 'the way' is this very way by which the cause may be destroyed, and this is the 'true way,' and there is no other. World-honoured one, the Bhikshus are firmly fixed in these doctrines: there is not the shadow of a doubt, there is no question or difference of opinion in the congregation respecting them. The only thought which affects the congregation is one of grief that the world-honoured one should be about to depart and enter Nirvāṇa, just as we have begun to enter on the practice of this law and understand its meaning; just as in the night a flash of lightning lights up the way for the weary traveller and then in gone, and he left to wander in the dark; this is the only thought which weighs on the mind of the congregation."

Notwithstanding the assurance of Aniruddha, the world-honoured one wishing that every member of the congregation should be strong in his belief, and attain perfect assurance, again out of his compassion addressed them, and said:—

"Bhikshus, lament not at my departure, nor feel any regret; for if I remained in the world through the *kalpa* (*i.e.* to the end of the world), then what would become of the church (assembly) ? it must perish without accomplishing its end ! and the end is this : 'by personal profit to profit others.' My law is perfectly sufficient for this end. If I were to continue in the world, it would be for no good; those who were to be saved are saved, whether gods or men; those who are not saved shall be saved, by the seeds of truth I have sown. From henceforth all my disciples practising their various duties shall prove that my true body, the Body of the Law (*dharmakava*), is everlasting and imperishable.

"Be assured of this, the world is transitory; dismiss your sorrow, and seek deliverance; by the light of wisdom destroy to gloom of all your doubts. The world is fast bound in fetters and oppressed with affliction; I now give it deliverance, as a physician who brings heavenly medicine. Put away every sin and all wickedness; remember that your 'body' is but a word coined to signify that which does not really exist – ford across the sea of death, old age, and diseases – Who is the wise man that does not rejoice in the destruction of these, as one rejoices when he slays the enemy who would rob him ?

"Bhikshus, keep your mind on this; all other things change, this changes not. No more shall I speak to you. I desire to depart. I desire Nirvāṇa. This is my last exhortation."

6. Another Sūtra worthy of notice is the *Chong-Lun,* or *Pranya-mud-śāstra-taika,* by Nagārjuna. I shall proceed to give the translation of the 25th section of this work on Nirvāṇa.

(1) If all things are unreal,
Then how is it possible to remove
From that which does not exist
Something which being removed leaves Nirvāṇa ?

This section argues that if all things are alike empty and unreal, then there is no such thing as birth and death; consequently there can be no removal of sorrow, and the destruction of the five elements of existence (limited existence), by removal of which we arrive at Nirvāṇa (what is called Nirvāṇa).

(2) But if all things are real,
Then how can we remove
Birth and death, real existence,
And so arrive at Nirvāṇa ?

This section argues that we cannot destroy that which has in itself real existence, and therefore, if all things have this real being, we cannot remove birth and death, and so arrive at Nirvāṇa; therefore, neither by the theory of *Bhava,* nor by the theory of *Sunyata* (emptiness), can we arrive at the just idea of Nirvāṇa.

(3) That which is not striven for, or "obtained,"
That which is not "for a time" or "eternal,"
That which is not born, nor dies,
This is that which is called Nirvāṇa.

"Not to be striven for," that is, in the way of religious action (*achārya*), and its result (fruit). "Not obtained" (or "arrived at"), that is, because there is no place or point at which to arrive. "Not for a time" (or not by way of interruption [*per saltum*]); for the five skandhas having been from the time of complete enlightenment proved to be unreal, and not part of true existence, then on entering final nirvāṇa (*anupadisesha nirvāṇa*) – What is there that breaks or interrupts the character of previous existence ? "Not for ever," or "everlasting," for if there were something to be obtained that admitted of distinctions whilst in the possession of it, then we might speak of an *etenal nirvāṇa;* but as in the condition of silent extinction (nirvāṇa) there can be no properties to distinguish, how can we speak of it as "everlasting ?" And so with reference to Birth and Death. Now that which is so characterized is what we call *Nirvāṇa.*

"Again, there is a sūtra which says, *Nirvāṇa* is the opposite of 'Being' and 'not Being;' it is the opposite of these two combined; it is the opposite of the absence of 'Being' and the absence of 'not Being.' So, in short, that which admits of no conditions such as are attached to limited existence, that is Nirvāna."

(4) Nirvāna cannot be called *"Bhava;"*
For if so, then it admits of old age and death,
I fact, both "being" and "not being" are phenomena,
And therefore are capable of being deprived of characteristics.

This means that as all things which the eye beholds are seen to begin and to end, and this is what the śloka calls "Life" and

"Death" (or birth and death). Now if Nirvāṇa is like this, then it would be possible to speak of removing these things and so arriving at something fixed – but here is a plain contradiction of terms – for Nirvāṇa is supposed to be that which is fixed and unchangeable.

(5) If Nirvāṇa is Bhava (existent).

Then it is *personal;*

But, in fact, that which cannot be individualized

Is spoken of as *not personal.*

This means that as all phenomenal existence comes from cause and consequent production, therefore all such things are rightly called "personal."

(6) If Nirvāṇa be Bhava,

Then it cannot be called "without sensation" (*anuvedana*);

For non-Being comes not from sensation,

And by this obtains its distinct name.

This means that as the sūtras describe Nirvāṇa as being "without sensation" (*anuvedana*), it cannot be *Bhava;* for then *abhava* would come from sensation. But now it ill be asked if Nirvāṇa is not *Bhava,* then that which is "not Bhava" (*abhava*), surely then is Nirvāṇa. To this we reply –

(7) If Nirvāṇa be not Bhava,

Much less is it nothing (*abhava*);

For if there be no room for "Being,"

What place can there be for "not Being"

This means that "not Being" is the opposite of "Being." If, then, "Being" be not admissible, how can we speak of "not Being ?" (its opposite).

(8) If, again, Nirvāṇa is Nothing,

How is it called "without sensation" (*anuvedana*) ?

For it would be wonderful indeed if everything not capable of sensation

Were forthwith spoken of as Nothing.

If, then, Nirvāṇa be neither "Being" nor "non-Being," what is it ?

(9) By participation in cause and effect
Comes the wheel of continual existence,
By non-participation in cause and effect
Comes Nirvāṇa.

As by knowing a thing to be straight we also know that which is crooked, so by the knowledge of the elements of finite existence comes the knowledge of continual life and death. Do away with those, and you do also away with those, and you do also away with the other.

(10) As Buddha says in the Sūtra,
Separate "Being," separate "not Being,"
This is Nirvāṇa,
The opposite of "Being," the opposite of "non Being."

"Being" here alludes to the three worlds of finite existence. The absence of these three worlds is "not Being." Get rid of both these ideas, this is Nirvāṇa. But it may now be asked, if Nirvāṇa is not "Being" and if it is not "absence of Being" – then perhaps it is the intermixture of the two.

(11) If it is said "Being" and "not Being"
By union, produce Nirvāṇa,
The two are then one;
But this is impossible.

Two unlike things cannot be joined so as to produce one different from either.

(12) If it is said "Being" and "not Being,"
United, make Nirvāṇa,
Then Nirvāṇa is not "without sensation,"
For these two things involve sensation.

(13) If it is said that "Being" and "not Being,"
United, produce Nirvāṇa,
Then Nirvāṇa is not Impersonal;
For these two things are Personal.

(14) "Being" and "not Being" joined in one,
How can this be Nirvāṇa?

These two things have nothing in common.

Can Darkness and Light be joined?

(15) If the opposite of "Being" and "not Being"

Is Nirvāṇa,

These opposites –

How are they distinguished?

(16) If they are distinguished,

And so, by union, become Nirvāṇa,

Then that which completes the idea of "Being" and "not Being,"

Also completes the idea of the opposite of both.

(17) Tathagata, after his departure,

Says nothing of "Being" and not Being:"

He says not that his "Being" is not, or the opposite of this.

Tathagata says nothing of these things or their opposites.

The question of Nirvāṇa sums itself up in this, that whether past, or present, or to come, it is one and the same condition of non-sensational existence. Tathagata is ever the same: if he be removed, then Nirvāṇa itself becomes a mere fancy.

The conclusion of the whole matter is that Nirvāṇa is identical with the nature of Tathagata, without bounds, and without place or time.

From this section of the *Chong-lun* we can understand the character of the entire work. It advocates the theory that the true condition of Being (*Nirvāṇa*), or the nature of Tathagata, is to be found in the conciliation of differences. Neither Eternal nor non-Eternal, personal nor impersonal – but above and beyond all such verbal limitations.

References

* Slightly abridged from Mr. Beal's official report.

1. Mr. Turner published a brief outline of the *Mahaparinibbana Sutta,* from the Pāli, in the *Asiatic Society's Journal of Bengal.*
2. The expression *aindrajāla* is a well-known one to signify "jugglery." If the net of Indra be the "curtain of stars" that enclose the atmosphere (as it were), we do not wonder that the idea of jugglery should be associated with it.
3. *Op. cit.,* p. 68.
4. *T'sin,* a feudal state occupying the region of the rivers Wei and King. See for the date *Jul.* I., p. 322.

2

Extracts from Taranatha's History of Buddhism in India

W.L. Heeley, B.C.S

The existence and importance of Tārānatha's work were first made known to Western students by Vassiliev, who used it freely in his work on Buddhism;[1] and the book itself was translated by Schiefner from the Tibetan, and published at St. Petersburg in 1869: but it seems to me by no means to have attracted the attention it deserve, and I have no doubt that the extracts which I have now translated from Schiefner's German will interest many readers, and serve to lead them to the book itself. Tāranātha steadily cites his authorities and shows an historical feeling very alien to the Oriental world generally; and his facts have therefore considerable historical weight. His lists of kings are full and contain many names not otherwise known. For the period after *Hiwen Thsang* his historical *data* are particularly valuable, as we are there left very much in the dark by historians, and future writers on mediæval India will have the task of comparing his statements with the monumental and numismatic evidence on which our knowledge of that period is mainly based.

Tāranātha's real name was Kun-snjing; he was born in 1575, and composed his work in 1608. He was a monk of the Jonang school, which after Tsongkapa's reforms was numbered among the heterodox schools, *i.e.* those opposed to the prevalent sect of the "Yellow mitres," though at a later period, after Tāranātha's death, it was attached to that sect.

I begin with the last chapter of the book, as perhaps the most generally interesting.

I – On Buddhist Art

"In former days human masters, who were endowed with miraculous power, produced astonishing works of art. It is expressly stated in the *Vinaya-āgama* and other works that the wall-paintings, &c. of these masters were such as to deceive by their likeness to the actual things depicted. For some centuries after the departure of the Teacher many such masters flourished. After they had ceased to flourish, many masters appeared who were Gods in human form; these erected the eight wonderful *chaityas* of Magadha, – the Mahābodhi, Manjuśridundubhīśvara, &c., and made many other objects. In the time of king Aśoka, Yaksha[2] artisans erected the *chaityas* of the eight great places, the inner enclosure of Vajrāsana, &c. In the time of Nāgārjuna also many works were performed by Nāga artisans. Thus the works of the Gods, Yakshas, and Nāgas for many years deceived men by their reality. When in process of time all this ceased to be, it seemed as if the knowledge of art had vanished from among men. Then for a long course of years appeared many artistic efforts brought to light by the striving of the individual genius, but no fixed school or succession of artists. Later, in the time of king Buddhapaksha, the sculpture and painting of the artist Bimbasāra were specially wonderful and resembled those early works of the Gods; the number of his followers was exceedingly great, and as he was born in Magadha the artists of his school were styled Madhyadeśa Artists. In the time of king Śīla lived an especially skilful delineator of the gods, born in Mārwār, named Śriñgadhara; he left behind him paintings and other master-pieces like those produced by the Yakshas. Those who followed his lead were called the Old Western school. In the time of kings Devapāla and Śrīmant Dharmapāla lived in Varendra [Northern Bengal] an especially skilful artist, named Dhīmān; his son was Bitpālo; both these produced many works in cast metal, as well as sculptures and paintings which resembled the works of the Nāgas. The father and son gave rise to distinct schools; as the son lived in Bengal, the cast images of gods produced by their followers were called gods of the Eastern style, whatever might be the birth-place of their actual designers. In painting, the followers of the father were called the Eastern school; those of the son, as they were most numerous in Magadha, were called followers of the Madhyadeśa school of painting. So in Nepāl, the earlier schools of art resembled the Old West school, but in the course of time a peculiar Nepālese school formed itself, which in painting and casting resembled rather the Eastern schools; the latest artists have no special character. In Kaśmir too, there were in former times followers of the Old Western school of Madhyadeśa; later on, a certain Hasurāja founded a new school in painting and sculpture, which is now called the Kaśmir school. Wherever Buddhism prevailed, skilful religious artists were found, while wherever the Mlechchas [Mahamadans] ruled, they disappeared; where, again, the Tirthya doctrines [orthodox Hinduism] prevailed, unskilful artists came to the front. Although in Pukam [Burma] and the southern countries the making of images is still going on, no specimens of the works appear to have reached Tibet. In the South three artists have had many followers: Jaya, Parojaya, and Vijaya."

II – *Pāṇini.* (From Chapter X)

"A companion of king Nanda was the Brāhmaṇ Pāṇini, who was born in the west in Bhīrukavana. When he asked a chiromantist whether he possessed the power of acquiring grammatical learning, and the chiromantist answered in the negative, he made the suitable lines on his hand with a sharp pair of scissors, and resorted to all the masters of grammatical lore on the earth, pursuing that study with the greatest eagerness; and as he was still discontented, he through perseverance succeeded in summoning his protecting deity to his help. When the deity to his help. When the deity showed his face and uttered the vowel-sounds *a, i,* and *u,* Pāṇini attained a knowledge of all the sounds that are to be found in the three worlds. The Heterodox [Brāhmaṇists] maintain that this deity was Īśvara, but have no special reasons for their belief; the Orthodox [Buddhist] on the contrary assert that it was Avalokiteśvara, and refer to the prediction from the *Manjuśrīmulatantra:* "The Brāhmaṇ's son Pāṇini will undoubtedly, through the perfect insight of a Śrāvaka, according to my prediction, invoke by his conjurations the majesty of the Lord of the world." This Pāṇini composed the grammatical Sūtra called the *Pāṇinivyākaraṇa,* composed of 2000 ślokas, namely 1000 ślokas on the formation of words, and 1000 of explanation. This is, moreover, the root of all grammars. Before him there were no *Śāstras* on the formation of words reduced to writing, and as no system existed which brought the subject under distinct points of view, individual grammarians, who brought special facts of language into connections of two and two, were esteemed as remarkably learned. Though it is said in Tibet that the *Indravyākatana* is older, yet, as we shall show below, though it may have penetrated earlier into the Celestial country, in India Pāṇini's grammar was the earliest. And though paṇḍits assert that the *Chandravyākaraṇa,* translated into Tibetan, agrees with Pāṇini, and the *Kalāpavyākaraṇa* with the *Indravyākaraṇa,* it is universally maintained that *Pāṇini's* grammar, in the copiousness of its explanations and the systematic completeness of its views, is something quite unique."

III – *Kālidāsa.* (From Chapter XV)

"Kālidāsa's biography is as follows : – At the time when the Brāhmaṇ Vararuchi was in honour at the court of Bhīmaśukla, king of Vārāṇasī, the king proposed to give his daughter Vāsantī to Vararuchi to wife. Vāsantī, however, out of pride, considering herself more learned of the two, refused to be Vararuchi's servant. On this Vararuchi determined to outwit her, and said to the king 'Invite my learned teacher, who is a hundred-fold cleverer then I, and give your daughter to him.' He saw a cowherd of Magadha, with a handsome figure, sitting on the end of a branch and cutting the lower part of the branch with an axe; judging that this man must be unusually stupid, he had him called and after some days rubbing and scrubbing, he carefully clothed him in the dress of a Brāhmaṇ Paṇḍit, got him as far as the expression *oṁsvasti,* and told him in case he found himself before the king and his court to throw flowers at the king and say *oṁ svasti,* but if any one else addressed him, by no means to answer. But in carrying this out when the rustic threw the flowers at the king he said *Uśaṭara.* This the Āchārya (Vararuchi) made out to be a blessing, thus explaining the sense of the four syllables – 'Umayā sahito Rudraḥ, Śaṁkarasahito Vishṇuḥ, ṭaṁkāraśūlapāṇischa rakshantu Śivaḥ sarvadā;' which is, being interpreted,

'May Rudra with Umā, Vishṇu with Śaṁkara, And Śiva holding the sounding trident evermore preserve (you)!'

"Upon this Vāsantī began to ask him the meaning of different words, and when he gave no answer, Vararuchi asked 'How can you expect my learned teacher to answer a woman's questions ?'; and when he had thus turned all their heads, he went away to the south. While the bridegroom was carried in triumph to all the temples, he spoke never a word, till seeing at last on the outer wall of a temple the picture of various animals and among them that of an ox, he was delighted, and put on the aspect and manners of a cowherd. Then Vāsantī said, 'Alas! it is a cowherd!' and saw that she had been played upon. She thought that if he were clever she might teach him the science of language, but on trial she found him very dull of comprehension. She became scornful, and sent her husband every day to gather flowers. In a certain locality of Magadha there was a figure of the goddess Kālī, the work of a divine artist. To this figure he carried every day an abundance of flowers, bowed before it an prayed full of thought. When Vāsantī on one occasion brought an offering to the goddess, and her husband had gone out at daybreak to pluck flowers, an attendant of hers concealed herself by way of a joke behind the pedestal of the goddess. She was chewing *pān* at the time, and when the cowherd as usual came to pray she handed him a piece of the betel she was chewing, which he took and swallowed, believing that the goddess herself had really given it. There and then he attained an unlimited intellectual power, and became an eminent authority in logic, in grammar, and in poetry. As he happened to hold in the right hand a day-lotus (*padma*) and in the left a night-lotus (*utpala*), Vāsantī asked him which he preferred, the beautiful day-lotus with its thick stalk, or the little night-lotus with its delicate stalk; he replied: 'In my right hand the day-lotus, in my left the night-lotus; whether with coarse or delicate stalk, take which thou wilt, O lotus-eyes!' As the lady now perceived that he had gained intelligence, she held him henceforward in high honour, and as he had shown so much reverence to the goddess Kālī he obtained the name of Kālidāsa, or the slave of the dark goddess. After this he became the crown-jewel of all poets, and composed the Eight Messengers, the Cloud-

Messenger (*Meghadūta*) and the others, the *Kumārasambhava,* and the other poetical Śāstras. Both he and Saptavarman belonged to the sect of the Heterodox [*i.e.* non-Buddhists]."

IV – *Authorities* (From the conclusion)

"If any one ask on what authorities this work depends, let him know that although many fragmentary histories of the origin of the (Buddhist) religion, and stories, have been composed in Tibet, I have not met with any complete and consecutive work; I have therefore, with the exception of a few passages, the credibility of which proves their truth, taken nothing from Tibetan sources. As, however, I have seen and heard the comments of several Gurū-Paṇḍitas on a work in two thousand *ślokas* composed by Kshemendrabhadra, a Paṇḍita of Magadha, which narrates the history as far as king Rāmapāla, I have taken this as my foundation, and have completed the history by means of two works, namely the *Buddhapurāṇa* composed by Paṇḍita Indradatta of a Kṣhatriya family, in which all the events up to the four Sena kings are fully recorded in 1200 *ślokas,* and the ancient History of the Succession of Teachers (āchāryas) composed by the Brāhmaṇ Paṇḍita Bhaṭ aghaṭī. In chronology too I have followed these three works, which agree except in some minor particulars. Their narrations have, as is obvious, as special reference to the rise of religion in the kingdoms of Aparāntaka [India proper], but I have not been able to describe its history in Kaśmir, Udyāna, [Swat], Tukhāra, Koki [the Indo-Chinese peninsula], and on the different islands, as I have never seen or heard of any books on the subject.'

References

1. Published in Russia in 1857; date of Schiefner's German translation, 1860.
2. In another place Aśoka is described as having subdued India by the aid of an army of Yaksha mercenaries; Vassiliev is inclined to connect the name Yaksha with the Yuei-chei, and suggests that they were Baktrian Greeks. The author, however, clearly treats the Yakshas as supernatural beings – a race of demigods, in the ordinary sense in which the word is used in the *Purāṇas.* A good deal may be said for Vassiliev's conjecture, if we bear in mind that Tāranātha also ascribes

as special artistic style to the Nāgas, who were without doubt a particular fraternity in Kaśmir, supposed to be under the special protection of the snake-gods. Works like the temple of Amravati, which shows an obvious Kaśmir influence, were probably ascribed to Nāga architects; and if the Græco-Baktrian school, traces of whose influence are visible in many parts of India, represented the Yaksha art, it remains only to ascertain what works were ascribed to the Devas, and who they were.

3

Biographies of Aśvagosha, Nāgarjuṇa, Āryadeva, and Vasubandhu

E. Lyall

Translated from Vassilief's work on Buddhism

1. Aśvagosha[1] (in Chinese *Ma-mine,* 'voice of the horse') was a disciple of the venerable Pārśva. Pārśva, on arriving in Central India from the North, learned that the clergy of that district dared not strike the *Gaṇṭā,*[2] a privilege, as we know, which had been granted to the religions which prevailed or which had obtained preponderance. The cause of this humiliation was Aśvagosha, who, belonging to the most learned Tīrthikas, had demanded that the Buddhists should not be permitted to strike the *Gaṇṭā* so long as they had not refuted him. Pārśva ordered it to be struck; he entered into discussion with Aśvagosha, and first asked him this simple question : – 'What is to be desired in order that the universe may enjoy peace, the sovereign long life, the countries abundance, and that people may no longer have to submit to miseries?' A turn so unexpected, to which it was necessary to reply, according to the laws of discussion, confounded Aśvagosha, and after the meeting he became a disciple of Pārśva, who counselled him to teach Buddhism, and then returned to his native town. Aśvagosha remained in Central India, and made himself celebrated by his superior talents.

It happened that the king of Little *Yu-chyi,* in Northern India, invaded Magadha, and demanded the cups of Buddha and Aśvagosha to be given up to him. The nobles grumbled against the king because he had set much too high a value on the latter; in order to convince them of their merit, the king took seven horses, and after having starved them for six days, he led them to the place in which Aśvagosha was teaching, and ordered fodder to be given to them, but when the horses heard the preacher they shed tears, and would not eat. Aśvagosha became celebrated because the horses had understood his voice, and because the horses had understood his voice, and because of this he received the name of Aśvagosha (voice of a horse).

2. Nāgārjuṇa was born in Southern India. He was descended from a Brahmanical family; he was naturally endowed with eminent qualities; and whilst yet a child he taught the four Vedas, each of which contained 40,000 *gāthas* (each of which is composed of 42 letters or syllables). He travelled into various kingdoms, and learned all the secular sciences, such as astronomy, geography, secret and magical powers; then he entered into friendship with three very distinguished men, and, having obtained power to render himself invisible, he glided with them into royal palaces, where he began to disgrace the women. Their presence was discovered by the print of their feet; the three companions of Nāgārjuṇa were hewn to pieces, and he himself was saved only by first making a vow to adopt the spiritual state (Buddhist). Accordingly, having arrived on the mountains, at the *stūpa* of Buddha, he uttered his vows, and in ninety days he learned the three *Piṭakas,* the deepest meaning of which he penetrated. Then he began to search for the other *Sūtras,* but he found them nowhere; it was only on the summit of the Snowy Mountains that a very old Bhikshu gave him *The Sūtra of Mahāyāna,* the depth of the meaning of which he comprehended, without being able to discover the detailed explanations of it. All the opinions of the Tīrthikas and Śramaṇas seemed to him worthless; in his pride he supposed himself a founder of a new religion, and invented new vows and a new costume for his disciples. Then Nāgarāja (King of the Dragons) concentrated himself in him, took him with him to his palace at the bottom of the sea, and showed him there seven deposits of precious objects, with the Vaipulya books and other Sūtras of a deep and mystical meaning; Nāgārjuṇa read them for ninety consecutive days, and then returned to the earth with a casket. There was at this time in

Southern India a king who knew very little of the true doctrine; Nāgārjuṇa, wishing to attract all his attention, appeared before him for seven years with a red flag, and when the king, in course of a prolonged conversation with him, asked him, as a proof of his universal knowledge, to tell him what was going on in heaven, Nāgārjuṇa declared that there was war between the Asuras and the Devas, and to confirm his words there fell from heaven an arm and some mutilated limbs of the Asuras. Then the king was convinced, and ten thousand Brāhmaṇs gave up wearing their hair in knots (that is to say, they were shaved), and made the vows of perfection (that is, of the spiritual calling). Then Nāgārjuṇa spread Buddhism widely in Southern India: he humbled the Tīrthikas, and to explain the doctrines of the Mahāyāna he composed the *Upadeśa,* of 100,000 *gāthas;* besides that, he composed *Chyuane iane fo lao lune,* 'The Sublime Path of Buddha,' consisting of 5,000 *gāthas; Da tzzi fane biane lune,* 'The Art of Pity,' consisting of 50 *gāthas* (5000 ?). It was by means of these that the doctrine of the Mahāyāna spread on all sides in Southern India. Besides these he composed *U veī lune,* 'Meditations on Intrepidity,' in 100,000 *gāthas.*[3] A Brāhmaṇ who had entered into discussion with him produced a magic pond in the middle of which was a water-lily with a thousand leaves, but Nāgārjuṇa produced a magic elephant which overturned the pond. At length, upon a chief of the Hīnayāna showing a desire that Nāgārjuṇa should die, he shut himself up in his solitary chamber and disappeared. For a hundred years temples were raised in his honour in all the kingdoms of India, and people began to worship him as they did Buddha. As his mother had borne him under an *Arjuṇa* tree, he received the name of Arjuṇa, and as after that a Nāga (dragon) had taken part in his conversion, the name Nāga was added, whence has resulted the name Nāgārjuṇa (in Chinese *Lune-chu*, dragon-tree; the Thibetans translate it 'converted by a dragon'). He was the thirteenth patriarch, and administered religion more than three hundred years.[4]

3. Deva (Āryadeva) was descended from a Brahmanical family of Southern India. He rendered himself celebrated by his general knowledge. There was in his kingdom a golden image

of Maheśvara two *sagenes*[5] high; whoever, in asking a favour, turned himself towards it, had his prayer granted in the present life. All who presented themselves were not admitted to the image, but Deva insisted that he should be allowed to enter, and when the angry spirit began to roll his eyes, he pulled one of them out. Another day Maheśvara appeared to him in a festival and promised him that the people should believe his words. Deva came to the pagoda of Nāgārjuṇa,[6] advanced into the spiritual state, and then began to enlighten the people. But that did not satisfy him; he was possessed with the desire to convert the king himself. For that purpose he went to the bodyguards, and after having gained their attention he asked permission to enter into discussion with some heretics, every one of whom he overcame. Deva composed *Bo-lune erl-chi ping,* 'The Hundred-fold Meditation,' and *Ci bo lune* (400 *gāthas*) for the overthrow of error, but a Tīrthika laid open his stomach and he died. As he had before this given one of his eyes to Maheśvara when he met him at the festival, he remained blind of an eye, and was surnamed Kānadeva.

4. Vasubandhu was born in the kingdom of Purushapura,[7] in Northern India. In the history of the god Vishṇu the following is related:–Vishṇu was the younger brother of Indra, who had sent him into Jambudvīpa to conquer the Asura: he was born as son to the king Vāsudeva. At this time the Asura existed under the name of Indramana[8] (conqueror of Indra), a name which he had received because of his war against Indra. In the *Vyākaraṇa*[9] it is said that the Asura asserts that it is not a good thing for people to amuse themselves by giving opposition to the gods who find enjoyment in well doing. This Asura had a sister named Prabhāvatī[10] (sovereign of light), who was very beautiful. The Asura, wishing to injure Vishṇu, placed his sister in a prominent position, and himself told her that if any one wished to marry her she was to propose that he should seek a quarrel with her brother. Vishṇu came to this place; he fell in love with Prabhāvatī, and, as all the gods had married daughters of the Asuras, he proposed marriage to her: he was in consequence forced to fight a duel with the Asura. Vishṇu, as the body of Nārāyaṇa, was invulnerable; the Asura also

continued to live though Vishṇu had cut off his head, hands, and other limbs, which returned anew to their places. The fight continued till night, and the strength of Vishṇu was beginning to fail, when his wife, fearing lest he should be beaten, took an *Utpala* leaf, and tearing it in two pieces, threw them on different sides, and began to walk in the middle. Vishṇu, understanding the meaning of this action, tore the body of the Asura into two pieces and passed between them; then the Asura died. He had formerly obtained from a Ṛishi the privilege that if any of his limbs should be cut off they should reunite, but the Ṛishi had not promised that his body would be joined together again if it should be torn asunder. As Vishṇu had shown here the courage of a man, the kingdom was thus named Purusha. There was in this kingdom a royal chief who was a Brāhmaṇ of the Kauśika[11] family. He had three sons who bore the single name Vasubandhu, which was common to them, and which signifies 'celestial parent' (*Tiane-tzine*). It is the custom in India to give all children only one name, which is common to them, and besides that, in order to distinguish them, another one is added as a special distinction. The third son Vasubandhu had advanced into the spiritual calling at the Sarvāstivāda school. He became an Arhana and was named Bi-lin-chi vatsya (*ba-po*); Bilinchi was his mother's name, and Vatsya signifies 'son;' but it is thus that the children of servants, cattle and specially calves are called. The eldest son Vasubandhu advanced equally in the spiritual calling at the Sarvāstivāda school, and although he might have escaped suffering he could not understand the idea, and wished to put himself to death; but the Arhana Pindola, who dwelt in the eastern Videhadvīpa, having seen him, came to him and instructed him in the contemplation of the void of the Hīnayāna; but Vasubandhu, not being satisfied with that, sent a messenger into the heaven named Tushita to make special inquiries of Maitreya, and after having received from him an explanation of the void of the Mahāyāna, he returned to Jambudvipa, where, having given himself up to study, he received the gift of foresight, and because of that he was surnamed Asañga (*U-thyo,* 'unimpeded'). He still went sometimes into Tushita to

Maitreya to make particular inquires about the meaning of the *Sūtras* of the Mahāyāna; but when he explained to others what he had learned they did not believe him, and he was obliged to ask Maitreya to return to the earth, to which he consented. For four months Maitreya was found in the temple of preaching, addressing the people upon the *Sūtra of Seventeen Worlds,* and explaining the meaning of it clearly; nobody but Asañga could see him, – the others could only hear the preaching, – and every one believed in the Mahāyāna. Maitreya taught Asañga the Samādhi of the solar ray; then everything became intelligible to him, and he composed in Jambudvīpa the *Upadeśa* upon the *Sūtras* of the Mahāyāna.

The second son Vasubandhu advanced also in the spiritual calling at the Sarvāstivāda school: in the extent of his learning, the number of the subjects which he understood, and his knowledge of books, he was unequalled. As his brothers had received other names, the name of Vasubandhu remained to him alone.

Towards the five-hundredth year after the *nirvāṇa* of Buddha, the Arhana Katyāyaṇaputra, who had advanced in the spiritual calling at the Sarvāstivāda school, lived. He was purely Indian, but in course of time he came into the kingdom of Kipine (Kofene, Cabul), which is on the north-west of India, where at the same time there were 500 Arhanas and 500 Bodhisatvas (?). He began to compose the *Abhidharma* of the Sarvāstivāda school, which consists of 8 *grantas*. A declaration was published everywhere that those who knew anything of the *Abhidharma* of Buddha should tell what they knew of it. Then men, gods, dragons, Yakshas, and even the inhabitants of the heaven Akanishṭa communicated everything that they knew, were it only a phrase of a verse. Katyāyaṇaputra, with the Arhanas and the Bodhisatvas, chose out of all what was not contradictory to the *Sūtras* and to the *Vinaya;* they formed of it a composition which they divided into eight parts, in which there were 50,000 ślokas. Then they wished to compose the *Vaibhāshya* to explain the *Abhidharma*. At this time Aśvagosha was living in India, a native of the *Po-dyi-do* country in the kingdom of Śravasti; he understood eight parts of the *Vyākaraṇa,* the four *Vedas,* the six sciences, and the three *Piṭ akas* of eighteen schools: so Katyāyaṇaputra sent an ambassador to Śravasti to invite Aśvaghosha to correct the writing of the proposed *Vaibhāshya.* For twelve consecutive years after his arrive in Kipine Aśvagosha was occupied with the work of which Katyāyaṇaputra and the other Arhanas and Bodhisatvas had given him charge; the whole *Vaibhāshya* contained a million of *gāthas*. After their composition, Katyāyaṇaputra engraved a command on stone that no person, knowing this doctrine, should cause it to spread out of Kipine, and also that the composition itself should not pass beyond the frontier. He also took care that the other schools and the Mahāyāna should not profane to change this pure doctrine. This command was also confirmed by the king. The kingdom of Kipine was surrounded on all sides by mountains, and there were gates only on one side; all the prelates had set their guard of Yakshas as sentinels to allow all those who wished to be instructed to pass in, but not to allow them to go out again. In the kingdom of Ayodhya lived the master Vasasubhadra,[12] who was gifted with intelligence and a good memory; as he wished to learn the *Vaibhāshya,* he feigned madness and repaired to Kipine, where the listened for twelve consecutive years. Sometimes while they were explaining to him he began to inquire about the *Rāmāyaṇa;* and on that account he was disdained by all, and was allowed to go out of Kipine, although the Yakshas had prevented to priests. After his return to his birthplace he declared that every one should hasten to learn of him the *Vaibhāshya* of Kipine, and, as he was old, his disciples wrote as quickly as he spoke, and in short everything was conducted towards a good end.

About the ninth century after the death of Buddha of Tīrthika Vindhyākavasa lived; he demanded the work *Sene-ge-lune* from the dragon who dwelt near the lake at the foot of the Vindhya mountains, and after having adapted it to his point of view, he came to Ayodhya and asked king Vikramāditya to allow him to enter into discussion with the Buddhist priests. At this time the great masters, such as Maṇiraṭa, Vasubandhu, and others, were away in other kingdoms. The only one remaining was Buddhamitra, the master of Vasubandhu, a very old and feeble man, but one who had deep knowledge; he was called to argue, but he could not repeat what the Tīrthika had said, and he was vanquished.

The king re-compensed the Tīrthika, who, upon returning to the Vindhya mountain, was changed into a pillar of stone, but his work *Sene-ge-lune* has been preserved till the present day. When, upon his return, Vasubandhu learned this circumstance, he caused a search to be made for the Tīrthika; but as he had been changed into stone; Vasubandhu composed the *Tzi-shi-chyane-shi-lune,* in which he refuted all the propositions of the *Sene-ge-lune,* and for that he received from the king a gift of three *lakshas* of gold, with which he set up three idols, – one for the Bhikshunīs, another for the Sarvāstivāda school, and the third for the school of the Mahāyāna; after that the true doctrine (that is to say Buddhism) was established anew. Vasubandhu first studied the meaning of the *Vaibhāshya;* then, having adopted this teaching, he composed every day a *gātha* in which was contained the meaning of all he had been teaching during that day; after having written this *gātha* on a leaf of copper, he caused it to be carried about on the head of an intoxicated elephant, and called by the beating of a drum those who wished to dispute the meaning of the *gātha;* but no one was found able to refute it. In this way more than 600 *gāthas* were composed, which contain all the meaning of the *Vaibhāshya;* it is the *Kośakarina,* or the *Kośa* in verse. When Vasubandhu had *added* to it fifty pounds in gold, he sent it to Kipine to all those who were masters of the *Abhidharma,* who were greatly rejoiced that their true doctrine was spread aborad; but as they found in the verses some incomprehensible passages, they themselves added other fifty pounds in gold, and desired Vasubandhu to write an explanation in prose; he then composed the *Abhidarmakośa,* in which he has introduced the Sarvāstivādine ideas, and refuted whatever deviated from the principles of the *Sūtras*. When this composition arrived at Kipine, the masters in these districts were irritated at seeing their opinions overturned.

The son of king Vikramāditya, who bore the name of Prāditya ('new sun') made his vows to Vasubandhu; and his mother, who entered the religious calling, became his pupil. When Prāditya mounted the throne, the mother and son besought Vasubandhu to stay at Ayodhya and enjoy their fortune, which he consented to do; but the brother-in-law of Prāditya, the Brāhmaṇ Vasurata, who had married his sister, was a master of the Tīrthikas and was versed in *Vyākaraṇa,* according to the principles of which he composed a refutation of the *Kośa,* a work of Vasubandhu, who for his defence wrote *Sane-shi-erle-piṅg* (32 Articles), in which he refuted all the objections. The *Vyākaraṇa* was lost, and there remained only the other composition. The king gave him as a reward a *laksha* of gold, and his mother gave him two; with this Vasubandhu erected an idol in each of the three kingdoms of Kipine, Purushapura, and Ayodhya. The Tīrthika, red with shame, wishing the humble Vasubandhu, brought from India to Ayodhya the master Siñhabhadra, who composed two works to refute the *Kośa:* in the one (*Gunane-sane-ma-lê*), in 10,000 *gāthas,* he explained the meaning of the *Vaibhāshya;* and in the other (*Sui-shi-lune*), in 12,000 *gāthas,* he defended himself and overturned the opinions of the *Kośa.* After having finished these works, Siñhabhadra provoked Vasubandhu to discussions, but the latter removed himself under pretext of his old age, referring them to wise people to judge them. At first this master, who had plunged into the study of the ideas of eighteen schools, had devoted himself to the Hīnayāna, and did not believe in the Mahāyāna,—he said that the doctrine of Buddha was not in it. Asañga, apprehending that his brother would write a refutation of the Mahāyāna, called Vasubandhu to Purushapura, where he himself dwelt, and converted him to the Mahāyāna. Vasubandhu repented of his former criticisms of the Mahāyāna and wished to cut out is tongue, but his brother sought to persuade him that it would be better to write an explanation of the Mahāyāna, which he indeed composed after the death of Asañga. It is to him that the commentaries on the *Avantansaka,* the *Nirvāṇa,* the *Saddharmapundarika,* the *Prajnāpāramitā,* the *Vimalakirti,* and other *Sūtras* belong; besides these he composed *Veī-shi-lune,* in which is contained the whole conception of the whole Mahāyāna, and also *Gane-lu-mine* and the other *Śāstras* of the Mahāyāna. All that was composed by this master is distinguished for excellence of style and ideas: it is for that reason that, not only in India, but also in other countries, beyond the frontiers, the partizans both of the Hīnayāna and the Mahāyāna have adopted his works as authoritative. Heretics grow pale with fear when they hear his name. He died at Ayodhya, at the age of 80 years.

References

1. The biographies of the first three were translated into Chinese under the dynasty of Yao-tzine, A.D. 384-417, by Kumāraśya (Kumāraśila ?); and the last, that of Vasubandu, appeared under the Chene dynasty (A.D. 557-588), by the celebrated Chene-ti. From these M. Vassilief derives the following abridged lives (pp. 210-222 of the Russian ed.).
2. A sort of bell for calling to religious exercises.
3. We do not find all these works of Nāgārjuna either in Chinese or Thibetan, though there are others that go under his name.
4. This note is found in the Chinese biography.
5. The 'sagene' is a Russian measure of 6 ft. 9.2 in.
6. Yet we do not know that Nāgārjuna was still alive, though the usual legends make Āryadeva the personal disciple of Nāgārjuna.
7. *Fu-lou-cha-fu-lo*.
8. *Ine-to-lo-to-ma-na; to-ma-na* signifying vanquisher.
9. *Bi-kia-lo*.
10. *Po-lo-po-no-di*.
11. *Kiao-chi-kia,* one of the names of Indra himself.
12. *Po-soso-siui-ba-to-lo*.

4

The Story of the Faithful Deer

S. Beal

There is, perhaps, no fable so frequently met with in Buddhist books, and also depicted on coins and in sculptures, as the story of Buddha when he was the king of the Deer. It is possible that this very story is that called the *Miga-Jātaka* at Bharhut, at any rate it is one that carries interest with it, both as it exemplifies the duty of wife-life devotion, and also exhibits in the simplest way the mode of instruction adopted by the founder of the Buddhist religion, to impress on the minds of his followers the moral lessons it was his aim to inculcate.

The Story of the Deer – king

I remember, in years gone by, there was in the neighbourhood of Banāras a certain enclosure (district: *arāṇya*), in which a Deer-king with his herd had found a place of pasture, and lived in contentment. At this time a hunter, having discovered the spot where these deer congregated, set a snare to entrap one or more of them, and as it happened he caught the king of the herd himself. At this time a certain hind, the wife of the Deer-king, big with young, seeing the Deer-king thus in the snare of the huntsman, stopped in the neighbourhood, and would not leave the spot where he was. Meantime, all the other deer having fled from the spot, the Deer-mother spake as follows in *Gāthās* which she addressed to the king :–

"Deer-king! exert your strength,
Push with yout head and your heel,
Break to pieces the trap which man
Has set to catch you, and escape."

Then the Deer-king answered in the following *Gāthās,* and said : –

"Although I used all my strength,
Yet I could not escape from this trap,
Made as it is with thongs of skin, sewed with silk,
In vain should I struggle to get away from such a snare.
Oh! ye mountain dells and sweetest fountains!
May none of your occupants henceforth,
Meet with such a misfortune as this!"

And the *Gāthās* continue as follows : –

"At this time those two deer,
Filled with alarm, and shedding bitter tears,
Beheld the wicked hunter approaching the spot.
With his knife and club in his hand (*ready to slay*)."

Then the Deer-king, seeing the hunter thus armed approaching the place, said to the mother-deer : –

"This is the hunter, coming here,
His face dark and forbidding, his doublet of skin.
He will come and strip off my hide,
Cut up my flesh in joints, and depart."

Then the female deer, gradually approaching the hunter, addressed him and said : –

"Most illustrious hunter ! listen !
You may arrange your seat of grass and prepare
First of all to kill me, and skin my hide from my body.
Then go and kill your prisoner – the Deer-king."

At this time the huntsman addressed the hind as follows: "Is this Deer-king related to you ?" Then the hind answered and said, "He is my husband. I love and revere him with all my heart, and therefore I am determined to share his fate; kill me first, then, hunter! and afterwards do as you list to him!"

Then the huntsman reflected and said:

"What a faithful and exemplary wife is this! seldom indeed is such a one to be found !" Then he addressed the hind and said, "Most respectable one ! your conduct is very commendable; I will let your lord go !"

Then there was great joy, and the huntsman said :–

"Seldom have I seen such faithfulness.

Go, then! Oh, Deer-king!

And as you owe your life to your mate,

Cherish and nourish her as you ought."

Then the huntsman loosed the snare, and let the Deer-king go, on which the hind overjoyed, addressed the huntsman, and said :–

"Most virtuous and illustrious huntsman!

May all your friends and relations,

As you have caused me to rejoice,

Seeing my husband escape, likewise so rejoice.

Then Buddha said, "This Deer-king was myself, and the hind was Yasodharā, who, on my account, experienced much sorrow, so much indeed, that for six years she carried Rahūla in her womb, till at last hearing that I was about to return and assume the dignity of a universal monarch (whereas my kingdom is of a spiritual character), overcome with joy she brought forth her son, Rahūla, and clothed and adorned him as became the child of a queen".[1]

References

1. From *The Oriental,* Nov. 6, 1875.

5
The Eighteen Schools of Buddhism

S. Beal, *B.A.*

One of the most interesting but intricate questions that can occupy the attention of the Buddhist student is the history of the eighteen sects into which the Buddhist Church was at an early date separated. A clear account of the causes that led to the schisms and the several tenets held by the separatists was, in the opinion of the late Mr. Spence Hardy, one of the great *desiderata* in the history of this religion. The Chinese and Tibetan books contain much valuable information on these points. Among other works in the northern copy of the *Tripiṭ aka,* common in the monasteries of China and Japan, is one which contains three translations from Sanskrit of the treatise, written by Vasumitra, on the eighteen schools. This Vasumitra[1] was one of the Buddhist patriarchs who lived probably about the time of Kanishka, that is, as far as we know at present with any certainty, about 42 B.C.[2] His aim was evidently to reconcile the differences that existed in traditions, customs, and acknowledged scriptures; and it was probably under his auspices, or by his influence, that the Great Council was held that re-arranged and revised the Buddhist Canon as it is known in the North. There are three translations of this treatise into Chinese; the first is anonymous, and is most obscure. The second is by Chin-ti, of the Tsin dynasty. The third is by Hiwen Thsang, of the Tang dynasty. It would be rash to attempt a translation of these tracts into English without aid or direction—nor would the present writer have undertaken such a task—but, unfortunately, there is a parallel translation from the Tibetan in Vassilief's *History of Buddhism* (Second Supplement, p. 222). This translation by the learned writer named above was prepared after careful comparison of the Tibetan text with the three Chinese versions. The result is no doubt an accurate, though most obscure, reproduction of the work by Vasumitra. It may perhaps be useful to attempt an independent version of the three Chinese translations. Not that we can hope to render all plain, but with the purpose of inducing scholars in China to look into this matter, and endeavour to throw some light on the subject by comparing these translations and working independently in the production of others. The matter may appear of little consequence to some, and needless labour to others, but in the presence of facts, which are daily coming to our knowledge, it becomes almost the duty of those who are interested in the religious development of the Eastern mind, not only in India, but in other countries more or less affected by Indian speculations, to search out the causes and the character of that development, and so connect it with the religious movements which occurred elsewhere about the same time. We proceed to give part of the translation by the anonymous Chinese writer, and which stands first in the Buddhist Canon.[3]

An Account of the Eighteen Principal Schools of Buddhism, from the original Treatise of Vasumitra, translated into Chinese by three separate authors

A treatise on the eighteen schools (translator's name unknown).

In the 15th section of the latter volume of the work known as the Queries of Manjuśrī (*Manjuśriparipṛichchhā*), the subject being "The division into schools." [It is thus written:]

At this time Manjuśrī questioned Buddha thus: "World-honoured! Explain, I pray you, what will be the different schools into which your followers will separated in the future after your *Nirvāṇa,* and from what original division these schools will be formed?"

Buddha answered Manjuśrī thus: "There will be twelve schools among my followers hereafter, in which (the separate interpretation of) my law will be preserved in the world. These schools will be the repositories of the diversified fruits of my

Scriptures (*piṭakas*) without priority or inferiority—just as the taste of sea-water is everywhere the same—or as the twelve sons of one man all honest and true, so will be the exposition of my doctrine advocated by these schools. Manjuśrī! the two original germs of these separate schools will be found in the rendering of my doctrine by the Mahāyāna and the Prajñāpāramitā systems. The Śrāvakas, Pratyeka, Buddhas, and different Buddhas (*i.e.*, the doctrine which teaches these three degrees of religious advancement) will come from the Prajñāpāramitā. Manjuśrī! as earth, water, fire, wind and space compose the material and visible universe, so the Mahāyāna and the Prajñāpāramitā compose the material of the system in which these different degrees of Śrāvakas, Pratyeka-Buddhas, and Buddhas are entertained."

Manjuśrī asked Buddha this question: "World-honoured! and by what names will these schools be known ?"

Buddha replied: "The two schools first formed will be 'the Mahāsāṁghikas[4] and the Pi-li'[5] (Sthaviras). Within a hundred years after my *Nirvāṇa* a school will be formed called 'Yeb-wu-in'[6] [Ekabhyohārikhās (Burnouf, tom. I, p. 357), or Ekavyavahārikās (according to Vassilief's *Buddhism,* p. 227, n.)]. Again, within a hundred years from the formation of this school, another will be formed called 'Ko-kiu-li'[7] [Kukkulikās]. Within a hundred years from this another school will arise called To-man[8] (Bāhuśrutiyas), Within a hundred years from this there will be another school formed, called 'Che-tai-ho'[9] [Chaitiyavādās]. Within another hundred years a school will arise called 'Eastern Mountain'[10] [Pūrvaśailās]. Within a hundred years another school will arise from this called 'Northern Mountain'[11] [Uttaraśailās]. These seven schools come from the Mahāsāṁghikās, and including the original Saṁgha, or congregation, they are classified as eight schools.

"From the Sthaviras were formed eleven schools. Within a hundred years from the origin of the above school, there arose another, called 'Yeh-tsai-wu-in'[12] (Sarvāstivādas). Within a hundred years from this school proceeded another, called 'Yun-shan"[13] (Haimavatās). Within a hundred years from this school another will arise, called 'Vātsiputriyas'[14] (sons of the calf).

Within a hundred years after this another school called 'Dharmottarīyas.'[15] Within a hundred years from this school will come another called 'Bhadrāyanīyas.'[16] Within a hundred years from this another called 'Yih-tsai-sho-kwei'[17] (Sammatīyas). Within a hundred years another school will arise from this, called 'Jing-shan'[18] (Jungle-hill, *i.e.,* Shāṇṇagarika). Within a hundred years after this arose another school called 'Tai-puh-ho-ki'[19] (Mahīśāsakas). Within a hundred years from this arose the school called 'Fau'[20] (Dharmaguptās). Within a hundred years another school arose called 'Ka-hi-pi'[21] (Kāśyapīyas). Within a hundred years from this another school arose named 'Sieon-to-lo-ku'[22] (Samkantikās or Sautrāntikās). The above are the eleven schools derived from the Sthaviras, and including their mother-school, comprise twelve distinct branches."

Buddha spoke the following *gāthas*:–

"The school of the Mahāsāṁghikas
Will divide into seven parts,
The Sthavirās into eleven,
This is what we term the twelve schools,[23]
The eighteen including the two original,
All these will arise from the Mahāyāna,
Which admits of neither affirmation or contradiction.
Now I say that in future time will appear,
The miscellaneous writings of the Master Kumārajiva
After the cessation (*nirvāṇa*) of the true Law,
Just one hundred years;
And by these various productions
The true Law will be gradually destroyed,
Everyone forming his own views,
Founding their opinions on heterodox sects,
Despising that which ought to be honoured.
A rebellious and discontented tone will arise
But now the *Sūtras* alone are the ground

On which to build the doctrine of Buddha,
Relying on the former truths.
Seeking a foundation on this solid basis,
Is like in the multitude of sand particles
Seeking for the truth gold.
Thus have I heard former sages,
Who appear like suns among men."

"One hundred and sixteen years after the *Nirvāṇa* of Buddha (*in a*) city called 'I-ta-fuh,' (*I* for *Pa,* therefore equivalent to Pa-ta-fuh, *i.e.,* Pātaliputra) there shall be a king called 'A-yu' (Aśoka) who shall gather (as in a square) the whole of Jambudwipa as his empire. In his time the division of the great congregation into schools shall begin. There shall arise a Bhikshu called 'Neng' (able), and another called 'Yin-un' (Nidāna), and another called 'To-man' (Bāhuśrutiya ?)—these shall assert the necessity of teaching five propositions as a basis for religious instruction. The five points are these:—

Profit and increase from others.
Ignorance.
Doubt.
Words according to the religious formula.
To obtain reason.

"It was from a consideration of these questions that the first two schools arose, to wit, the Mahāsāṁghikās and the Sthavīras.[24]

In the middle of the century (*following*) the Mahāsāṁghikās other schools arose as follows:— (1) 'Yih-shwo' [Ekavyavahārikās], (2) 'Chu-shai-kan-shwo' [Lokottaravādins], (3) 'Kiu-ku' [Gokulikas or Kukkuṭikas]. Again, in the middle of a century or so after the Mahāsāṁghikas will originate other schools, called 'Shi-chi-lun.'[25]

"Again, in the middle of the two hundred years, the heretical followers of the Mahādêva, taking on themselves the vows of religious ascetics, fixed their abode in Mount Chaitiya. Again, from the Mahāsāṁghika arose three other schools, viz. Chetika, 'Huh-pi-lo' (Apara), and Uttaraśaila. Thus from the Mahāsāṁghika arose nine schools, viz. (1) Mahāsāṁghikas, (2) Ekavyavahārika, (3) Lokottaravādin, (4) Gokulika, (5) Bāhuśrutīya, (6) Shi-chi, (7) Yan-ka, (8) Ho-lo, (9) Uttaraśaila."

"In the middle of the three hundred years from the Sthavira school, arose from controversies connected with the Canon of the *Abhidharma,* different schools, as follows : (1) Sarvāstivādin, also called Hetuvāda, (2) Haimavatas. In the middle of the three hundred years again there arose another school called Vātsiputrīyās, from this school sprang another, called Dharma gupta (or Dharmottarīyas), another called Dharmagupta (or Dharmotarīyas), another called Bhadrāyanīyas, and again, another called Mi-lī (where *li* is evidently a mistake for *ti*), otherwise named San-mi-ti (Sammatīyas), another school called the school of the six cities (Shannagarikas). Again, in the three hundreth year, the Sarvāstivādins produced another school; viz., Mahīśāsakas, from which sprang the Dharmaguptas (so called from the Master of the school, whose name was In-chi-lin).[26] Again, in this three hundredth year, another school sprang from the Sarvāstivādins, called Yan-li-sha (Varsha), likewise named Kāśyapīyas. In the four hundredth year from the Sarvāstavādins sprang another school called Seng-kai-lin-to (Saṁkrānti), so called from the name of its founder Yeou-to-lo (Uttara), this school was also known as Sautrāntika."

"Thus, from the school of the Mahāsthaviras branched off twelve schools, viz. (1) Mahāsthaviras, (2) Haimavatas, (3) Sarvāstivādins, (4) Vātsiputrīyās, (5) Dharmottarīyas, (6) Bhadrāyanīyas, (7) Sammatīyas, (8) The school of six Cities, (9) Mahīśāsikas, (10) Dharmaguptas, (11) Kāśyapīyas; (12) Sautrāntikas."

We will now proceed to speak of the distinguishing tents of these various schools, both to their radical differences and also those held[27] in common.

The following schools, Mahasāṁghikas, Ekavyavāhārikas, Lokottaras, Kukkutikas, hold the views we are about to mention. They all say that the traditions respecting the Buddhas having been bore into the world (*as men*) are incorrect—that the law is Tathāgata, and the only one in the world. They all say that the (*system of religion known as*) 'turning the Wheel of the Law' is at an end. They say that "things exist," "relationships exist," "truth exists." They say that Tathāgata is infinitely extended, immeasurably glorious, eternal in duration, that to his power of recollection (*nim, smriti*) his power of faith (*srāddhabala*), his experience of joy, and his life, there is no end; he sleeps not, he speaks, asks, reflects not; they say that his existence is ever one and uniform (*one heart*), that all things born may obtain deliverance by having his instruction, that in his essential existence (one heart, *ekachitta*) Tathāgata comprehends all subjects (*laws*) in a moment by his own wisdom.

References

1. *Ind. Ant.* vol. IV, p. 363.
2. By some he is placed rather later—ED. *I.A.*
3. This translation is denoted as *C* by Vassilier.
4. This word means the great congregation, composed of young and old alike, the same as the school of "various and miscellaneous Moral Rules."—[Ch. Ed.]
5. This word means the congregation of old men only, it is the same as that which acknowledges the authority of the (*original*) *Vinaya* only.
6. So called because they agreed in the main with the Mahāsanghikas,—[Ch. Ed.]
7. From the name of the master who formed it—[Ch. Ed.]
8. So called from the "*famous* wisdom" of its founder—[Ch. Ed.]
9. So called from the locality in which the founder lived.
10. So called from the locality in which the founder lived.
11. Likewise from the abode of the founder.
12. So called because the founder of the school held the positive existence of all things in the three worlds—[Ch. Ed.]
13. So called from the abode of the founder.

14. From the name of the founder.
15. From the name of the founder.
16. From the name of the founder.
17. So called from the great esteem in which the master was held among men.
18. So called from the character of the place where the founder lived. The name in Sanskrit however means "of six towns," and so in Tibetan; see Vassilief, p. 231 – J.B.
19. So called because the founder of this school was, when a child, cast into a well by his mother, and when his father sent to recover his body he was found uninjured.
20. The founder's name.
21. The founder's name.
22. The founder rested his deductions on the Sūtras.
23. That is the twelve schools that sprang from the Mahāsthavirās.
24. In Chinese, "high-seat."
25. I cannot explain this title at present – S.B.
26. *Vide* Vassilief, p. 232 n. 5.
27. So I would translate "Chung-kan."

6

The Chong-Lun or Pranyamūla-Śāstra-Tika of Nāgārjuna

S. Beal, *M.A., Rector of Wark*

I shall here give a translation of the 25th section of the *Chong-Lun Sūtra* or *Pranyamūla-śāstra-tika,* by Nāgārjuna, on *Nirvāṇa.*

(1) If all things are unreal,
Then how is it possible to remove
From that which does not exist
Something, which, being removed, leaves *Nirvāṇa* ?

This section argues that if all things are alike empty and unreal, then there is no such thing as Birth and Death; consequently there can be no removal from sorrow, and the destruction of the five elements of existence (limited existence), by removal of which we arrive at Nirvāṇa (what is called Nirvāṇa).

(2) But if all things are real,
Then how can we remove
Birth and Death, real existence,
And so arrive at *Nirvāṇa* ?

This section argues that we cannot destroy that which has in itself real existence, and therefore, if all things have this real being, we cannot remove Birth and Death, and so arrive at *Nirvāṇa*; therefore, neither by the theory of *Bhava,* nor by the theory of *Sunyata* (emptiness), can we arrive at the just idea of *Nirvāṇa.*

(3) That which is not striven for or "obtained,"
That which is not "for a time" or "eternal,"

That which is not born, nor dies,

This is that which is called *Nirvāṇa.*

"Not to be striven for," that is, in the way of religious action (*achārya*), and its result (*fruit*).

"Not obtained" (or "arrived at"), that is, because there is no place or point at which to arrive.

"Not for a time" (or not by way of interruption) [*per saltum*] for the five skandhas having been from the time of complete enlightenment proved to be unreal, and not part of true existence, then on entering final *Nirvāṇa* (*anupadiśesha Nirvāṇa*) – What is there that breaks or interrupts the character of previous existence ?

"Not for ever," or "everlasting," for if there were something to be obtained that admitted of distinctions whilst in the possession of it, then we might speak of an *eternal nirvāṇa,* but as in the condition of silent extinction (*Nirvāṇa*) there can be no properties to distinguish, how can we speak of it as "everlasting ?"

And so with reference to Birth and Death.

Now that which is so characterised is what we call *Nirvāṇa.*

Again, there is a *Sūtra* which says, "*Nirvāṇa* is the opposite of 'Being' and 'not Being'; it is the opposite of these two combined, it is the opposite of the absence of 'Being', and the absence of 'not Being'.

So, in short, that which admits of no conditions such as are attached to limited existence; that is *Nirvāṇa.*

(4) *Nirvāṇa* cannot be called *Bhava;*

For if so, then it admits of old age and death,

In fact both "being" and "not being" are phenomena,

And therefore are capable of being deprived of characteristics (*lakshanam*).

This means that as all things which the eye beholds are seen to begin and to end, and this is what the Ślōka calls "Life" and "Death" (or birth and death). Now if *Nirvāṇa* is like this, then it would be possible to speak of removing these things and so arriving at something fixed – but here is a plain contradiction of terms – for Nirvāṇa is supposed to be that which is fixed and unchangeable.

(5) If *Nirvāṇa* is *Bhava* (existent),

Then it is *personal;*

But, in fact, that which cannot be individualized

Is spoken of as not "personal."

This means that as all phenomenal existence comes from cause and consequent production, therefore all such things are rightly called "personal."

(6) If *Nirvāṇa* be *Bhava,*

Then it cannot be called "without sensation" (*anuvedana*);

For non-Being comes not from sensation,

And by this obtains its distinct name.

This means that as the *Sūtras* describe *Nirvāṇa* as being "without sensation" (*anuvedana*), it cannot be *Bhava;* for then *Abhava* would come from sensation. But now it will be asked, if *Nirvāṇa* is not *Bhava,* then that which is "not *Bhava*" (*abhava*), surely then is *Nirvāṇa*. To this we reply—

(7) If *Nirvāṇa* be not *Bhava,*

Much less is it nothing (*abhava*);

For if there be no room for "Being,"

What place can there be for "not Being."

This means that "not Being" is the opposite of "Being." If, then, "Being" is not admissible, how can we speak of "Not Being"? (its opposite).

(8) If again *Nirvāṇa* is nothing,

How is it called without "sensation ?" (*anuvedana*),

For it would be wonderful indeed if everything not capable of sensation,

Were forthwith spoken of as nothing.

If then *Nirvāṇa* be neither "Being," nor "non-Being," what is it ?

(9) By participation in cause and effect

Comes the wheel of continual existence,

By non-participation in cause and effect
Comes *Nirvāṇa.*

As by knowing a thing to be straight we also know that which is crooked, so by the knowledge of the elements of finite existence comes the knowledge of continual life and death. Do away with those, and you do away also with the other.

(10) As Buddha says in the *Sūtra,* –

Separate "Being," separate "not Being,"
This is *Nirvāṇa,*
The opposite of "Being," the opposite of "not Being."

"Being" here alludes to the three worlds of finite existence. The absence of these three worlds is "Not Being." Get rid of both these ideas, this is Nirvāṇa. But it may now be asked, if Nirvāṇa is not "Being," and if it is not "Absence of Being," then perhaps it is the intermixture of the two.

(11) If it is said that "Being" and "Not Being,"
By union, produces *Nirvāṇa,*
The two are then one;
But this is impossible.

Two unlike things cannot be joined so as to produce one different from either.

(12) If it is said "Being" and "Not Being"
United make *Nirvāṇa,*
Then *Nirvāṇa* is not "without sensation;"
For these two things involve sensation.

(13) If it is said that "Being" and "Not Being,"
United, produce *Nirvāṇa,*
Then *Nirvāṇa* is not Impersonal;
For these two things are personal.

(14) "Being" and "Not Being," joined in one,
How can this be *Nirvāṇa* ?
These two things have nothing in common,
Can Darkness and Light be joined ?

(15) If the opposites of "Being" and "Not Being,"
Is *Nirvāṇa,*
These opposites –
How are they distinguished ?

(16) If they are distinguished ?
And so, by union, become *Nirvāṇa,*
Then that which completes the idea of "Being" and "Not Being"
Also completes the idea of the opposite of both.

(17) Tathāgata, after his departure,
Says nothing of "Being" and "Not Being."
He says not that his "Being" is not, or the opposite of this.

Tathagata says nothing of these things or their opposites. The conclusion of the whole matter is, that *Nirvāṇa* is identical with the nature of Tathāgata, without bound, and without place or time.[1]

References

1. *The Oriental,* October 9, 1875.

7
The Age and Writings of Nagarjunā-Bodhisattva

S. Beal

From an examination of Chinese documents relating to Nāgārjuna, it seems evident that he is not the same person as Nāgasêna.

It has been hitherto commonly held that these two names denote one person. But the Chinese version of the *Melinda-Praśna* (Nanjio's *Catalogue,* No. 1358) describes Nāgasêna as a native of North India, and simply terms him a *Bhikshu;* whilst the *Life* of Nāgārjuna by Kumārajīva (*id.* No. 1461) places him in South India, and speaks of him as an eminent *Bôdhisattva.*

Again, the time when these two writers flourished is not the same. Nāgasêna was contemporary with Menander, who flourished about B.C. 140; whilst Nāgārjuna was certainly subsequent to the date of Kanishka, and, according to the latest conclusions, lived towards the end of the second century A.D.

Again, the characters of the two seem to be wholly different. Nāgasêna was a skilful disputant, but a loyal follower of the primitive doctrine of the great Teacher; but Nāgārjuna was the founder of a new school, an ambitious innovator, and an adept in conjuration and magic.

On all grounds, then, we must distinguish these two-writers, and be content to let Nāgasêna alone, judging him only by his one work, *The Questionings of Melinda.*

I will, however, make one or two remarks about the Chinese versions of this book. I call them versions, but they are only abridgments of the original work, if that work is fairly represented by the Pāli translation. The first was made by an unknown hand during the Eastern Tsin dynasty, *i.e.* between A.D. 317 and 400; it is called *Na-sien-pi-khu-king* or "the *Sūtra* of the *Bhikshu* Nāgasêna." After some introductory matter relating to previous births, we are told that there were two Brāhmaṇs, who had practised together their rules of austerity in the same mountain. One of these had expressed a wish that he might be born as a king; the other desired that he might be re-born in a condition to arrive at *nirvāṇa*. Accordingly, the first became the son of a king whose kingdom was by the sea-shore; and when the time came to name him, he was called *Mi-lan.* The other was born in the country of *Ki-pin* (Cophene) and he was called *To-la;* but, because a royal elephant belonging to the family was born on the same day as the child, he was also called *Na-sin,* "for (the narrative adds) the Indian word for 'elephant' is *Na"* (? Nāga). Having become a *Bhikshu,* he attained celebrity, and after a while came to the country of *She-kie* in India, and took up his residence in the *Shi-ti-kia* temple. We must restore *She-kie* to Śākala,[1] and *Shi-ti-kia* to Jêtika. So that the plot of the discussion which follows, is laid in the same place as in the Southern or Pāli account. Meanwhile, the Prince *Mi-lan* had succeeded to his father's maritime kingdom; and, being an adept in religious and philosophical questions, he requested his ministers to inquire for one worthy to enter the lists with him in disputation. The reply was that in the Northern region, in the country *Ta-ts'in,*[2] in the kingdom of *She-kie,* and in the palace of an old king of that country, there was dwelling a *Shaman* well able to dispute with the royal scholar. Then follows a description of the city of Śākala, the noble character of the people, the richly ornamented gates, the sculptured palaces, the apartments of the court ladies, the streets and suburbs, the elephants, horses and chariots, the artizans and scholars, and the tribute paid to this city by all the small countries round about.[3] The clothing of the people is described as being of the five colours, glistening and bright,—the women, of white complexion, and wearing jewels and costly ornaments,—the soil, rich and productive, &c., &c. This was the capital of the country of *Mi-lan.* The king, therefore, proceeds thither, and the disputation is narrated in two long chapters of twenty and fourteen double pages respectively.

From a superficial examination, the description appears to be, in its general character, identical with that found in the *Melinda-pañho;* but, as I do not possess the English translation of this work, published, I understand, by Mr. Trenckner, I have not been able to make any exact comparison.

The only remark on the foregoing that need be made, is that the kingdom of Menander may properly be described as a maritime one, as the conquest of Pattalene is ascribed to him; and, as "he reigned over an extensive tract form the foot of the Paropamisus to the sea,"[4] we may accept the Chinese account that, whilst his kingdom bordered on the sea, its chief city was Śākala. This country the Chinese writer identifies with *Ta-ts'in,* which is generally referred to the Roman Empire, but may, I think, be also equivalent to the countries ruled by the Baktrian satraps. On all sides, at least, this Chinese book supports the identification of Melinda (*Mi-lan*) with the Menander of the Greeks.

There is another short work, in the Chinese collection of books, relating to this subject. It comprises the 101st tale, or story, in the *Tsah-pao-ts'ang-king* (the *Saṁyuktaratnapiṭ akasūtra*).[5] The tale is called *Na-sien-Nan-to-wang-king, i.e.* "the *Sūtra* of Nāgasêna and Nandarāja." The contents are similar to the former work noticed. The king's name is given as Nanda, instead of *Mi-lan.* But I see no difficulty in supposing Nanda to be a contraction of Menander, or of the Pāli Minanda.

On the whole we may conclude that Nāgasêna, the *Bhikshu,* was contemporary with Menander, and that his discussion with the Greek ruler may have given rise to the story of Plutarch about the distribution of his (Menander's) relics and the monuments placed over them.

We now come to Nāgārjuna, respecting whom there is abundance of information, of a mixed character, to be found scattered throughout the Buddhist literature of China. The chief difficulty is how to connect these scattered notices into anything like a reliable narrative.

Taking Hiuen-Tsiang's notices first,[6]—we find that, according to him, Nāgārjuna lived during the time of a king called *Ṣo-to-p'o-ho,*[7] in Southern Kôsala. He practised the art of converting inferior substances into gold, and also gained a knowledge of the elixir of life. By means of the latter, he had extended his own and the king's years over several centuries. The King built for him, or excavated from the rock, a *saṁghārāma;* the rock or mountain was called *Po-lo-mo-lo-ki-li* and it was 300 *li* south of the country.[8] We cannot fix the site of the capital city, visited by Hiuen Tsiang; and so the *Po-lo-mo-lo* hill is not known for certain. One thing, however, we know that it must be restored to Bhramara, or "the black bee," and was called after Durgā or Pārvatī; and that it is the same as the Śrī-parvata-Paramalagiri named by Scheifner in his Translation of *Tāranātha*, p. 304. On this hill Nāgārjuna is said to have passed one hundred and twenty-nine years of his life (Scheifner, *Tāranātha,* p. 73). We must then, it appears, given up the old story of Fa-hian[9] about the pigeon (*pārāvata*) monastery, and substitute for it the Śrīparvata dedicated to Durgā. I have been told by Dr. Burgess that he was good reason for identifying this rock with the celebrated Śrīśāila, on the river Kṛishṇā.[10]

But now the question arises who was this king *So-to-p'o-ho,* and what his probable date?

The Chinese explanation of the king's name is, "he who draws, or pulls well."[11] This, however, gives us but little help, beyond suggesting, as the original Sanskṛit word, Sadvaha,—a name which we do not know of from Sanskṛit sources, and which does not seem a very probable one. But we are told by I-tsing[12] that this monarch was also called *Shi-yen-te-kia,* which might be restored to Sindhuka; moreover, the same writer says that Nāgārjuna wrote to him as the king of a country called *Shing-t'u* (Sindh ?). All this is obscure; it is true the *Vāyu-Purāṇa* gives us the name Sindhuka as the first of the Andhras; but his date is much too early for Nāgārjuna. Under these circumstances, I can find no clue to the settlement of the date from this part of my enquiry; and must rest satisfied with the suggestion that the Chinese translation of the Sanskṛit name is wrong,—that the original name was Śātavāha(na), which is equally deducible from the transliteration, and the sound of which might easily be confused by the Chinese with the sound of Sadvaha,—and that the king is to be identified with one of the Śātavāhana or Andhra kings, and possibly with the Yajñaśrī-Śātakarṇi, who seems to have flourished about A.D. 178 to 207.

If we come now to consider the succession of Buddhist Patriarchs as they are named in the Northern Books, we find that Nāgārjuna is the thirteenth in the order, and Pārśva the ninth. If this Pārśva was the one who presided over the council summoned by Kanishka, then we may reasonably place him about 300 years after Aśôka, or A.D. 70 or 75; for this seems to be the meaning of the 400 years after the *nirvāṇa,* alluded to by Hiuen Tsiang.[13] His successors were Puṇyayaśas, Aśvaghôsha, Kapimala, and then Nāgārjuna. Respecting these, there is no reliable observation found in Chinese Books, except that Aśvaghôsha was contemporary with Kanishka. As there has been some doubt expressed about this, I will refer to stories 93 and 94 in the above named work called *Samyuktaratnapiṭaka*. In these stories we have mention made of the king called *Chandan-Kanika,* which I can only restore to Kanishka of Gāndhāra. He was a great conqueror, and was converted to Buddhism. In story 94 he is said to have had three friends,—Aśvaghôsha, his spiritual adviser;—*Mo-cha-lo* (Madra), his great minister;—and *Chay-lo-kia* (Jurka ?), his chief physician. We are then told how Kanishka, after a great slaughter of his enemies, relented and desired to pursue a more peaceful life; on which his chief minister intimated that such a desire could scarcely be carried out by such a man as he had been. The king then orders a caldron full of water to be heated to the boiling point, and, this done, he flung into the water his ring, ordering his minister immediately to take it out with his hand. The officer begs to be excused, but in vain; at last, on condition he would take it out, the king permits him to adopt his own method. Of course he takes from under the caldron the fire, and allows the water to cool. Then he removes the ring. "And so," replied the monarch, "even I may gain the treasure of the Law, by extinguishing within me the three fires of lust, hatred, and doubt."

I only refer to this story to shew that Aśvaghôsha was contemporary with Kanishka. But he was probably a young man, and may have succeeded Puṇyayaśas in his old age. At any rate, we cannot accommodate this succession to any date for Nāgārjuna earlier than the latter end of the second century A.D.

According to Tibetan accounts, Nāgārjuna lived some 600 years after Buddha; for this is the only reasonable way of explaining the statement that according to some his life was 71 years short of 600, and according to others 29 years short of that period.[14] This is supposed to be a mistake for 71 or 29 years short of 600 years after Buddha; and if we assume the date of Buddha (according to Tibetan accounts) to be 100 years before Aśôka, this again would give us a date for Nāgārjuna from about a.D. 166 to A.D. 200.

I think we may safely regard this as the nearest approximate date to be got from Chinese or Tibetan sources. I will merely add that the change introduced by Nāgārjuna into the code of Buddhist doctrine was so great that it is said he claimed himself to be the "all-knowing one" (the Omniscient), and that, after his death, *Stūpas* were raised to him, and he was worshipped as Buddha ![15]

References

1. The modern Saṅgalawālāṭibbā in the Pañjāb: see page 246 above, note 9—J.F.F.
2. *Ta-t'sin* in this place must denote the Græeco-Baktrian Empire.
3. Śākala, therefore, at this time was the seat of Greek influence and civilization in North India.
4. Wilson: *Arian Antiq.* page 280.
5. Nanjio's *Catalogue,* No. 1329.
6. *Buddha. Rec. West. World,* Vol. II. p. 210 ff.
7. This is a phonetic representation, and is explained as meaning "he who draws the good," which of course suggests Sadvaha or Sadvahana as the original Sanskṛit word.
8. This expression probably means that it was 300 *li* from the capital of the kingdom.

9. *Buddh. Rec. West World,* Introd. p. lxviii. ff.

10. It seems worth nothing that a Buddhist *Bhadanta* named Nāgārjunachārya is mentioned in one of the inscriptions at the Jaggayyapêṭa *Stūpa,* thirty miles north-west of the well-known Amarāvatī in the Kistna (Kṛishṇā) district (*Archæol. Surv. South Ind.* Vol. III, p. 57). This inscription, however, is in Sanskrit; and, partly for that reason, partly on palæographical grounds, has to be allotted to about the beginning of the seventh century A.D.; and it thus gives about A.D. 650 as the date of this Nāgārjunāchārya—J.F.F.

11. *ching yin; lit.* 'right-drawing.' At one time I thought this was equivalent to the Greek $\sum \omega\tau\eta\rho$.

12. *Nan-hai-khi-kwei-chun,* K. iv. p. 5. I-tsing tells us that the king's title (*ho*) was *Sha-to-po-han-na,* his private or personal name (*ming*) being *Shi-yen-te-kia.*

13. *Buddh. Rec. West World,* Vol. I. p. 151.

14. Vassilief (French Ed.) p. 201 n.

15. Records of the Patriarchs (*Nanjio's Catalogue,* No. 1840) K. v. p. 20. b.

8

The Vicissitudes of the Buddhist Literature of Ceylon

T. Foulkes

The great influence which the historical books of Ceylon have had in the formation of the prevailing views of some portions of the ancient history of India, and especially of its chronology, makes it very desirable that as much as is possible should be known of the history of the literature to which they belong. The recent rapidly accumulating additions from other Buddhist literatures have taken the books of Ceylon out of the isolation in which they formerly stood, and help to throw light upon the legends of the Sinhalese; and they themselves contain an incidental record of the many vicissitudes to which this particular literature was exposed in the midst of the political and religious changes which mark the history of the island. The object of this paper is to bring together that scattered information, and to gather from it whatever it may teach us of the history of this interesting literature.

The authorities here referred to are the Dīpavaṁsa, the Mahāvaṁsa, the Rājaratnākari, the Rājāvali, and some other works which are occasionally quoted below, but need not be separately named here. Of these the *Rājaratnākari* and the *Rājāvali* are written in the Sinhalese language, and are of comparatively recent date.[1] The *Dīpavaṁsa* and the *Mahāvaṁśa* are in the Pāli language, and have both been supposed to belong to the 5th century, A.D.[2] But while there is good evidence in support of the claim of the *Dīpavaṁsa,* in its original form, to that early date, there are strong reasons for regarding the *Mahāvaṁsa* as a work of a considerably later period. Turnour erroneously regarded these two books as identical, and was unable to throw off the idea, although he subsequently had the *Dīpavaṁsa* in his hands, and made an analysis of its contents.[3] The text and an English translation of the *Dīpavaṁsa* were published in 1879 by Professor Oldenberg; and a retranslation of a portion of it by Mr. Donald Ferguson appeared in this journal, *ante,* Vol. XIII, p. 33ff. Oldenberg[4] has shown that the *Dīpavaṁsa* quoted by Buddhaghôsha in the 5th century, A.D., differed in some details from the existing work of that name; still there is sufficient probability on the side of the supposition that the existing recension is at least a close recast of the original work. We have the *Mahāvaṁsa* in two different recensions; one of them is an English translation edited by Upham in 1833, and made for Sir Alexander Johnston, a former Chief Justice of Ceylon; and the other, published in 1837, by the Hon. George Turnour, of the Ceylon Civil Service. Turnour's translation has the great advantage of being accompanied by the Pāli text; but it extends only as far as the 38th chapter, bringing the history down no later than A.D. 477; while the Upham recension contains eighty-eight out of the hundred chapters of which the work consists, and brings the history down to A.D. 1319. The unpublished chapters[5] continue the history down to the latter half of the 18th century.

The traditions to be considered in this paper may be conveniently grouped under the following five periods: –

I From the death of Buddha to the 1st century B.C., forming the so-called unwritten period.

II From the 1st century B.C. to the 5th century A.D., forming the first written period of these legends.

III From the 5th century A.D. to the subversion of Buddhism in Ceylon in the 11th century A.D.

IV From the Buddhist revival in the 11th century A.D. to the second subversion of Buddhism in the 13th century.

V From the second Buddhist revival in the 13th century A.D. to the present time.

Period I

From the death of Buddha to the 1st century B.C.—This period is covered by the following legend of the *Dīpavaṁsa* belonging to the time of king Abhaya Vaṭṭagāmaṇi, whose reign Turnour places in 104 to 76 B.C.[6] "Before this time the wise Bhikkhus had orally handed down the text of the three *Piṭakas* and also the *Aṭṭhakathā*. At this time the Bhikkhus who perceived the decay of created beings, assembled; and in order that the religion might endure for a long time they recorded (the above-mentioned texts) in written books." The text of the Turnour recension of the *Mahāvaṁsa*[7] is, with the exception of one unimportant word, precisely the same here as the *Dīpavaṁsa;* but Turnour's translation has introduced a new element into its meaning;—"The profoundly wise (inspired) priests had therefore orally perpetuated the Pāli *Piṭakattaya* and its *aṭṭhakathā* (commentaries). At this period," &c. His text says nothing whatever of the language of these scriptures; but, as is evident from his use of the capital letter *P* in his text in the word *Pālincha,* he has taken the temporal adverb *pālim,* "before this time" of Oldenberg's version, which is opposed to the similar adverb *hānim,* "at this time," of the succeeding sentence, to mean "the Pāli" language. As this is the first appearance of the Pāli language in the record, it deserves to be noted that it is brought in here quite by mistake.[8] The Upham recension of the *Mahāvaṁsa* and the *Rājāratnākari*[9] repeat the tradition with the addition of a few amplifying words; unless the words "for want to the Pāli books which contained them" in the former of these two authorities mean that these books had formerly existed and had been lost. By the 13th century this legend had acquired a still more distinct form. "The Buddha's doctrines, being written in the Pāli language, which aforetime had been borne by heart by those great learned priests, had been committed to books at the time of the king Walagam-abha."[10] And out of this has ultimately grown the still later tradition,[11] that this king Vaṭṭagāmaṇi was the inventor of the art of writing.

The tradition of the exclusively oral transmission of the whole of the Buddhist canon during the first five centuries after the death of Buddha belongs to the legends of the Southern

Buddhists alone, which have their ultimate source in Ceylon: and assuming the *Dīpavaṁsa,* quoted by Buddhaghôsha, to be substantially the same as Oldenberg's, this tradition was prevalent in the 5th century of the Christian era. Now these scriptures are about twice the size of our Bible,[12] and contain 1,237,000 verses of thirty-two syllables each,[13] occupying 78,871 lines of *talipot* leaf manuscript from 1 ft. 7 in. to 3 feet in length.[14] The enormous memory which the retention of this immense quantity of matter involves presents no difficulty to the Buddhists themselves, who attribute it to the supernatural powers possessed by their teachers during their age of miracles.[15] Amongst European critics, Hardy[16] declined to credit the statement, and, together with Prof. Max Müller,[17] proposed to distribute the contents of the books among many memories. Turnour himself declared that it was "founded on superstitious imposture.[18] Professors Rhys Davids[19] and Oldenberg[20] accept the tradition.

On the other hand, the traditions of the Northern Buddhists, including their Chinese offshoot, regard their canonical scriptures as a written literature preserved in books from Buddha's own days downwards. Buddha himself was a highly educated man according to the manner of the princes of his times.[21] Instance are given of his epistolary correspondence.[22] He was, moreover, an accomplished Sanskṛit scholar,[23] and learned in the philosophies of the Brāhmaṇs. Although his teaching consisted largely of popular oral discourses, it by no means follows that he did not commit anything to writing; and there is actually one record, albeit a solitary one, of a manuscript being found at his death which had been written with his own hand.[24] We cannot ignore the statements which speak of written books in the time of Aśôka in the 3rd century B.C. and even earlier, nor set aside the long stream of indirect evidence which all along assumes and sometimes declares the existence of written books from the beginning. The legends of the Sinhalese themselves are not without some substantial evidence of a more direct kind to the existence of this early written literature,[25] though it is subversive of the general drift of their other traditions; for it is stated in one of their principal historical books that religious books formed a portion of the complimentary presents which Aśoka sent to the king of Ceylon;[26] and the names of some of these books, or of some others which Mahinda, the converter of Ceylon, then brought with him, and the use which he made of them in the course of his teaching, are distinctly mentioned.[27] The same authority[28] also refers to the existence of a portion of the *Sūtra-piṭaka* in Ceylon in a written form in the middle of the 2nd century B.C. It tells us that on a certain occasion king Duṭṭhagāmaṇi assumed the preaching chair and "began to read the book *Maṅgala-sūtra*," with a large assembly of monks for his audience; and it also tells us that this prince possessed other manuscripts besides those of the Buddhist canon; for he "saw once amongst the writings of his ancestors a prediction delivered to his grandfather, king Dêvenipiyatissa by the priest Mihidu-mahāterunvahanse." Again the *Dīpavaṁsa*[29] has a list of eminent Buddhist nuns on the continent of India, who were well versed in the *Vinaya* and other scriptures, from the foster-mother of Buddha downwards, and another similar list, headed by Saṅghamittā, king Aśoka's daughter, who came from India to Ceylon, and taught the whole of the Buddhist canon in Anurādhapura, from the 3rd century of the Buddhist era down to the days of king Abhaya in the dawn of the Christian era. It would be extremely difficult to understand this tradition on any other supposition than that the *Piṭakas* existed during the whole of this time in a written form, and that these written books were in the hands of these learned female teachers.

In the presence of this amount of direct and indirect evidence, which has, moreover, all natural probability on its side, we may be justified in regarding the improbable legend of the exclusively oral transmission of the *Tṛipiṭaka* as a fable put into a form which was calculated to satisfy the faith of the friendly and to silence the taunts of the unbelieving, invented to account for the earliest known traces of written books in Ceylon in the first century B.C. We may further regard the books originally brought to Ceylon as having been lost or destroyed at some time between the death of Mahinda and this date, through the carelessness of the local monks, or the hostility of the foreign rulers of the island, or both combined; for the legend itself admits the increasing ignorance and incapacity of the monks, and the history records the local trials of

Buddhism during this interval. The *Dīpavaṁsa,* in which we first meet with the fable, was not written even in its earliest form until about five centuries after the times of which the legend speaks; and its plausibility would receive additional support from the well-known circumstance that in all ages both the students of the *Vêdas* and the disciples of Buddhism alike received their only legitimate teaching from the living voice of a master, even when written books were abundantly accessible.

The legends regarding the translations of the commentaries on the *Tripiṭaka* in the Sinhalese language, and more particularly the additional Aṭṭhakathā of Mahinda himself, belong to this period of the history of this literature. This tradition appears in the notice of Buddhaghôsha in the Turnour recension of the *Mahāvaṁsa:*[30] – "The Sinhalese *Aṭṭhakathā* are genuine. They were composed in the Sinhalese language by the inspired and profoundly wise Mahinda." But the other authorities do not mention it at all. The more modern tradition is thus stated by Turnour:[31] – "The *Piṭakattaya,* as well as the *Aṭṭhakathā* propounded up to the period of the third convocation in India, were brought to Ceylon by Mahindo, who promulgated them orally here – the *Piṭakattaya,* in Pāli, and the *Aṭṭhakathā* in Sinhalese, together with additional *Aṭṭhakathā* of his own. His inspired disciples and his successors continued to propound them also orally, till the age of inspiration passed away, which took place in this island (as already stated) in the reign of Vattagāmini, between B.C. 104 and B.C. 76. They were then embodied into books, the text in the Pāli and the commentaries in the Sinhalese language. The event is thus recorded in the thiry-third chapter of the *Mahawanso,* p. 207: – 'The profoundly wise,' &c. In the reign of the Rāja Mahānāmo, between A.D. 410 and 432, Buddhaghôsha transposed the Sinhalese *Aṭṭhakathā* also into Pāli. The circumstances is narrated in detail in the 37th chapter of the *Mahāwanso,* p. 250. This Pāli version of the *Piṭakattaya* and the *Aṭṭhakathā* is that which is now extent in Ceylon, and it is identically the same with the Siamese and Burmese versions." The tradition is thus made to rest upon two passages in the Turnour recension of the *Mahāvaṁsa.* The former of these passages, however, neither mentions Mahinda nor his Sinhalese commentaries: on the contrary, it distinctly states that both the text and the commentary of the *Pīṭaka,* which were then committed to writing, were in the Pāli language.[32] The whole legend, indeed, seems clearly to belong to much more modern times, when Sinhalese books had ceased to be a novelty. It reads by the side of the other legends rather as an elaborated invention than an original tradition; and with our present knowledge of the earliest literature of Buddhism, the question of the existence of these Sinhalese commentaries of Mahinda cannot any serious consideration.

Period II

From the 1st century B.C. to the 5th century A.D.—This period opens with the restoration of the legitimate king Vaṭṭ agāmaṇi, Valakan-abha, or Valagambā, in B.C. 88,[33] after a period of usurpation by the Tamils of Southern India.[34] Following a time of civil and religious commotion.[35] The loss of the earlier literature may safely be attributed to these disturbances; and the rise of the new literature, which now replaced it, was one of the results of the royal patronage of the seeding monks of this king's new Monastery of Abhayagiri.[36] The origin of this new literature is thus states in the *Dīpavaṁsa:*[37]—"At this time the Bhikkhus, who perceived the decay of created things, assembled; and in order that the religion might endure for a long time, they recorded the three *Piṭakas* and their commentaries (*aṭṭhakathā*) in written books." The text of the corresponding passage of Turnour's *Mahavaṁsa,*[38] as stated above, is precisely the same, with the exception of an unimportant particle, as the text of Oldenberg's *Dīpavaṁsa:* as also apparently were the equivalent texts of Upham's *Malāvaṁsa*[39] and the *Rājaralnākari*[40] before the glosses were worked into them.[41] The language in which these books are assumed to have been written in those glosses is Pāli; but this, as already out,[42] is due to a palpable error. It is, moreover, at variance with the subsequent traditions that the Ceylonese *aṭṭhakathā* were written in the Sinhalese language, into which Mahinda had translated them. The language of the books of this Abhayagiri revival cannot be determined at present; though the drift of the present evidence points rather strongly towards Sanskṛit, and the sources from which the new recension of the *Piṭakas* and their commentaries was made must also remain over for future investigation.

The *Rājāvali* has no reference whatever to this remarkable event of Vaṭṭagāmaṇi's reign; although it relates the principal circumstances of his reign much like the other authorities. But, if the legend is a corrupted survival of the same tradition, it transfers the transaction to the reign of Vaṭṭagāmaṇi's successor, and converts it into the more commonplace formation of a central library, into which he gathered a good many Buddhist religious books, which were heretofore scattered abroad. "The next king was Maha Dileyaw Tissa Rajah. He entertained five hundred rahatoons, and caused the books concerning the religion of Buddha to be collected and deposited in one place."[43] The *Dīpavaṁsa* and the *Mahāvaṁsa* do not mention this library, and the *Rājaratnākari* omits this king's reign.

It is quite possible that some of these books were recovered from the monasteries of the southern and eastern districts of the island, into which the power of the invaders did not penetrate at this time, and that others were obtained from Southern India. However this may be, we are here clearly in contact with the earliest written books of Ceylon, of which the local memory had any cognizance at the time when these legends were written in their present form.

To this period belongs the thrice-repeated destruction of the books of the heretical Vaitulyas, the first occasion being in the beginning of the third century A.D[44] They made head again during the succeeding half century, and their books were again committed to the flames.[45] From the way they are spoken of, these books seem to have been numerous; but there is no clue to the language in which they were written.

The *Rājaratnākari*[46] states that king Mahāsêna, A.D. 275 to 302, caused a complete copy of Buddha's sermons to be written, which occupied 30,000 volumes; and that he deposited these books in a chest or bookcase made purposely to contain them. He also brought a learned monk from a foreign country to Ceylon, with a retinue of thirty-five companions or disciples, for the purposes of instructing the monks of his own monasteries in the *Vinaya* and the Pāli language. None of the other authorities mention this legend. This circumstances takes something out of the weight of the record; and it may possibly be only an anticipation of the legend of Buddhaghôsha, placed by mistake in the reign of Mahāsêna, instead of in that of Mahānāma.

(*To be continued*)

References

1. Upham's *Sacred and Historical Books of Ceylon,* Intod. pp. viii. xvi.: Turnour's *Mahāwanso,* Introd. p. ii.: Hardy's *Manual of Buddhism,* 519.
2. Turnour, *op. cit.* Intod. p. liv., and notes on pp. xci. and 257.
3. See *Journal* of the Bengal Asiatic Society for 1838, Vol. VII. 919 ff.
4. Introd. p. 9.
5. Turnour's *Synopsis,* Introd. p. xcii.
6. Oldenberg, 211; Turnour, *Mahawanso,* Introd. p. lxi.
7. Turnour, 207.
8. As Upham's version (i. 219) has the same forced construction of the word *pāliṁ* it is probably to be attributed to a native commentary.
9. Upham, I.219; II.43. The *Rājāvali* does not mention it.
10. Upham, I. 332.
11. Upham, III. 161.
12. Prof. Rhys Davids in *Encycl. Brit.* IV. 438.
13. Upham, III. 30.
14. *Journ. As. Soc. Beng.*, VI. 509, 527: Turnour, Introd. (Appendix III), p. lxxv, Hardy's *East. Monach.* 167.
15. *Journ. As. Soc. Beng.*, VI. 506, Turnour, Introd., p. xxviii, xxix.
16. *Eastern Monachism,* 185, 186, 187.
17. *Sacred Books of the East,* X, Introd. p. xxv.
18. Turnour, Introd., p. lvii.
19. *Sacred Books of the East,* XIII.
20. Introd. p. xxxv.
21. Hardy's *Manual of Buddhism,* 147: Rajendralāla Mitra's *Lalitavistara,* 205, 213: Beal's *Romantic History of Buddha,* 68, 85ff: Rockhill's *Life of the Buddha,* 19.

22. Körös' *Tibetan Grammar,* 164: Rockhill, 59.
23. Hardy, *Man. Bud.,* 164ff.: Max. Müller's *Hist. of Ancient Sanskṛit Literature,* 261: Weber's *History of Indian Literature,* 291: Bigandet's *Life of Gaudama,* 65: *Rom. Hist. Bud.,* 155ff: Rockhill, 27ff: Mutu Coomara Swamy's *Dāṭhavaṁsa,* 28: Fytche's *Burma,* II. 152.
24. Kæmpfer's *History of Japan,* I. 245.
25. See., *e.g. Journal As. Soc. Beng.* VII. 282, 922: Upham I. 43, 37, 38: Ward's *Hindoos* (3rd edition), II. 211: Bigandet, 120, note, 350 note, 360 note: *Sacred Books of the East,* X. Introd. p. xii.
26. Ward's *Hindoos,* 1 c. sup.
27. Upham's *Mahavaṁsa,* I. 83: Lindlay's *Fa Hian,* 37, 42.
28. Upham, I. 90, 92, 94.
29. *Ibid.,* p. 200.
30. *Journal As. Soc. Ben.* VII. 932, 933: Oldenberg, 204ff.
31. Turnour, 251.
32. Introd. p. xxix.
33. See also Upham, I. 322.
34. The *Rajāvali* (Uph. II. 224 with 226) puts his date considerably later.
35. Oldenberg's *Dīp.* 207, 211: Upham, I. 218: II. 43, 224: Turnour, 207, and Introd. p. lxi. All the dates in this paper unless specially mentioned, are taken, for the sake of uniformity, from Turnour's Introduction, Appendix, p. lxff.
36. Hiuen Tsiang, (Beal II. 247) tells us that the monks of the Abhayagiri studied both vehicles, and widely diffused the *Tripiṭaka.*
37. Oldenberg, 211.
38. Turnour, 207.
39. Uph. I. 219 with 332.
40. Uph. II. 43.
41. See also Upham, III. 115.
42. *Ante,* p. 101.
43. Upham, II, 224.
44. Upham, I. 231; II. 61, 65ff.
45. *Ibid.* I. 234; II. 65. Turmour's recension (p. 227, 232) records the repeated suppression of this sect; but it does not mention the books.
46. Upham, II. 129.

9

The Vicissitudes of the Buddhist Literature of Ceylon

T. Foulkes

Another noteworthy event of this period is the production of a medical work in the Sanskṛit language by king Buddhadāsa, who reigned in the middle of the 4th century A.D.,[1] which was still extant when the *Mahāvaṁsa* was written. The special significance of this book is, that its royal author, living at a time when, with this single exception, the existence of Sanskṛit books in Ceylon is not mentioned by the native authorities, should have chosen this language for a book whose practical subject shows that he wrote it for more or less public use. It affords reason for the conclusion that, whether known or unknown to the chroniclers, the Sanskṛit language was cultivated in Ceylon at this time, and that books written in that language were sufficiently well-known there in the 4th century A.D.

Both recensions of the *Mahāvaṁsa* attribute to this king's reign translations of some unmentioned portions of the sacred books of Buddhism into the vernacular Sinhalese languages.[2] The Upham recension adds that these translations were made from Pāli texts; but the Turnour recension and the *Rājaratnākari*[3] do not uphold this latter statement; and, if Buddhaghôsha's Pāli texts were the earliest appearance of books in that language in Ceylon, that statement cannot be accepted. The *Rājāvali* does not mention these translations; but it states[4] that this king provided books and preachers for the villages in his dominions.

We have now reached a very interesting epoch in this history of this literature, namely, the visits of the Chinese Buddhist pilgrim Fa-Hian and the famous Pāli scholar Buddhaghôsha. Fa-Hian went to Ceylon in A.D. 411 by the sea-route, from the mouth of the Ganges, and spent two years in the island.[5] He had come to India from China by the long land-route to the north of the Himālayas, in order to search for an authentic copy of the *Vinaya,* one of the three great divisions of the Buddhist canonical scriptures;[6] and although he had visited many monasteries in his route, he had been unsuccessful in his search until, after five years' wanderings, he reached Pāṭaliputra, the modern Pātna, the home of the great Aśoka and his missionary son Mahinda, where he found in one of its monasteries a venerable copy of that work in the Sanskṛit language, which had originally belonged to Buddha's own famous Jêtavana monastery at Śrāvasti.[7] He remained three years at this place studying the Sanskṛit language, reading Sanskṛit books, and copying this great work and other Buddhist books in the same language which he found there. He subsequently spent two years at Tāmraliptī, copying similar books and sketching Buddhist images, and he then embarked for Ceylon.[8]

It is important to remark here that the very ancient copy of the Vinaya, which Fa-Hian found in the capital of the Magadha country – the supposed home of the Pāli language, "the speech of Magadha," and the alleged vernacular of Buddha's own discourses – was written in the Sanskṛit language, as were also the other Buddhist scriptures which he found there. It is equally clear that such imperfect portions of the *Vinaya* as had reached China before Fa-Hian started on this journey were also written in that language[9] and the books which he subsequently copied in Tāmraliptī and Ceylon were in the same language; all of which he "edited" on his return home, with the assistance of the Chinese Sanskṛit scholars of Nankin.[10] All this may not be absolutely decisive of the question of the original language of the Buddhist canonical scriptures: but it has considerable importance in the investigation of that question, especially as no equally trustworthy evidence has yet been discovered of the existence of any portion of the Buddhist canon in the Pāli language as early as this period.[11]

It is also worth while pausing to remark that Fa-Hian found the teachers of the Buddhist monasteries of Mongolia, Afghānistan, the Pañjāb, and North-Western India, as far down as Pāṭaliputra, teaching their pupils the standard works of their religion by word of mouth,[12] although it was from these same countries that the books which they so taught had been brought to China during the previous four centuries, and copies of them were still in existence in Pāṭaliputra, Tāmraliptī and Ceylon at this very time. This circumstance affords to my mind a sufficient solution of the Sinhalese paradox of the exclusively oral transmission of these books down to be 1st century B.C. The kind of oral teaching which Fa-Hian had himself passed through in his youth in China,[13] and which he now found in use amongst the northern Buddhists, while the books were there also, may be accepted as the practice which we still find in all indigenous Hindu schools, and which has existed in them at all times; but at no time did this kind of teaching necessarily presuppose the contemporaneous or previous non-existence of the books which were so taught.

Fa-Hian made some important additions to his previous literary acquisitions during the two years which he spent in Ceylon,[14] and he expressly states that the books which he found there were written in the Sanskṛit language, and the these books were large portions of the *Tripiṭaka*. Moreover, though the argument from silence is not be pressed beyond its value, he does not appear to have seen any books there in the Pāli or any other language but Sanskṛit.

The visit of Buddhaghôsha followed soon after that of Fa-Hian, according to the date which is commonly assigned to him. Various dates, however, have been given to him, ranging from B.C. 307 to A.D. 307. All the details also in the descriptions of his visit differ largely in the different authorities respecting the place from whence he came and the country to which he returned, what his connection were during his stay, and what his object and motive for going to Ceylon, whether he enriched the existing literature of the island by additions which he brought with him, or borrowed from its books to enrich the literature of his own country, or wrote original works of his own. The account which has been commonly received of him is that which is given of him in Turnour's recension of the *Mahāvaṁsa*. This account, however, not only stands alone and unsupported, and differs materially from the statements of the other authorities, but its elaborate details strongly suggest that it is the interpolated work of some suggest that it is the interpolated work of some later commentator rather than the original words of the continuator of the *Māhāvaṁsa*. To enter fully into these conflicting statements would occupy too much space here, but that which arises out of the spirit of the whole of the traditions regarding him is the predominating circumstances of his intimate connection with the traditions of the Pāli language.

He appears also to have been the first to present the Buddhist canonical scriptures in the Pāli dress in which they have since his time been preserved by the Southern Buddhist nations. The Turnour *Mahāvaṁsa* makes his work to be a translation of these scriptures into Pāli, from a version made into Sinhalese by the royal monk Mahinda in the 3rd century B.C.; but this statement[15] does great violence to the whole current of the other more consistent traditions. We shall not be in error probably in supposing the books which he found in Ceylon to be the very same, or similar, Sanskṛit books as Fa-Hian had seen there so recently before, and that Buddha-ghôsha's special work, apart from his original compositions, consisted in transliterating the *Tripiṭaka* and its commentaries out of the Sanskṛit language into the more amenable form of the Pāli Prākṛit, and so adapting them for popular use. The practical service which he would thus have rendered to all future generations of his co-religionists would be amply sufficient to secure for him the high position which he has ever since continued to occupy in their traditions as one of their foremost literary benefactors.

Period III

From the 5th to the 11th centuty A.D. – Very little remains on record on the constructive side of the literature during this period. Soon after Buddhaghôsha's visit a succession of twelve irruptions of the Tamils of the opposite continent of India commences, which form the special subject of the Rājāvali, resulting, notwithstanding some alternating revivals, in the overthrow of the ancient monuments and monasteries of the island, and the repeated suppression of Buddhism, and culminating in the dispersion of its monks and the complete destruction of its ancient literature.

After one of these catastrophes king Dhātusêna, A.D. 459 to 477, inaugurated a restoration of the old religion by convening a council, after the example of Aśôka, to settle anew the text of the canonical books.[16] He also caused the *Dīpavaṁsa* to be publicly read on the site of Mahinda's funeral pyre,[17] in order to stimulate the religious zeal of his people.

Towards the middle of the sixth century, the books of the heretical Vaitulyas were publicly burnt of the heretical Vaitulyas were publicly burnt for the third time.[18] And then a long barren period succeeds down to the middle of the 9th century, which is only broken by the appearance of the Laṅkāvistariyaye, a Sinhalese work which Sir Emerson Tennent attributes to the 7th century,[19] and by the despatch of the Brāhmaṇ priest, in A.D. 746, by the king of Ceylon, on an embassy to the emperor of China, bearing, together with other royal presents, a copy of the great Prajñā-sūtra.[20]

The poet-king Mutwāle-Sêna, A.D. 838 to 858, explained the *Sūtra-piṭaka* in public,[21] according to the legend of the Upham *Mahāvaṁsa.* The *Rājaratnākari,* however, from the traditions of a different school, states that this king, under the influence of a heterodox monk from India, was turned away from the orthodox creed, and "rejected and laid aside the precepts taught by the books and sermons of Buddha, and adopted the maxims of other systems of religion."[22]

His successor, Kāśyapa IV. or Madisên-Sêna, A.D. 858 to 891, did his best to counteract this evil. He "encouraged the priests of Buddha to re-establish their religion and to oppose the false religion throughout all his dominions, caused the coasts of the island to be diligently watched to prevent the approach of Buddha's enemies, and reigned as a good king; but, notwithstanding all this precaution, it was only like enclosing a field of corn after driving oxen into the same to eat it up, for a number of unbelievers were already in the island."[23]

The end was not far off now. The *Mahāvaṁsa* states that at the close of this period the "religion" "was overthrown by the Malabars during the term of eighty-six years."[24] The *Rājaratrākari*[25] similarly states that during the nineteen reigns which preceded that of Mahalu-Vijayabāhu, in A.D. 1071, "the Malabars kept up a continual was with the Ceylonese, and had filled by this time every city and village in the whole island," and that these Malabars, "as far as they did prevail, abolished the laws and religion of Budha."[26] So also that *Rājāvali*[27] states that they "vanquished Ceylon and subverted the religion of Budha."

Soon afterwards, in the reign of Udaya II, A.D. 926 to 937, the open wickedness of this immoral sect attracted the attention of the king, who, after an examination of their books, "shut them all together in a house, with their books, and, setting fire to the same, burnt the whole to ashes."[28]

In the latter half of the 10th century the rich and learned king Kāśyapa VI, A.D. 954 to 964, caused the *Abhidharma-piṭaka* to be engraved on golden plates and adored it with precious stones.[29]

Period IV

From the 11th to the 13th century A.D.: king Mahalu-Vijayabāhu, A.D. 1071 to 1126, vanquished these Malabars, and "united the three kingdoms of Ceylon under the same banner;"[30] and he then set about the restoration of Buddhism. At this time "there were not five monks left" in Ceylon, or, as the *Rājāvali* more emphatically says, "the Malabars had completely extirpated the priests of Buddha, so that a yellow robe was no more to be found.[31]

He therefore sent large presents to the king of Aramana,[32] on the coast of Coromandel, and obtained from him a mission of twenty or twenty-nine monks, to confer ordination on the ministry of the revived church; and these foreign monks brought with them their books to form the nucleus of its new literature.

Sir Emerson Tennent guesses that this kingdom of Aramana may be a part of the Indo-Chinese Peninsula, probably between Arracan and Siam,[33] and Turnoun[34] had already, without giving any authority, fixed it an Arracan; but the passages in the *Rājaratdākari,*[35] the *Rājāvali*[36] and the *Mahāvaṁsa,*[37] in which it is mentioned, clearly locate it on the Coromandel coast; and, as it is not Pāṇḍya nor Chôḷa, the only part of that coast which remains is that which lies between Chôḷa and Kaliṅga, namely, the old dominions of the Pallavas.

It is possible that the following passage in General Fytche's *Burma*[38] may in some may be connected with this Ceylonese legend: – "In 1080 A.D. [which falls in the reign of Mahala

Vijayabāhu] the Talaings were conquered by Anauratā, the Burmese king of Pagān, who burnt and sacked Thatūn, and took away with him to Pagān the Buddhist scriptures brought by Buddhaghôsha, as also the most learned of the priesthood;" since, besides the coincidence of time, the name of this Burmese king corresponds with that of "the foreign king," 'Anoorudda,' the friend of Vijayabāhu, as given in the *Mahāvaṁsa* version of the tradition.[39]

His son Parākramabāhu, A.D. 1153 to 1186, maintained this revival on the orthodox basis of the *Tripiṭaka,*[40] even in the midst of the excitement of rebellions, invasions and counter-invasions,[41] he provided two libraries in the palace which he erected for the head of the Mahāvīra monastery,[42] and restored a hundred and twenty-eight libraries elsewhere.[43] The Abhidhānappadīpika, a Pāli dictionary, was complied in his reign.[44]

His queen, Līlāvatī, was a Pāṇḍyan princess[45] and a patroness of learning; and during her triple reign, A.D. 1197, 1209 and 1211, she specially patronized the author of the *Dāṭ hāvaṁsa*. This work is mentioned in the Turnour recension of the *Mahāvaṁsa,*[46] and, that being so, the date of this recension of the *Mahāvaṁsa* has to be brought down to some time later than the reign of queen Līlāvatī in the 12th and 13th centuries, instead of standing in the 5th century A.D. as its commentator tried to persuade his readers. A commentary on the Sanskṛit grammar of Chandragāmi glosses on the *Samanta-pāsādikā* commentary on the *Viṇaya* and on a commentary on the *Anguttara,* the *Vinaya-saṅgaha,* and other works in the Pāli and Sinhalese languages, were written in her reign,[47] which was a period of unusual literary activity, her Pāṇḍyan friends probably contributing their share of materials for it.

Paṇḍit Vijayachakka, A.D. 1186, was a learned prince and a Pāli scholar, and he composed poems in that language.[48] Hardy[49], doubtfully supposes this king to be the author of a commentary on Buddhaghôsha's *Visuddhimārga,* but his short reign precludes the supposition that he could have written a work of that magnitude while he occupied the throne. Perhaps it belongs to the reign of one of the other Vijayachakkas.

The new life which had thus been given to Ceylonese Buddhism was not destined to last much longer; a series of weak reigns, with a fresh series of invasions from the continent of India, followed rapidly upon each other from A.D. 1196 to 1235; and these invaders "began to destroy both the country and religion;" the monks were "hunted from place to place and had lost all their book by the Malabars;" and, to crown the destruction, the last of these invaders made the reigning king prisoner, put out his eyes, "and extirpated the established religion." The recently resuscitated literature of the island naturally fell in for its share of these calamites: and at length "all the books which had been written [from the time of Valagam Abhaya] had been from time to time destroyed by the Malabars," so that on their recall "the priests for want of books to remind them of their duty had forgotten to know good from evil.[50]

Period V

From the 13th century A.D. to the present time—Kalinga Vijayachakka, A.D. 1235 to 1266, succeeded in rescuing Ceylon from these usurpers,[51] and he made great efforts to revise its old theology and to restore its lost literature.[52] He caused copies of the *Tripiṭaka* to be made at great expense, and placed one of them in every village throughout the island; he employed the more learned to teach the younger and more ignorant of his monks, and he sent to India for ten monks to confer ordination in his confer ordination in his new church[53] Thus a complete re-establishment of Buddhism was effected in his dominions after its complete extirpation in the preceding reigns. This new order was once more built upon a foreign basis, and its new literature, which may be regarded as the nucleus of all the present literature of the island, was in the first instance obtained from the Chôḷas of Southern India, who had by this time annexed the Pallava and Eastern Chālukya provinces on the coast to their original dominions in the basin of the Kāvêrī.

His valiant son, Parākramabāhu III, A.D. 1266 to 1301, maintained and greatly extended his father's work; he procured learned monks from the Chôḷa country to teach the *Tripiṭaka* to his people; he obtained books also from Southern India, and he settled a new local canon of the Buddhist scriptures.[54]

Moreover, he himself taught his brother the orthodox doctrines of his religion, and caused him to teach them to the monks in his monasteries, and he still further popularized the revival by causing several portions of the scriptures to be translated into (apparently) the vernacular Sinhalese.[55] The Pūjavaliya, one of the Sinhalese historical authorities, was written in his reign,[56] so also was the continuation of the *Mahāvaṁsa* from the reign either of Mahāsêna or the Mahānāma down to the present reign,[57] and I do not see any reason to suppose that he did not, at the same time, at least recast the earlier portions of that work.

Bhuvanêkabāhu I, A.D. 1303 to 1314, made the contents of the *Tripiṭaka* still more widely known by multiplying copies of it and distributing them to all the monasteries of his kingdom,[58] and another legend[59] states that the copies which he so multiplied were of two only of three *Piṭakas,* which a third legend[60] confines them to the *Sūtrapiṭaka* alone.

Upon his death the old clouds began again to roll up darkly over the island; a Pāṇḍyan army landed upon its shores, "and began to lay waste the country and extirpate the religion of Buddha."[61] This time, however, the troubles lasted but a short time, and the new king, Parākramabāhu IV, A.D. 1314 to 1319, succeeded in making peace with the enemy.[62] This prince's tutor taught him to be interested in the Jātakas, or legends of Buddha's numerous incarnations; he had them translated into the Sinhalese language, and, after the translation had been revised by competent scholars, he distributed copies of these legends throughout his dominions, placing the original in the custody of his chief priest.[63]

For nearly a century after the close of this king's reign in the Ceylonese legends are barren of all literary notices, with the single exception of the appearance of the Nikāya-saṅgraha, one of the minor historical authorities in the Sinhalese language, which is assigned,[64] to the reign of Bhuvanêkabāhu IV, A.D. 1347 to 1361.

In the 15th century Parākramabāhu VII, A.D. 1410 to 1462, caused new commentaries to be written upon the Buddhist scriptures, apparently in the Sinhalese language, and he rewarded the authors of these expositions with grants of land and promoted them to higher orders.[65] Possibly these may be the Sinhalese commentaries on Buddhaghôsha's Visuddhi-mārga: if, as is probable, they were written at this time.[66] The Saddharmālaṅkāra also belongs to this king's reign.[67]

There are no indications in these books that Ceylon derived any of its literature from India at a later date than this; the last embers of Buddhism were then fast expiring there. The more recent sources of this literature were the Buddhist countries to the east of the Bay of Bengal, which had originally obtained their religious book from Ceylon.[68] There was a constant commercial intercourse with these countries from early times, frequent interchanges of complimentary and religious embassies also took place between their sovereigns,[69] and their canonical scriptures are identical with those of Ceylon.[70] The monasteries of the maritime districts of the island enriched their libraries from time to time by fresh additions of manuscripts brought to them by ship; and it is still in these seaside monasteries alone that the *Tripiṭaka* is to be found complete.[71] Some of these contributions were probably enough a restoration of some of the lost books of Ceylon, which had been carried to those countries by the Ceylonese monks when fleeting from thesis persecutions at home, and others were copies of the older manuscripts transliterated in the characters of their new homes. Professor Oldenberg has informed us[72] that all the manuscript copies of the *Dīpavaṁsa* which he used for his work bear marks of having been derived from one and the same Burmese original; and the first discovered copy of that work was written in the Burmese character, and was found by Mr. Turnour amongst some manuscripts which had been brought to Ceylon from Siam.[73] It was also from that collection of Siamese manuscripts that he obtained a reliable copy of the commentary on the *Mahāvaṁsa* which he used for his translation of that work. The Colonial Library of Ceylon contains manuscripts which were presented by the king of Burma,[74] and the monastery-libraries of the island possess manuscripts which were "brought from the Camboja country," written in the character which is used there.[75] The Mutaliyār, George Nadoris, brought back to Ceylon a valuable collection of Pāli books on his return from Siam in A.D. 1812.[76] Previous to this time an embassy of Buddhist priests from Siam arrived in Ceylon in A.D. 1758, bringing presents of books with them, and similar earlier religious missions from that country brought similar complimentary presents with them.[77]

References

1. A.D. 339 to 368. Turnour, 245; Introd., p. lxii. The record of this work is confined to the Turnour *Mahāvaṁsa*.
2. Upham, I. 238; Turnour, 247.
3. Upham, II. 129.
4. *Ib.* II. 241.
5. *Fa-Hian's Travels,* Chap. XXXII. By means of these general references to the chapters of Fa-Hian's book the reader will be able to consult any one of the versions which may be most convenient to himself.
6. *Fa-Hian,* chap. XXXVI.
7. *Fa-Hian,* chap. XXXVI.
8. *Fa-Hian,* chap. XXXVII.
9. For illustrations of Fa-Hian's statements on this subject, see the Rev. Samuel Beal's Introduction to his translations of the works of this Chinese traveller and of Hiuen Tsiang; and also Dr. Edkins' *Chinese Buddhism,* p. 401ff.
10. *Fa-Hian,* chap. XL.
11. The supposition that Pāli books existed in China, which originated in an error of Gutzlaff (*Sketch of Chinese History,* I. 250, and another work quoted in Fortune's *Wanderings,* p. 186), may now be regarded as exploded. [See Medhurst's *China, its State and Prospects,* p. 206, and Edkins *op. cit. sup.* p. 402]. It seems also high time to discard the idea that the Pāli of the Southern Buddhists was at any time the spoken language of Magadha.
12. *Fa-Hian,* chap. XXXVI.
13. He was able to recite the *Sūrānga Sūtra* from memory on the spot where Buddha had delivered it (*Fa-Hian,* chap. XXIX) before he learnt Sanskṛit systematically at Pāṭaliputra.
14. *Fa-Hian,* chap. XL.
15. See *ante,* p. 103.

16. Upham, I. 241; II. 75: Turnour, 256.
17. Turnour, 257.
18. Upham, I. 242; II. 61, 65, 77.
19. Tennet's *Ceylon,* I. 494.
20. *Ibid.,* I. 621, note 2.
21. *Ibid.,* I. 249.
22. Upham, II. 81, 82.
23. Upham, II. 251.
24. Upham, I. 253.
25. Upham, II. 85.
26. Upham, II. 84.
27. Upham, II. 251.
28. Upham, II. 83.
29. Upham, I. 218.
30. Upham, I, 252; II. 85, 252.
31. Upham, II. 252.
32. Upham, I. 253; II. 85, 86, 252; Davy's *Ceylon,* 301.
33. Introd. p. xv.
34. *Ceylon,* I. 406, note.
35. Upham, II. 86, 87.
36. *Ib.* II. 147, 252, 254.
37. Upham, I. 293.
38. Vol. II. 170.
39. Upham, I. 253. The intermediate reign of Vikramabāhu, A.D. 1127, is passed over lightly in the legends. His daughter is the heroine of the *Ratnāvali* (*Wilson, Hindu Theatre,* II. 314). [Phayre, *History of Burma,* p. 37, dates that Anaurathā is said to have communicated with Ceylon direct, and that he invaded Arracan (pp. 37, 46)—ED].
40. Upham, I. 271, 298: II. 86, 252.
41. Upham, I. 280, 287, 292, 296, 298; II. 87, 253.
42. Upham, I. 300.
43. Upham, I. 312.
44. Turnour, Introd., p. xxxvii.

45. *Journal As. Soc. Beng.* VI. 258. Mutu Coomāra Swāmy's *Dāṭhāvaṁsa,* 24. Turnour (*loc. cit.*) sometimes confounds the Pāli *Dāṭhāvaṁsa* with the Sinhalese *Daladāvaṁsa.*
46. Turnour, 241.
47. *Dāṭhāvaṁsa,* Introd. p. xix. 80.
48. Upham, I. 313.
49. *Man. Bud.,* 512.
50. Upham, I. 318, 319, 322, 323; II. 93, 95, 97, 98, 256, 257, 259.
51. Upham, I. 319; II. 94, 257.
52. Upham, I. 322; II. 97ff, 258.
53. Upham, I. 324; II. 98, 106, 257, 259.
54. Upham, I. 330, 331; II. 106, 261.
55. Upham, I. 344.
56. Turnour, Introd. p. ii.; Hardy's Man. Bud., 518.
57. Turnour, Introd., p. ii.
58. Upham, I. 354; III. 354.
59. Upham, II. 107.
60. Upham, II. 250.
61. Upham, I. 355; II. 108, 263.
62. Upham, I. 355; II. 108.
63. Upham, I. 356; Upham's *History of Buddhism,* 32.
64. Turnour, Introd. p. ii.
65. Upham, I. 113.
66. Hardy, *Man. Bud.* 512.
67. *Ibid.,* 518.
68. Turnour, Introd. p. xxx: Hardy, *E. Monach,* 365, Bigandet, Introd. p. ix: Tennent's *Ceylon,* i. 416.
69. Tennent's *Ceylon,* I. 416, 607 ff.
70. *Journal As. Soc. Beng.* vi. 503: Turnour, Introd. p. xxx, Hardy's *E. Monach.,* 330.
71. Turnour, Introd., p. xxx.
72. *Dīpavaṁsa,* Introd. p. 11.
73. *Jour. As. Soc. Beng.,* vi. 790; vii. 922.
74. Oldenberg's *Dīpavaṁsa,* Introd. p. 10.

75. Upham, III. 171, 185.

76. *Journal As. Soc. Beng.*, vi. 790: Turnour, Introd. p. xxxi: Hardy, *E. Monach,* 328.

77. Turnour, Introd. p. ii.

10

Ārya Śūra's Jātakamālā and the Frescoes of Ajaṇṭā

Heinrich Lüders, *Ph. D.*

Translated from the Nachrichten von der Königl, Gesellschaft der Wissenschaften zu Göttingen, Phil.-hist. Kl, 1902, pp. 758 to 762

[The following is a translation of a paper read to the Göttingen Royal Society, 13th December, 1902. As will be seen it is based on a passage in No. 10 of the Miscellaneous publications of the Archæological Survey of Western India (Bombay, 1881). There, at page 81, a lithograph of tracings of inscriptions in Cave II, is given, and in the text Paṇḍit Bhagwānlāl Indraji's readings and remarks on the inscriptions are interspersed with my account of their positions in relation to the accompanying frescoes. The epigraphs are often so faint that it was almost impossible to trace them correctly, and mistakes were almost unavoidable; for example, in the case of No. 7 on the plate (Dr. Lüders's last), the abrasion of the upper left arm of the *m* left only *ch*. In other cases mislections seem to have been made in the transcripts, and in the following I shall not follow Dr. Lüders in repeating these and then correcting them by the facsimiles, but substitute at once the readings of the latter in place of the transcriptions, along with his parallel quotations from the *Jātakamālā*. The paintings and inscriptions in question are in a small chamber outside and to the left of Cave II, and unfortunately the former are as much destroyed as the latter, and Mr. Griffths made no copies of the frescoes in this apartment – J. Burgess.]

The twenty-eighth story of the Jātakamāla – the Kshāntijātaka,[1] – is a version of the legend of Kshāntivādin found in the Pāli collection of the Jātakas (No. 313)[2] and in the Mahāvastu (tom. III. p. 357). The contents of the Jātaka, according to the representation of Ārya-Śūtra, are briefly as follows: –

The Boddhisattva lived in a forest as a pious hermit. As he was fond of making forbearance the subject of his discourses, people called him Kshāntivādin – the preacher of patience. Now once on a hot summer day the king of the country with his harem were walking in that forest. Becoming tired from the walk and the drinking freely of wine, he lay down to sleep. When the women saw that their lord had fallen asleep, they wandered about at pleasure in the wood and came to the hermitage of Kshāntivādin, who at once employed the opportunity to give them an edifying sermon on patience. Meanwhile the king awoke, sought for the women, and when he found them as they were sitting in a circle round the hermit, listening to his discourse, he fell into a terrible rage. The women seek to soothe him, but their pleading is in vain, and – filled with fear – they draw back. Meanwhile Kshāntivādin remains quite calm: he warns the king against too hasty action and advises him to cultivate patience. In fierce wrath the king draws his sword and strikes off the hermit's right hand, but his patience is not disturbed by this; even when the king hacks off one limb after another he has only a feeling of pity for the angry man. The merited punishment overtakes the latter: as he is just about to leave the wood, the earth opens and swallows him. The people of the country dreaded a like fate for themselves; but Kshāntivādin calmed their fears and, remaining true to his principles till death, when dying he blessed his murderers.

This story was pictorially represented in the frescoes of a small chamber outside and to be left of Cave II. at Ajaṇṭā. In the *Inscriptions from the Cave-Temples of Western India,* p. 81,[3] Burgess says that "on the back wall to the right of a door in it, a man is represented seated on a stool (*bhadrāsana*) in a plain dress indicative of a Sādhu or Brāhmaṇ; his head is destroyed."

Under his seat, in letters of about the sixth century, is one word which Bhagwānlāl Indraji read *Kshāntivādiḥ* and translated "a discourse on forbearance." This is surprising seeing that in a foot-note[4] it is remarked that Kshāntivādin was the name of Gautama Buddha in one of his previous birtha. It is, of course, the name of the person represented above, as also for example in Cave XVII, the figures are marked by accompanying inscriptions – as king Śibi or Indra.

Facing Kashāntivādin, according to Burgess, is represented another seated figure, and below is a stripe of green colour on which an inscription is painted in two lines, so mutilated as to be untranslateable. Sergius F. Oldenburg has already expressed the surmise[5] that this inscription contains verses from a version of the Jataka. I believe I can prove that the inscription is taken from stanzas 4, 15 and 19 of the Kshāntijātaka of the Jātakamālā.

In the following I have printed the stanzas named, whilst immediately below I have passed the text of the inscription from Bhagwānlāl Indraji's *lithographed tracings*[6]: –

nivasanti hi yatraiva santaḥ sadguṇabhūshaṇāḥ |

. . . . ha *yatrava rānta sadgu . .bhushaṇā*

tan maṅgalyaṁ manojñaṁ cha tat tīrthaṁ tat tapovanam | | 4 | |

tan ma . . . . . . nājña na . . . .

ngarhitāṁ jātīm avāpya mānushīm anūnabhāvaṁ paṭubhis tathendriyaiḥ |

agahi . . nītim avāpya mānusha . . . . .pāṭu . . s tachendriyai

avaśyamṛityur nna karoti yaḥ śubhaṁ pramādabhāk pratyaham esha vaṁchyate | | 15 | |

avakyamṛityu nnaṁ karoti yaḥ śubhaṁ prem[ā]da*chā . . kyacham ema* daṁ*nyate.*

alaṁkriyante kusumair mahīruhās taḍidguṇais toyavilambino ghaṇāh |

. . *śāyanta kusumair mahirubās* ta *dāguse . . . ntin*[o] *ghanā*

sarāṁsī mattabhramarais saroruhair guṇait vviśeshādhigatais tu dehinaḥ | | 19 | |

*sarāsi mantabhramates saro*ru . . . . . *rvvichāva . . . . kshā hīṇa . .*

It hardly needs further proof that the two texts are identical, and in every case where the inscription differs from the Jātakamālā, it is evidently an incorrect copy.[7] The contents of these three stanzas clearly indicate what was the subject of the picture above. The first stanza praises the place in the wood where Kshāntivādin had settled; the other two verses are taken from the discourse which he delivered to the king's wives. Thus the picture evidently represented this sermon, and the figure sitting opposite to the hermit, of which Burgess speaks, was probably one of the royal women.

Under this picture there was another which Burgess describes thus : – "Below this is a Brāhmaṇ or Pāśupata, seated on a stool in plain dress and with a *rudrāksha* rosary about his neck. Opposite him is another male figure, and between them a woman is seated, with her hands joined towards the former, whilst she is speaking to the second." Under these figures again is an inscription, which proves to be a rendering of śloka 56 of the Kshāntijātaka. With the correct text it runs thus: –

gātrachchhedepy akshatakshāntidhīraṁ chittaṁ tasya prekshamāṇasya sādhoḥ |

nātrachchhedity akshatakshāntichiraṁ chit[t]*a tasya preksha* . . . .

nāsīd duḥkhaṁ pritiyogān nṛipaṁ tu bhrāshṭaṁ dharmād vīkshya santāpam āpa | |56| |

. . . .*prītisaṁnyāna maha tāṁ nasa* . . . . . *nātra nādevādh āra*

It is scarcely possible without an examination of the fresco itself, to determine what part of the story the picture represented was, to which these verses belong. They glorify rest of spirit which did not forsake the Kshāntivādin, even under the fearful tortures inflicted by the king, and from this it might be inferred that the scene of the mutilation was represented. Burgess' description of the people, in whom we have no difficulty in recognising Kshāntivādin, the king, and one of the wives praying for mercy on the ascetic – seems, on the other hand, to indicate that the scene preceding the actual mutilation was depicted.

The Kshāntijātaka is not the only story from the Jātakamālā which has served the Ajaṇṭā artists as a subject. On the right side wall of the same chamber, near the front corner, there is, according to Burgess,[8] the figure of a king seated on a throne, which bears an inscription that Bhagwānlāl Indraji doubtfully read as *Chaitrivalorkīrājā,* and explained as 'King Chaitra of Valorka.'

The correct reading, however, is certainly *Maitrībalo . . . rājā,*[9] and the picture represents the Boḍhisattva in his former birth as Maitrībala. The history of this king forms the subject of the eighth story of the Jatakamālā.[10] Maitrābala is there held up as a pattern of human kindness; he goes so far in his goodness that once he satisfied with his own flesh and blood five Yakshas who asked him for food.

The correctness of my explanation is proved by the inscription which, according to Burgess, is round above the representation of the king. It is much mutilated, but sufficient is left to identify it undoubtedly with śloka 44 of the Maitribalajātaka. The stanza and Bhagwānlāl Indraji's tracing of the text run thus:—

hriyamāṇāvakāśaṁ tu dānapritya punaḥ punaḥ |

. . . . *nā*

na prasehe manas tasya chchhedaduḥkhaṁ vigāhitum | |

*na prasehe manas vasyā traivaduḥkhā vigāhi*tum

I-tsing tells us how widespread and popular was the Jātakamālā in India at the end of the seventh century. The inscriptions at Ajaṇṭā, in characters that belong to about the sixth century, prove that the work held as high a reputation a hundred years earlier.

Other Jātakas in the Ajaṇṭā Frescoes[11]

Dr. Sergius F. Oldenburg in 1895 published a paper on the representations of the Jātakas on Buddhist monuments. His results are of the utmost value, and the communication was translated from the Russian in the *Journal of the American Oriental Society* (Vol. XVIII. pp. 183ff), 1897. In this Dr. Oldenburg expressed the difficulty of satisfactory identification of the scenes in the almost complete absence of reproductions (*ib.* pp. 195, 196). Mr. Griffiths' work, *The Paintings in the Buddhist Caves of Ajaṇṭā* (1886), had not then appeared. But even this great work does not remove all impediments; for, of the 320 pieces, large and small, copied between 1872 and 1885, half were destroyed by fire at South Kensington Museum soon after they were hung up, and the 159 plates in Mr. Gṛiffiths' work represents about eighty-five of his canvases, and the these fully 40 per cent. are decorative details—contained in the second volume. To study the subjects of the very interesting paintings in the Ajaṇṭā Caves, a more complete series of the scenes, drawn in outline and lithographed, should be in the hands of scholars. Meanwhile the meagre information available has been carefully studied; and Dr. S.F. Oldenburg, solely on the basis of the description in *Notes on the Bauddha Rock-Temples of Ajaṇṭā, their paintings an sculptures, &c.,*[12] has made the following identification: –

1. Cave II., Nos. viii, ix, page 32 (*cf.* below No. 5) ...534[13] Mahā-Haṁsa jātaka.
2. Cave II., No. xxvii, p. 38 ... ... 482 Ruru.
3. Cave IX., No. i, p. 47 (*cf.* below No. 11) ... 499 Sivi.[14]
4. Cave X., p. 50 ... ... 514 Chad-danta.[14,15]
5. Cave XVII., No. xix, pp. 65-66 (*cf.* above No. 1)534 Mahā-haṁsa
6. Cave XVII., Nos. xxii-xxiv, pp. 66-67 ... ... W. 539 Mahā-vessantara (?).
7. Cave XVII., N. xxv, p. 67 ... ... 516 Mahā-kapi.
8. Cave XVII., Nos. xxxvi-xxxvii, p. 70 ... . 455 Māti-posaka.
9. Cave XVII., No. xxxviii, p. 71 ... ... W. 532 Sāma (?).
10. Cave XVII., xxxix, p. 71... ... ... 278 Mahisa.
11. Cave XVII., No. liv, pp. 75-76 (*cf.* above 3) ... 499 Sivi.[16]
12. Cave II., Outside chamber to the left, pp. 81-82 313 Khanti-vādi.

References

1. [Kern's edition in Lanman's Harvard Oriental Series, pp. 181-192–J.B.]
2. [*The Jāṭaka,* ed. by E.B. Cowell, Vol. XII. pp. 26-29. –J.B.]
3. The paintings referred to here are not contained in the fine work by J. Griffiths–*The Paintings of the Buddhist Cave-Temples of Ajanta.* I have therefore been throughout confined to the publication by Burgess and Bhagwānlāl Indraji. –[See above–J.B.]
4. [This footnote was added by me–J.B.]
5. *Jour. Amer. Or. Soc.* Vol. XVIII. p. 196–[See below.]

6. [I have, as stated above, changed the transcribed readings for those of the facsimiles, printing the more doubtful syllables in roman type – J.B.]
7. [The original is so faded and indistinct that a correct copy is impossible. The corrections made from the facsimile are indicated by roman letters. I omit some remarks by Dr. Lüders on the discrepancies here – J.B.]
8. *Loc. cit.*, p. 82.
9. The *rki* standing between the two words, looks more like *ki* in the facsimile. It cannot, of course, be right, but I cannot propose a satisfactory correction.
10. [Kern's ed. pp. 41-50 – J.B.]
11. [I add the following as connected with Dr. Lüders's paper, and of interest to such as may not have seen Dr. Oldenburg's paper – J.B.]
12. *Archæological Survey of Western India,* No. 9, Bombay, 1879.
13. These numerals refer to the current numbers of the Jātaka-tales in Fausböil's edition or to those of Westergaard's Catalogue.
14. Pointed out by Burgess.
15. See Burgess, *Report on the Buddhist Cave-Temples, &c. Arch. Sur. West India,* Vol. IV. pp. 45-46. *Cf.* L. Feer, Le Chaddants-jātaka, *Jour. As.* IX Ser. tom. V. (1895), pp. 31-35 and 189-228. [See also Cunningham *Bharhut Stūpa,* pl. xxvi, fig. 6.]
16. See Burgess, *Report on the Buddhist Cave-Temples, &c. Arch. Sur. West India,* Vol. IV. pp. 45-46. *Cf.* L. Feer, Le Chaddants-jātaka, *Jour. As.* IX Ser. tom. V. (1895), pp. 31-35 and 189-228. [See also Cunningham *Bharhut Stūpa,* pl. xxvi, fig. 6.]

11

The Dīpavamsa and the Mahavamsa and the Historical Tradition in Ceylon

Wilhelm Geiger; *Erlangen*

A condensed translation by Miss C.A. Nicolson, M.A.

[The great value of Dr. Geiger's researchers into the development of the historical literature of Ceylon, and the importance of that literature in connexion with the evolution of chronological details, both historical and religious, are so well known, that we cannot doubt that all readers of the *Indian Antiquary* will welcome the condensed translation here given, with the permission kindly accorded by him, of his latest writing on these topics, and that many of them will be led to look into the German work itself for the full treatment of the themes.

While dealing chiefly with the Dīpavaṁsa and the Mahāvaṁsa, – the two works which must always rank foremost in this line until any of the older compositions may be recovered, – and with the Commentary on the Mahāvaṁsa, Dr. Geiger has here handled also other writings which, arranged in chronological order, are as follows: –

1. Samanta-Pāsādikā of Buddhaghosa (first third of 5th century).
2. Mahābodhivaṁsa (last quarter of 10th century).
3. Dāṭhāvaṁsa (shortly after 1211), with Daḷadāpūjāvali (about 1300).
4. Pāli Thūpavaṁsa (about 1250), and Singhalese Thūpavaṁsa (shortly before 1260).
5. Dhātuvaṁsa (date unknown).
6. Pūjāvali (second half of 13th century).

7. Nikāyasaṅgraha (end of 14th century).
8. Rājaratnākara (middle of 16th century).
9. Rājāvali (beginning of 18th century).

In the original work, an appendix (pages 120–146) gives a comparative analysis of the Dīpavaṁsa and the Mahāvaṁsa, with references to parallel passages in the other literature. This most valuable appendix must be consulted in the original, where it is presented in such a form as to be easily capable of being used even by those who do not read German–Editor]

Introduction

Introd. pp. 1–4

There is hardly any part of the mainland of India, respecting whose history we are so well informed as that of the Island of Ceylon. Two chronicles in Pāli verse–the Dipavaṁsa and the Mahāvaṁsa, the former composed in the 4th century, the latter about the end of the 5th–form our most important authorities. They contain the same material, and mainly in the same arrangement. They begin with the history of Gotama Buddha and his three visits to Laṅkā. After this, a genealogical section is inserted, which traces back the family of Buddha to the mythical king Mahāsammata. Then the two chronicles follow out the history of Buddhism to the third Council under king Aśoka. Thereafter, the narrative goes back to the ancient history of Ceylon and the first settlement of the island by Aryan immigrants under the leadership of Vijaya, and then it follows the line of ancient Singhalese kings to the death of Mahāsena at the beginning of the 4th century A.D. The reign of Aśoka's contemporary, king Devānampiyatissa, is treated with especial detail; it was in his time that Mahinda, Aśoka's son, introduced Buddhist learning into Ceylon. The Mahāvaṁsa recounts with similar detail the deeds of Duṭṭhagāmani, whose reign in the 2nd century B.C. represents the heroic epoch in Ceylon.

In India the writing of history has not been quite separated from poetry, so we need not be surprised that the two Ceylonese chronicles likewise contain a medley of myths, legends, tales and historical material. The further back into the past we go, the more mythical do the statements sound. Similarly, as we approach the time of the authors, their credibility increases. Even the later sections, however, naturally demand historic criticism.

Whoever may write the history of Ceylon, has to extract the kernel of the actual from these traditions. The literary historian will, however, rejoice in the very veil in which the myths have clothed events. He will trace the origin of epic tradition, its development, and its survival in later literature. These are the problems of whose solution we would apply the following investigation.

We are here in the almost unique position of tracing how an epic sets out an a literary course. We are in a position to form for ourselves a picture of the contents and form of the chronicle which was the ground-work of the epic poem, and of the diverse elements out of which it was composed. We can still observe the traces and signs of the originally oral tradition, which, however, lies far back in time, and the co-mingling of prosaic and matrical forms. The Dīpavaṁsa represents the first clumsy effort to fashion an epic poem out of the material already available. It is a document which arouses our attention, from the very incompleteness of its composition and its inherent defects of style. We stand as yet on the very threshold of the epic. In like manner, the stiff outlines of the Apollo of Tenea are more interesting for the historian of art than many a far-famed example of the fully developed art of Greece.

The Mahāvaṁsa deserves at once the name of a real epic. It is the acknowledged work of a poet. And we are enabled in some measure to watch this poet at work in his workshop. Accordingly, dependent as he is on his model, to which he is at pains to cling as closely as possible, he also passes criticism on it, realizes its faults and inequalities, and seek to improve and equalize them.

Not only has the Mahāvaṁsa found continuators who have brought down the chronicle to their own time, but the old work itself was submitted to revision. This took place because the redactor of the poem, without reference even to essential rearrangements, inserted episodes at places where it seemed to him suitable or necessary, and thus almost doubled the extent of the poem. The sources from which he took these episodes are as a rule assignable. The revision is accordingly accomplished on literary lines. It is not "The People" who takes on to or changes the composition, but an individual who does not follow the dictates of free fancy but takes over fixed material and with artistic ingenuity adapts it to new requirements.

Finally, we can observe how the epic material passes into later literature, assuming a historic character, and is enriched here and there, in small measure of course, by new accretions from a tradition standing apart from the epos. These additions and amplifications shew in many ways by their folk-tale and legendary character their origin in popular tradition. It can hardly however be maintained that they were taken from takes orally transmitted. This certainly is not impossible, but it is not necessary. Perhaps, they differed in individual cases, and may very well have had their origin in literary sources which are no longer or not yet accessible.

We will not assert that the development of the epos, as we observe it in Ceylon, is typical. It need not necessarily have been the same at all times and among all nations. But whenever the epic question is raised, the Dīpavaṁsa and the Mahāvaṁsa will serve as valuable analogies, first for the Indian epic, but also for those of other nations. Its chief value consists in the fact that in the case of the Ceylonese epics we have not to deal with possibilities and hypothetical constructions, but we can follow the actual process of development. The foundation, it is true, is unfortunately no longer accessible, and must be inferred. There are, however, valuable means of help at our disposal, and the epos itself lies before us in three stages of development, which we are enabled to compare with one another and of which we can investigate the origin and growth.

I. The Dipavamsa and the Mahavamsa in Relation to each other

1 – The Composition of the Dīpavaṁsa

(p. 4./ p. 5)

In spite of its grandiloquent proem, we cannot call the Dīpavaṁsa a work of art. It appears rather as a collocation of fragments arranged on the system we have indicated. In addition we have the clumsiness and incorrectness of speech, and a number of other phenomena, which require a special discussion. To these belongs the peculiarity that the same subject is frequently treated twice or three times, *e.g.* the story of the first Council after Buddha's death is told in IV. 1–26 and again in V. 1–15, the second being a more orderly and finished picture. The chief difference is that, in the second account, greater importance is laid on the personality of Mahākassapa, the convener of the assembly. So, too, the story of the second Council, caused by the heretical teachings of the Vajjiputta-monks, is related in IV. 47–53 and in V. 16–38. Again the first version is more fragmentary, while the second looks like a working up of a sketch. In the first version there is a prose insertion, a list of the ten points of difference, which the orthodox Theras contest. This is versified in the second version.

P. 6

Two versions also exist of the third Council and its cause, *viz.* VII. 34–43 and VII. 44–59, in which greater discrepancies are seen. The second version mentions a new fact, wanting in the first—the deed of violence of one of Aśoka's ministers, which is told more particularly in the Mahāvaṁsa, V. 240ff. One circumstance is indicative of the copying tendency of the Dīpavaṁsa or the whole tradition. The second version is associated in certain particulars with the description of the first Council, as it is found in V. 1 ff. Single verses are almost identical. Evidently these are stereotyped turns of speech, which were employed again and again in narratives of this sort.

P. 7

The history of the gifts which king Aśoka sent to Ceylon to king Devānampiyatissa, with the addition of an invitation to accept Buddhism, is found in XI. 32–40 and again in XII. 1–7. A third account even is given in XVII. 83 ff. The call of Mahinda and the appearance to him of the god Sakka (Indra) who commands him to make a journey are told in XII. 16–28 and 29–40. Several verses are verbally repeated, and in the second version a piece of prose is inserted. Finally, in the last chapter a "contamination" of two versions is certain.

P. 8

Further peculiarities in the composition of the Dīpavaṁsa are the gaps which the narrative repeatedly shows, the immediate tacking on the one another of the episodes, the frequent interchange of speech and counter-speech without the speakers being named. One other phenomenon is of especial importance, and on this I must dwell at some length. A whole series of verses is met with in the Dīpavaṁsa, which contain only the heads of some narrative. They are ranged side by side in catchwords, after the manner of headings, often without proper construction. These I designate as mnemonic verses.

P. 9

An interesting example of such is found in XVII. 3ff., in the story of the last four Buddhas and their visits to Ceylon. The events took place each time in the same way, according to legend. The island is visited by some "affliction." This causes the Buddha to journey thither. He descends on a mountain in the island and frees the people from the "affection." Then he preaches to the prince and the people in the capital. He receives a park as a present, and plants in it a branch of his sacred tree, which a nun fetches from India. The Buddha leaves as objects of veneration relies which are kept in a Thūpa or tope. On his departure he appoints one his disciples to be the chief of the newly founded community. This is the course of events, which differs only as to the names of the Buddha, the island, the king, the capital, &c. The narrative of the history of the Buddha-visits to Ceylon begins in the Dīpavaṁsa with the following remarkable verse:–

"The island, the town and the king, the plague and the relics,

The tope, the island and the mountain, the park, the Bodhi tree, the nun,

The monk and the best of Buddhas. These are the thirteen subjects."

This is obviously a kind of heading, naming all the subjects to come under consideration in the story. The text then continues, taking up the subjects in order: "Ojadīpa, Varadīpa, Maṇḍadīpa are the names of the beautiful island of Laṅkā, which is also known as Tambapaṇṇi. Abjayapura, Vaḍḍhamāna, Visāla, Anurādhapura are the four named of the town at the times of the preaching of the four Buddhas," &c. This, then, is only a list of names, raw material for the narrative, but not itself a connected account. From v. 26 onward, however, the story of the first Buddha Kakusandha follows in orderly narration and systematic detail.

P. 10

Mnemonic verses, again, met with in Dīpavaṁsa, XIX. 2, 3, where the materials mentioned in the founding of the Great Tope in Anurādhapura are enumerated. The detailed description is found in the Mahāvaṁsa, XXIX. 1ff. Among other examples may be mentioned a singular verse in Dīpavaṁsa, I. 29 :–

"The throne, the Animisa, the cloister, the jewel-house, the Ajapāla-tree and the Mucalinda tree with the Khīrapāla grove."

The verse refers to what happened immediately after the night of enlightenment. It fills up a gap between this even and the first preaching at Benares.

P. 11

From these considerations it is plain that the Dīpavaṁsa represents a primitive stage of epic poetry. When we find two versions of the same story placed side by side, we have obviously to deal with the deposit of an originally oral tradition. Such versions are accountable only on the assumption that, while certain phrases and verses became stereotyped by custom, greater freedom was allowed to the narrator in other parts. It cannot indeed be maintained that the Dīpavaṁsa is merely this verbal tradition put directly in writing. The author has doubtless used one or more literary sources, but these again bear traces of an originally oral tradition. The collocation of versions must, in any case, have been intentional.

P. 12

The Dīpavaṁsa in many points recalls the form of the early Indian Ākhyāna poetry, the peculiarity of which is that the whole narrative did not formally take shape, but only certain parts were metrically fixed and so became more secure from further distortions in the course of transmission. Such parts were, especially, direct speeches. These were united by explanatory prose passages giving the names and the situation. When this prose became versified, the result was a poem of the ballad type, which forms the materials for an epic. Rhys Davids rightly notices that these separate stage of the Akhyana poetry are to be found in the canonical books of the Buddhists. In the Thera and Therīgāthās we have only the speeches preserved—the narrative framework must be taken from the commentaries. In the Suttantas of the second book of the Dīgha-Nīkāya, both the speeches in verse and the narrative in prose are contained. Finally, we find ballads in which the narrative also is transmitted in metrical form. We stand thus on the threshold of real epic poetry.

P. 13

The Dīpavaṁsa stands at this stage of development: it is not a fully developed epic, although single episodes, *e.g.*, the visit of Kakusandha, are worked out in ballad style; in many parts the prose narrative is assumed. At such points the mnemonic verses are inserted as an aid to the memory. This explains the presence of dialogue without the speakers' name. In many places the explanation of the narrator is necessary to the understanding of the story; *e.g.*, we have in the Dīpavaṁsa a prophecy about Moggaliputta with no indication of the author or occasion of the prophetic utterance. From the Mahāvaṁsa, V. 98 ff., we can infer that it was the Presbyters of the second Council who foresaw the future fall of Buddhist learning and the restoration of the faith by Moggaliputta. Again, in the Dīpavaṁsa we find introduced quite abruptly (XII. 64) :"The Thera, standing on the summit of the mountain, said to the carriage-driver, 'No, a carriage is not allowed: the Holy One has forbidden it.'" This only becomes intelligible when we add from the Mahāvaṁsa, XIV. 42, that in the meantime night has passed and that in the morning the king sends his charioteer to the Missaka mountain to conduct thence Mahinda and his friends into the town. Many verses in the Dīpavaṁsa are unintelligible without a commentary.

2 – THE MAHĀVAMSA IN COMPARISON WITH THE DĪPAVAMSA

P. 14

The Mahāvaṁsa and the Dīpavaṁsa agree not only in matter, but also in arrangement. This agreement is so close as to preclude any theory of a purely accidental congruity. Two alternatives remain: – (1) that the Mahāvaṁsa (which is undoubtly later than the Dīpavaṁsa) has taken matter and arranagement from the Dīpavaṁsa; or (2) that both have drawn from the same source. The later assumption is , as we shall see, the correct one.

P. 16

Only in two cases is there difference of order in the events treated, the Mahāvaṁsa following a tradition neglected in the earlier poem. Quite a number of verses are verbally identical; others, though not identical, closely resemble each other. It is quite likely that the author of the Mahāvaṁsa knew and copied the author of the Dīpavaṁsa, but it is more probable that for both authors many verses has, as it were, the official impress of tradition. Compare the words in which Aśoka communicates to Devānampiyatissa his attachment to Buddhism (D. XII. 5= M. XI. 34): "I have taken my refuge in the Buddha, the Dhamma and the Saṁgha; I have avowed myself a lay pupil of the doctrine of the Sakyaputta," and also the words in which Mahinda announces his mission to the king (D. XII. 51 = M. XIV. 8): "We are monks, O great king, pupils of the King of Truth. Out of compassion towards thee have we repaired hither from Jambudīpa."

In spite of these points of agreement, there is a wide gulf between the Dīpavaṁsa and the Mahāvaṁsa. The composition of the former is clumsy and inartistic. The latter is a work of art, a *kāvya* according to the conception of Indian poetry. This difference is seen at the outset by a comparison of the somewhat turgid the boastful tone of the Dīpavaṁsa with the more moderate tone of the Mahāvaṁsa, the author of which, however, claims for his work freedom from the faults which characterised the older compositions.

P. 19

The MSS. of the Mahāvaṁsa give at XXXVII. 50 the words *Mahāvaṃso niṭṭhito*. The Commentary, too, stops at this point. It corresponds further with the second last verse of the Dīpavaṁsa, XXII. 75. These arguments alone are sufficient to prove that the old work actually closely with these words, and that the succeeding chapters are the work of a later hand. In the later chapters occurs a series of words not found in the older Mahāvaṁsa . Again, at XXXVII. 93 there is made mention of the Dāṭhādhātuvaṁsa, in which the history of the tooth-relic is told. If this be the poem of that name now extant, as I think probable, and not its Singhalese prototype, the second half of the 37th chapter must have been written after the year 1219. Another instance of agreement is found in the fact that the continuation of the Mahāvaṁsa begins with the closing words of the Dīpavaṁsa.

P. 20

Apart from the formal differences in the poems, we find important differences in the subject-matter. While the outlines are essentially the same, the Mahāvaṁsa amplifies old material and introduces new.

Viewed as a whole, the Mahāvaṁsa falls into two principal divisions, the first being chapters I–XX, this again admitting a subdivision into two, *viz.*, I–X, and XI–XX. The latter subdivision deals with the history of Devānampiyatissa and the conversion of Ceylon; the earlier chapters form a sort of double introduction.

P. 23

The second chief division is entered on at Chapter XXI. with the accession of Mahāsiva. In the Dīpavaṁsa we reach Mahāsiva at XVIII. 45; and what follows embraces only 192 more verses. This disparity is explained by the presence in the Mahāvaṁsa of the history of king Duṭṭhagamani, which is here worked into a completely independent poem, filling ten chapters, while in the Dīpavaṁsa only 13 verses are devoted to this king. At Chapter XXV, we note the union of the two streams of tradition–the priestly and the popular. After the narration of war and bloodshed, the scene is shifted to the palace and cloister, and the warrior-hero becomes and Defender of the Buddhist faith. He devotes himself, in expiation of his sins, to the founding of monastic institutions, but before the completion of the Great Tope he falls sick and dies. This history is summarized in Dīpavaṁsa, the mnemonic verses XIX 2–9 shewing that all the events were known to its author.

The accession of popular tradition is further brought out by the introduction in the Mahāvaṁsa of shorter episodes, omitted or dismissed in the sentence by the Dīpavaṁsa. These episodes either are of the secular and political type of consist of anecdotes, tales, stories, and legends. These occur more frequently in the latter half of the poem. A genuinely Indian narrative of a popular character is the early history of Nigrodha (M.V. 43–63) who is known to the Dīpavaṁsa only as the monk who converted Aśoka. Another popular tale is that of the price Tissa (M.V. 155ff.) which finds an analogy in the Kathāsaritṣāgara (Ch. 27) and has the same underlying idea as the story of the Sword of Damocles.

P. 25

To the same class belongs the story of Vijaya and the sorceress Kuveri (M. VII. 96ff.). This bears a remarkable resemblance to the Circe-legend of the Odyssey, while many other episodes bear the mark of legendary and popular origin, and often resemble in a striking manner the legends of the European nations.

3 – The amplified Mahāvaṁsa

Pp. 28-29

The Mahāvaṁsa, however, does not complete the course of development of the epos; we possess in "amplified Mahāvaṁsa," embodying new material in addition to the original text. This discovery we owe to E. Hardy[1] in a Kambodiam manuscript. While its æsthetic value may be slight, its interest from the point of view of literary history is considerable as shewing how a ready-made work is extended by new additions. In the Kambodian MS, 5,791 verses are found, as against 2,915 in the original Mahāvaṁsas. It is of special interest that we can as a rule, fix the sources from which the author has taken his materials for this extension. He himself names the Buddhavaṁsa and the Thūpavaṁsa. The latter exists in Singhalese and Pāli. The Pāli commentary on the Mahāvaṁsa is also largely used. These three works resemble one another very closely, and from them the author of the Kambodian Mahāvaṁsa beats out his verses. Frequently, the mention of a name in the original Mahāvaṁsa is the occasion for a versified history of the person. Even without the earlier work, however, one could probably detect the interpolations from the presence of certain linguistic peculiarities and other signs that the interpolators was the less skilled poet. Yet, even admitting this, we should be far from establishing the original text. Apart from actual interpolations, there are in the Kambodian MS. detailed explanations of short statements in the older poem, also single lines inserted and slight alterations made for the sake of clearness.

P. 33

The author of this manuscript calls himself Moggalāna. Of his date we can say nothing with certainty, but from certain clerical errors in the text we infer that it was copied from an original in Singhalese. Other indications suggest that the author lived in Ceylon. In this connection it may be mentioned that in the later Mahāvaṁsa, LXXVIII. 9, a priest is introduced who lived in the 12th century under Parakkamabāhu the Great, and clearly was one of the then prominent ecclesiastics.

II – The Dipavamsa and the Mahavamsa in Relation to their sources.

4 – The Commentary and the author of the Mahāvaṁsa

Pp. 34-36

Turnour's identification of the author of the Mahāvaṁsa with that of the Commentary rests on a wrong interpretation of the closing words of the Commentary. In the Commentary, the author of the Mahāvaṁsa is designated as *ācariyo ayaṁ ācariya,* "the teacher, master of savant." A difference in time is clearly indicated in the Commentary, 447, 26, on Mahāvaṁsa, XXXIII. 53, where it is said that the Samagalla mentioned in the Mahāvaṁsa was now (*idāni*), *i.e.,* in the time of the writer of the Commentary, called Moragalla. More important for fixing a date is the passage (referred to by Snyder) at V. 13 where the Dhammaruchi and the

Sāgaliya are mentioned as schismatic sects. In commenting on this, the Commentary mentions later monastic strifes which took place in the reign of Dāṭhopatissa, "the nephew." The author of the Commentary, then, lived after the reign of Dāṭhopatissa II, *i.e.*, roughly speaking, after 670 A.D. Still narrower limits are drawn if the Mahābodhivaṁsakathā is identical with the Mahābodhivaṁsa. This, as I can prove, is a work not of the fifth century, as has been hitherto assumed, but of the end of the tenth. The Commentary on the Mahāvaṁsa therefore, cannot have been written before the beginning of the eleventh century.

P. 37

A lower limit is fixed from the fact that the author of the Commentary did not know the later continuation of the Mahāvaṁsa, and so must have lived before the second half of the thirteenth century; also notably from the fact that the Pāli Thūpavaṁsa, which was composed in the middle of the century, is made abundant use of in the Commentary. The date then for the Commentary is 1000 – 1250.

As regards contents, the Commentary adds to the Mahāvaṁsa, apart from exegetic and dogmatic statements, a mass of historical and legendary material, folklore, and romance. It bears the same relation to the Mahāvaṁsa as the Mahāvaṁsa does to the Dīpavaṁsa; so that the Mahāvaṁsa had not exhausted the store of available epic material.

P. 38

From legendary sources comes the history of the earlier Buddhas, which serves in the Commentary, 35ff., as an elucidation of Mahāvaṁsa, I. 6ff., where only the names are given. The history of Gotama-Buddha is treated more in detail than in the epic. These Buddha-legends undoubtedly come down from the church tradition, and we may assume the same authority for the different notes which amplify the account of the festival at the laying of the foundation-stone of the Great Tope. Another history bearing the stamp of genuine monastic tradition is that of Nanduttara, an earlier incarnation of Soṇuttara who was entrusted with the collection of relics for the Great Tope. The same holds good of the history of the relics and the dialogue between the dying Duṭṭagāmani and the monk Theraputtābhaya, as spun out in the Commentary.

Pp. 39–44

In the commentary there is no lack, however, of passages which seem to be derived from popular tradition. Quite a romance is formed by the tale of the love of Sālirājakumāra, a son of Duṭṭhagāmani, for a Caṇḍāla maiden. The Mahāvaṁsa merely states that the prince, for the sake of this girl, had resigned the throne, and that the two had been united in a previous state of existence. The Commentary elucidates this in a longer narrative. Other outlines are similarly supplemented, notably those of the Indian kings before Aśoka. The story of Susunāga belongs to that class of folktale which depicts the founders of new dynasties as having been exposed in infancy, and having been tended by some wild animal until the arrival of men who bring them up. Susunāga is tended by a serpent, while Candagutta, whose history is told at length in the Commentary, 119, 8ff., is brought up by a steer called Canda. A continuous analysis of the two poems shews the degree to which the "monastic" tradition is supplemented by the "Secular."

Pp. 44-45

Mahānāma is named in the closing words of the Commentary as author of the Mahāvaṁsa, and is said to have lived at the monastery built by the general Dīghasanda, who was a general under Devānampiyatissa. Turnour assumes that this Mahānāma was the uncle of the king Dhātusena, who is said to have lived in the institution built by Dīghasanda. Turnour[2] has taken the name of this individual from Mahāvaṁsa, XXXIX. 42, where we are told that Moggalāna I. (497–515) had transferred the monastery of Sīhagiri to Mahānāma, the presbyter of the Dīghasanda monastery. But the two Mahānāmas are not necessarily identical. Chronology is against it. Dhātusena entered the institution in the time of the Damila Paṇḍu (436–441) when his uncle was already "Thera" and therefore considerably older than his nephew. It is extremely improbable from considerations of age that that two Māhanāmas represent the same person. Turnour thinks that the uncle was author of the Mahāvaṁsa, basing his argument on the statement (Mahāvaṁsa, XXXVIII. 59) that on the occasion of a festival at the cremation of Mahinda, Dhātusena had ordered the Dīpavaṁsa to be read through. Turnour says without hesitation that the Mahāvaṁsa is meant, Snyder, however, has disposed of this identification. My own view is that we must entirely dissociate the Mahānāma named in Mahāvaṁsa, XXXIX.42 from the uncle of Dhātusena. Much points to him as the author of the Mahāvaṁsa, but of course we have to deal with a supposition which contains a certain probability, not with a certainty. Two points coincide: the name and the locality. In that case, the date of the composition would be the last quarter of the fifth century, a result which may at least have plausibility.

P. 47

With regard to the period of composition of the Dīpavaṁsa, we have Oldenberg's arguments for ascribing it to the time between the beginning of the fourth and the first third of the fifth centuries A.D. (1) The upper limit is fixed at 302–304, by internal evidence. (2) A lower limit is found in the fact that Buddhaghosa (beginning of fifth century) knew a version of the Dīpavaṁsa, which differed somewhat from ours. (3) The Dīpavaṁsa was publicly read under king Dhātusena (second half of fifth century). Besides, the Commentary mentions a "Dīpavaṁsaṭṭhakathā". Comparing these results with those reached about the Mahāvaṁsa, it seems probable that the two works are separated from each other by an interval of 100 to 150 years. The great difference in the matter of style which exists between them, is explained by the fact that in this period occurs the activity of Buddhaghosa, which forms a turning point in the entire literary life of Ceylon.

5–The Authorities

P. 48

Various passages in the Commentary deal with the authorities on which our Mahāvaṁsa rests and the relation it bears to them. These are :– (*a*) Comm. 21, 31–22, 21; (*b*) Comm. 25, 31–26, 1; (*c*) Comm. 18–26; (*d*) Comm. 29, 19–34; (*e*) Comm. 502,

34–503, 4. From these we gather that : (1) Our Mahāvaṁsa is the translation of a work, composed in Singhalese, into the Māgadhī or literary language, *i.e.*, into Pāli, by rendering the original prose into verse. From this it takes its name "Padyapadoruvaṁsa." (2) The translation, while exact was used to remedy the faults of omissions and repetitions found in the original. (3) Several names were attached to the original. It is called "Sīhalaṭṭhakathā" (Singhalese commentary) or Porāṇaṭṭ hakathā (commentary of the Ancients) and even "In the style of the Inhabitants of the Mahāvihāra," and, lastly, it is more particularly designated as the "old Mahāvaṁsa of the Sīhalaṭṭ hakathā" or the "Mahāvaṁsa of the Sīhalaṭṭhakathā composed by the ancients in the Singhalese language."

P. 40

It appear that at the Mahāvihāra in Anurādhapura an old commentary to the canonical writings was preserved, while was designated "Aṭṭhakathā." A part of this formed the "ancient Mahāvaṁsa," on which the monk of Mahānāma rests. Materially, the new work agrees with the old, but is more poetically and evenly set forth.

P. 50

We have now to consider the nature and compass of the literature which the author of our Mahāvaṁsa had before him, more especially of the Sihalaṭṭhakathā-Mahāvaṁsa and what position of the latter occupied in that literature. The Mahāvaṁsa speaks (Proem, I. 2) of a Mahāvaṁsa of the ancients, *porāṇehi kato p'eso* (scil. *mahāvaṁsa*). Clearly this refers to the work which formed the basis, known also to the Commentary by the same time. It is further briefly referred to as *Porāṇā,* "the Ancients," which name is mentioned seven times in the Commentary. Each time occur the word *tenāhu porāṇā* and one or more Pāli verses follow. Frequent mention of the *Porāṇā* is found in Buddhaghosa's Commentaries, also with Pāli verses, annexed. The authority, then on which the Mahāvaṁsa drew, was interspersed with Pāli verses, but was at the same time not merely a collection. The Sumaṅgala-Vilāsinī cites three Pāli verses, but also a series of prose passages which emphatically bear the stamp of notes from a commentary. The *Porāṇā* was then a regular Aṭṭhakathā, in Singhalese prose with Pāli verses, a form still seen in modern Singhalese works. From many passages in the Commentary it is clear that *Porāṇā* and Aṭṭhakathā refer to the same work, and that Sīhalaṭṭhakathā is only a more exact designation for the authority known more briefly as Aṭṭhakathā.

Apart from the two commentaries of Buddhaghosa, nine other works are cited in the Commentary, the most important of which are the Uttaravihāraṭṭhakathā and the Uttaravihāra-Mahāvaṁsa. The whole shews that a rich literature was at the disposal of the author; for at that time there still existed the vast collection preserved in the different monasteries in the shape of commentaries on the canonical writings. A secondary literature, too, had already begun, in which isolated subjects, such as the story of the Bodhi tree, the Topes, and so on, found a place. This literature the Commentary has used at all events for subsidiary incidents, the chief of these being drawn from the Sīhalaṭṭhakathā of the Mahāvihāra.

6 – The Contents of the Sources

P. 57

The Mahāvaṁsa follows closely, on the whole, the Aṭṭ hakathā: the Commentary amplifies and supplements from it: hence a combination of the two will give a nearer view of the nature and compass of the basis of the Mahāvaṁsa.

The passages we know to be cited from the Aṭṭhakathā may be divided into six classes, *viz.* :–

I – Early History, comprising the legends of the earlier Buddhas, though these may be taken only indirectly from the Aṭṭhakathā through the medium of the Jātaka-Nidānakathā. The text of the Commentary and of the Jātaka-Nidānakathā is simply a rendering of the old Singhalese original. Specially interesting is the narrative of the three visits of Buddha to Ceylon. These visits formed an important subject for both the Dīpavaṁsa and Mahāvaṁsa and both copy closely their original. The points of agreement between the Commentary and the Dīpavaṁsa are also numerous and significant, and shew, too, how detailed the Aṭṭnakathā must have been, while the author of the Commentary was able, with great exactitude, to check the Mahāvaṁsa by the Aṭṭhakathā.

II—History of India up to Aśoka—The additions of the Commentary to Indian history for which the Aṭṭhakathā is expressly named as authority are not numerous, but enough to shew that Indian history was reviewed in that work, as far as it concerned the development of Buddhism. But the Commentary brings into this section a mass of new materials of a genuinely popular character, nominally relating to the history of Candagutta. These narratives are taken partly from the Aṭṭ hakathā, partly from the Uttaravihāraṭṭhakathā, the latter being expressly cited as the source for the story of Susunāga, for that of the nine Nanda princes, and for Candagutta. The Commentary unfortunately does not name the authority for the tales immediately following; perhaps we may infer that, when no source is named, the Aṭṭhakathā is meant.

P. 63

III, IV—The Commentary contributes few additions to the History of the Councils and Theras, none at all to that of Devānampiyatissa and Mahinda. Here the Dīpavaṁsa and Mahāvaṁsa (in almost perfect agreement) both closely copy the Aṭṭhakathā, which must have contained the accounts of the Councils and the prominent ecclesiastical chiefs with even greater detail than we find in the later works.

P. 64

V—Two references only are found to the later kings (except Duṭṭhagāmani) in the Commentary: one in connection with Sūratissa, the successor of Mahāsiva, the other with Kaniṭṭhat ssa; the latter being important as shewing that the Mahāvaṁsa part of the Aṭṭhakathā extended to atleast the close of the second century A.D.: probably like the Dīpavaṁsa and Mahāvaṁsa it extended to Mahāsena.

P. 65

Many references to the Aṭṭhakathā relate to the time of Duṭ ṭhagāmani, which must have been treated in detail.The account of the festival at the laying of the foundation-stone of the Great Tope is particularly interesting because we can see from it how the Pāli verses may have been divided. At the end it is entitled *iti Aṭṭhakathāya vuttaṁ, vuttam pi c'etaṁ;* and then follows the mnemonic verse, Dīpavaṁsa, XIX. 8, which contains nothing but the names of the twelve Theras. It may reasonably be assumed that the verse stood exactly so in the Aṭṭhakathā and was transferred into the Dīpavaṁsa. Several sections of purely epic import are explicitly referred to the Aṭṭhakathā, but it is probable that such explicit references by no means indicate all the material derived from Aṭṭhakathā. Many isolated notes are given without any source being named; these probably, though not necessarily, are from this source. For instance, names are frequently given in the Commentary, which are wanting in the text of the Mahāvaṁsa. A series of brief notes introduced by *vuttaṁ hoti* indicate that they are quoted. The narrative of Bhaddaji, Commentary, 405–407, a more extended account of Mahāvaṁsa, XXXI. 5–14, considering its style, may come from the Aṭṭhakathā.

7–Results

P. 69

From the above investigation we reach the following conclusions:– (1) Before Buddhaghosa's time there was a wealth of literary commentary under the general name of Aṭṭ hakathā, called also the work of "the Ancients." (2) Such Aṭṭ hakathāṣ were preserved in the various monasteries; notably in the Mahāvihāra and Uttaravihāra. (3) A definite historic part of the Aṭṭhakathā of both institutions was called Mahāvaṁsa, the editions differing in details. (4) Our Mahāvaṁsa rests on the authority of the Mahāvaṁsa of the Mahāvihāra, (5) and is a fairly close copy of its original, with the faults of irregularity and redundance corrected. (6) The Commentary mentions other works besides the Aṭṭhakathā, many belonging to the literature of the *Porāṇā,* others to later works. Buddhaghosa's commentaries are also mentioned.

P. 70

Two questions now confronts us :– (1) What rôle does the old Mahāvaṁsa play in the literature of the Aṭṭhakathā, and of what elements is it composed? (2) How did the Epic Poetry of Ceylon, as represented by the Dīpavaṁsa and our Mahāvaṁsa, arise our of the old Mahāvaṁsa of the Aṭṭhakathā?

Oldenberg's view is that the Sīhalaṭṭhakathā-Mahāvaṁsa forms a historical introduction to the dogmatic part of the Aṭṭ hakathā, just as Buddhaghosa gives a similar-historical preface to his commentaries on the Dīgha-Nikāya. Many considerations point in another direction. Its very scope and fullness look unlike a "historic introduction," which would have ended with the establishment of Buddhism in Ceylon. More probably the Mahāvaṁsa of the Ancients was an independent work brought down by the Mahāvihāra monks to the time of Mahāsena, and interrupted at that time by wars. It may, of course, have grown out of such a historical introduction. The preface to the Dīpavaṁsa says as much, but it belongs to an epoch in which the scope of the work has less than at the time when Mahānāma worked out the material in a poetic way, or when the Dīpavaṁsa arose. The old frame was burst, and from the "historical introduction" to the Aṭṭhakaṭhā there grew the Mahāvaṁsa of the Ancients—the comprehensive chronicle of the Mahāvihāra.

P. 72

We have seen how a double strain of sacred and secular tradition appears in both the Dīpavaṁsa and the Mahāvaṁsa. From what the Commentary says of the relation of the Mahāvaṁsa to its basis, we must infer that already in the Aṭṭ hakahā-Mahāvaṁsa there appeared both phenomena, an originally oral tradition,. and the fusion of a "church" and a "secular" tradition. The legends naturally varied with the reciter, and variants were inserted, side by side, by the monks. The work gradually assumed the shape in which Mahānāma found it.

Pp. 73-76

Coming now to the Dīpavaṁsa, we find that in many places it is plainly a collection of the introductory and mnemonic verses contained in the Aṭṭhakathā-Mahāvaṁsa, but with some attempt at artistic treatment. It is in fact the bridge between the Aṭṭhakathā-Mahāvaṁsa and the Mahāvaṁsa. As the Pāli verses occur seldom or never in popular tradition and the Dīpavaṁsa contains so many, it must have deliberately preferred the monastic part of its basis. This is one of the striking points of contrast between the two works, the Dīpavaṁsa and the Mahāvaṁsa. It is to be noted that the "repetitions" are not always *verbatin;* they frequently look like two versions of the same narrative. The basis-work, the Aṭṭhakathā-Mahāvaṁsa, would naturally have preserved such: but it is just possible that a further source, resembling the Aṭṭhakathā-Mahāvaṁsa in plan and content, was drawn on by the complier of the Dīpavaṁsa.

P. 77

The development of the epos in Ceylon, then, came about by the following stages. About the middle of the fifth century was extant that comprehensive chronicle called "the Mahāvaṁsa of the Ancients"—a constituent part of the Aṭṭ hakathā. It was a king of Encyclopædia of all the legends and traditions bearing on the history of Ceylon. The Dīpavaṁsa, on the other hand, represents the first clumsy effort to give form to the mass of material stored in that chronicle. A noteworthy circumstance is the rejection of the old Singhalese dialect for Pāli, the new church-language. With the fifth century, Buddhaghosa's activity gave a great impetus to literary life in Ceylon. Pāli becomes forthwith the speech of the church and the scholar. Mahānāma is better equipped for his work. True, he has not yet surmounted his material, and transfers much of the original bodily into his work. He is no genius, and his work is no literary contribution of the first rank, but it shews, as compared with the Dīpavaṁas, a great step in advance.

The stage of epic form is reached with the Mahāvaṁsa, but the process of literary development is not ended. The Commentary amplifies and supplements from other works material relating to this subject. And now, from this material, Moggalāna has, at a later time, produced the amplified Mahāvaṁsa of the Kambodian manuscript, while at places he has embodied in Mahānāma's epic new episodes which he thought cognate. It would be interesting to know if other MSS. exits, in Ceylon or South India, which contain similar retouchings of the Mahāvaṁsa.

III – Historical Tradition apart from the Epic

8 – The Introduction of the Samanta-Pāsādikā, the Mahābodhivaṁsa, the Dāṭhāvaṁsa, and the Thūpavaṁsa

P. 78

Of much interest for us is the historical introduction which Buddhaghosa prefixes to his Samauta-Pāsādikā. This work lies between the epics in age, its contents coincide so exactly with those of the Mahāvaṁsa that there can be no question of their common origin. Both drew largely on the Aṭṭhakathā, and both reproduced their authority with considerable exactitude. The Samanta-Pāsādikā (Smp.) begins with the events immediately following Buddha's death, and deals with the story of the two Councils. The circumstance is peculiar in so far as an account of these Councils is also given in the Chullavagga XI and XII.[3] Buddhaghosa's account of the first Council rests on Chv. XI. 1–8, whence he copies whole passages *verbatim,* and amplifies them, presumably, from the old Singhalese Aṭṭhakatṇā. It is significant that even in the passages which occurs in the Smp., and not in Chv., verbal agreements are found. The account of the second Council is given similarly in Chv., Smp., and the Mahāvaṁsa. Buddhaghosa cites the Dīpavaṁsa, besides other authorities for passages which differ somewhat from the text now extant.

Pp. 79–81

Notable instances of agreement between the Samanta-Pāsādikā and the Mahāvaṁsa are :– Smp. 294, 2, the story of Moggaliputtatissa, who conducted the third Council, is in close agreement with M.V. 98ff. Then, Smp. 299, 17, History of Aśoka, =M.V. 9–34, D. VI. 1–14. The episodes of the Nāga king Kāla in 300, 12ff. and of Nigrodha 300, 32ff. are found in M.V. 89 and V. 36, D. VI. 24ff. The Dedication Festival of Aśoka, the entrance of Mahinda and Seṅghamittā into the Order, =M.V. 174–213, D. VII. 1–31. The narrative 306, 18ff. of the Thera Kontiputtatissa=M.V. 213–230, the fall of the Church= M.V. 231–243, Tissa and his conversion, M.V. 155–174,–all find a place in both works. These are a few examples where the verbal agreement between them is noticeable. Certainly in some parts

Smp. agrees even more closely with D. than with M. These, however, are cases where Mahānāma's artistic personality led him to deviate from his original.

It is of importance to note that the Samanta-Pāsādikā was frequently made use of in later literature. It is mentioned in the Commentary on the Mahāvaṁsa, which contains whole passages verbally identical with it.

Here and there the Samanta-Pāsādikā fills gaps in the epics; *e.g.*, Smp. 310, 12ff. narrates a dream of Aśoka before the arrival of Moggaliputtatissa (*cf.* M.V. 246ff.). Again, in 311, 32 ff. the Tittitajātaka told by Tissa to the king is briefly summarised.

P. 83

The assumption, then, that the Mahāvaṁsa of the Sīhalaṭṭ hakathā was the source for the introduction of the Samanta-Pāsādikā may be accepted as correct. Of course, Buddhaghosa has limited himself to what seemed important for his particular object. He holds as closely to his original as Mahānāma did at a later time. Indeed, it is not impossible that Mahānāman even consulted the Samanta-Pāsādikā and schooled himself in Buddhaghosa's classic Pāli.

The Mahābodhivaṁsa begins with the story of the Buddha Dīpaṅkara, enumerates shortly the existence of the Bodhisatta, and then relates the life of Gotama-Buddha until the night of enlightenment. This forms the first chapter and bears an unmistakable likeness to the introduction of the Jātakas, the Jātaka-Nidānakathā. The Mahābodhivaṁsa is shorter and more succint, but much more artistic, and often ornate in style. The Jātaka-Nidānakathā rests on the authority of the Aṭṭhakathā, and forms the medium through which the Buddhist history, especially that of Gotama, passed into the Mahābodhivaṁsa and thence into later literature.

P. 85

The second chapter of the Mahābodhivaṁsa rests on the Jātaka-Nidānakathā, also, and is entitled Ānandabodhikathā, as being the account of how Ānanda planted at the Jetavana a fruit of the holy tree from Uruvelā. The subsequent chapters are more directly dependent on the Samanta-Pāsādikā and Mahāvaṁsa, most being taken from the former—so much so that one might almost think that the two were independent translations of their old Singhalese forerunner. But the two texts coincide so in wording that the theory of a direct derivation seems necessary. Moreover, the style of the Maḥābodhivaṁsa is more elaborate and yet compressed, and has the air of an epitome of the Samanta-Püsādikā. The presence of the Mahāvaṁsa is seen in the brief additions to the parts taken from the Samanta-Pāsādikā, and also in the division and arrangement of material. The closing words of the Mahāvaṁsa are also utilised for closing the corresponding chapters of the Mahābodhivaṁsa. These were certainly composed by Mahānāma and were not in the Aṭṭhakathā. As regards various isolated notes, it is not improbable that the Aṭṭhakathā was directly responsible for many.

P. 88

The introduction tells us that the work is the translation of the Singhalese work into Māgadhī. If it be admitted that the Mahāvaṁsa preceded the Mahabōdhivaṁsa, then Strong's theory,[4] which makes the author of the latter a contemporary of Buddhaghosa, breaks down, his error being the identification of Dāṭhānāga, a Thera of the time of Mahinda IV, with Dāṭṭha, who, according to the Gandhavaṁsa, commissioned Buddhaghosa to write the Commentary to the Dīgha-Nikāya. The Mabābodhivaṁsa belongs to Mahinda IV's time, and was therefore composed in the last quarter of the tenth century. The translation was not made directly from a Singhalese text but through a Pāli version.

P. 89

As regard the age of the Dāṭhāvaṁsa we are sufficiently informed. The author in the closing verse calls himself Dhammakitti. His work was a translation of a Sinhalese original into Māgadhī at the instrance of the General Parakkama, by whose means Līlāvatī, the widow of Parakkamabāhu, was raised to the throne. This happened in 1211 A.D. The Dāṭhāvaṁsa must therefore have appeared shortly after that time. The contents deal with the previous existence of the Bodhisatta, Buddha's visits to Ceylon (where the Mahāvaṁsa is closely copied), the division of the relics, especially of the tooth-relic and its advent to Ceylon. With this part we overstep the beaten track of tradition. We notice two constituent parts of this tradition. The first is of Indian origin, and comprises the early history of the Buddhas, the life of Gotama-Buddha, the story of the first and partially of the second Council, the names of deeds of Indian kings. This tradition, being largely derived from the Aṭṭhakathā,is fixed and definite. The second ingredient is the local tradition of Ceylon, treating of Buddha's visits to Ceylon, the myths of Vijaya and the earliest kings of Laṅkā, the third Council and the mission of Mahinda, the already partly historical tradition of Duṭṭhagāmani and his journeys. This latter division was liable to almost indefinite extension from popular narratives or local chronicles.

P. 91

The materials of the Dāṭhāvaṁsa appear in a small work entitled Daḷadāpūjāvali, which is a very close paraphrase of the former.

P. 92

The Thūpavaṁsa, which comes down to us in Singhalese and in Pāli, is closely allied to the Mahābodhivaṁsa and preserves the epic form. Its contents range from the history of the early Buddhas to the death of Duṭṭhagāmani.

Pp. 93–95

As regards the relation between the two versions, we may say that on the whole the Singhalese is broader and more detailed than the Pāli. In Chapters X–XVI, the one seems a mere translation of the other; but in the history of Buddha the Singhalese makes considerable additions and amplifications. The author in his epilogue calls himself Vāchissara and mentions that he is connected with the Dhammāgāra of the king Parakkama, giving the names of a number of other works composed by him in Singhalese. He had two Thūpavaṁsas before him—one in Singhalese, and hence of use only for the natives of Ceylon; the other in Pāli, but so defective as to necessitate a fresh working out. I am of opinion that this Vāchissara was none other than the famous Thera of that name, spoken of in Mahāvaṁsa, LXXXI. 18 ff. He was an ecclesiastical chief under Vijayabāhu III, (1236–1240) and his power may well have continued under the next king Parakkamabāhu II. (1240–1275). We have thus secured a date for the Pāli Thūpavaṁsa, *viz.,* the middle of the thirteenth century A.D. the Singhalese version is to be regarded as a later extension of the Pāli text : for priority cannot be proved, and internal evidence points otherwise, as does the analogy of the Mahābodhivaṁsa. It must have followed quickly after the Pāli version; for Parākrama Paṇḍita, the author of our Singhalese version, is mentioned in the Rājaratnākara in the list of learned priests and laymen who flourished between the time of Buddhaghosa and 1809 after Buddha=1266 A.D. This work must have been, composed, therefore, between 1250 and 1260.

The usual sources were drawn from in the composition of the Pāli Thūpavaṁsa, *viz.,* the Jātaka-Nidānakathā, the Samanta-Pāsādikā, and the Mahāvaṁsa: and more sparingly the Commentary on the Mahāvaṁsa. Other sources, as in the case of the Mahābodhivaṁsa, may be traced, and it is not impossible that, where an authority is not named, the Aṭṭ hakathā may have been consulted, either directly or by the medium of the old Pāli Thūpavaṁsa (probably the Chetiyavaṁsaṭṭbakathā, which at all events was in close accord with the Aṭṭhakathā literature).

9 – Singhalese Writings

P. 99

The most comprehensive of these is the Pūjāvali, which is not yet completely edited, but which, as we can see from Wickremasinghe's analysis, consists of the usual material in the usual arrangement. The author, Mayūrapāda Thera, wrote in the second half of the 13th century and was a contemporary of Dhammakitti Thera by whom the Mahāvaṁsa was continued.

P. 99ff

The Nikāyasaṅgraha of Dhammakitti shews in the general arrangement of material and in particular instances it; dependence on the same sources. The history of the sects is treated in greater detail here. We learn, for example, that the Sāgaliya sect branched off from the Dhammaruchi of the Abhayagirivihāra and bore the name of their leader Thera Sāgala. They had their seat in the Dakkhiṇagirivihāra. This took place under Goṭ hābhaya, 795 years after Buddha's Nirvāṇa, *i.e.,* in 252 A.D. The record of the writings of the separate sects is entirely new. The source for these additions I cannot name, but merely remark that the Kathāvatthu-ppakaraṇa-Aṭṭhakathā does not so much as mention the Sāgaliyā.

Of especial interest is the dream of Kālāsoka and his dialogue with the Therī Nandā. This is taken directly or indirectly through an unknown source from the Aṭṭhakathā (*cf.* the Commentary, 108, 8 on Mahāvaṁsa, IV. 38ff.).

P. 102

The Dhātuvaṁsa[5] belongs to the myth-cycle of Malaya and Rohaṇa. It contains much popular tradition wanting in the works of the Aṭṭhakathā cycle. Otherwise, its dependence on the Mahāvaṁsa is easily recognised. The Dhātuvaṁsa, however, does not seem to be an independent work, but corresponds to a Pāli work existing only in manuscript, entitled Nalāṭ adhātuvaṁsa: it is only a Singhalese translation, then, of this work, like those of the Mahābōdhivaṁsa and Thūpavaṁsa. The author of the Singhlese Dhātuvaṁsa is Kakusandha: when he lived is not ascertainable.

Pp. 103 – 107

From several chronicles, especially the Rājāvali, Rājaratnākara, and Pūjāvali, we have accounts of the early history till Vijaya. The Rājāvali, the most recent of these, belongs probably to the beginning of the 18th century, and shews that its author made copious use of older sources. The introduction and the mythological parts are original. After a cosmological and geographical review, the dynastic list of kings follows down to Siddartha, the Buddha. It is, however, the introduction of new material not hitherto utilised in the epics that gives to the Rājāvali an independent value. For instance, the reign of Mahāsammata is depicted as a "golden age." Of king Chetiya it is told that he was the first to bring falsehood on earth and that as a punishment the earth swallowed him. Under Mahāpratāpa, murder and other crimes forced their way in, and the span of life of the princes was from that time shorter. After an account (taken from the Mahāvaṁsa-Commentary. 84, 4ff.) of the founding of the Sakya dynasty, an episode from another source follows: – The eldest sister of the exiled sons of Ariṭṭa, "the third Okkāka", attacked by leprosy, is placed by her brothers in a deep grave and covered with brushwood. The king of Benares, stricken by the same disease, had sought refuge in the same forest. He cures himself by an herb, finds the princess, cures her and makes her his wife. Rāma's son hearing of his father's abode builds there the town of Koliya. The 32 sons of Rāma and the princess marry the 32 daughters of the four kings of Kapilavatthu, and thenceforward the princes of Koliya and Kapilavatthu were united into one clan. The rest of this work is taken from the Mahāvaṁsa.

P. 108

The Rājaratnākara, belonging probably to the middle of the 16th century, is likewise specially detailed upon the history of Vijaya. The general scheme corresponds to that of the Rājāvali, and adds nothing to the Vijaya myth. The Pūjāvali in Chapter XXXIII treats the Vijaya history quite briefly, disposing of it in a single section.

P. 115

Generally, it may be said that, of the three chronicles, the Rājaratnākara stands nearest to the Mahāvaṁsa and draws upon it most largely. The other two stand in closer relation to one another, as follows from several important coincidences. We can see, also, that the Rājaratnākara has had recourse to the Pūjāvali, and occasionally copied from it and likewise from the Nikāyasaṅgraha. The Rājāvali shews some originality, and adds details bearing the mark of popular origin, as in the Kuveṇi-legend. It also brings new particulars to the story of Kāvantissa, the father of Duṭṭhagāmani, while following in the main the narrative in the Mahāvaṁsa, XXII. 13ff. Popular accretions are visible in the history of the *Beminiṭi* famine under Coranāga, when, as the result of a curse, Jambudvīpa was visited for twelve years with famine. Finally, in the story of the death of Siri Saṅghabodhi. 40, 22 f., are several features absent from the account in the Mahāvaṁsa XXXVI. 92, *e.g.*, the allusion to the future Buddhahood of Saṅghabodhi, and the recognition of the several head as his. The Rājāvali, moreover (like the Mahābodhivaṁsa), mentions after the king Paṇḍukābhaya a king Gaṇatissa, who is absent from the lists in the Dīpavaṁsa and the Mahāvaṁsa. He is given a reign of 40 years, while Paṇḍukābhaya is given one of 30. According to the Mahāvaṁsa and also to the Pūjāvali, Paṇḍukābhaya reigned the whole 70 years.

The Singhalese chronicles agree with remarkable closeness on the subject of Gajabāhu, of whom the Mahāvaṁsa merely says that he built or consecrated monasteries, erected Thūpas and planned the Gāmanissa pond. A detailed account of this monarch is found in the Singhalese chronicles, especially the Rājāvali, the new matter being unmistakably from popular sources.

References

1. *Cf. J.R.A.S.* 1902, p. 171; *J.P.T.S.,* 1902-3, pp. 61ff.
2. *Cf. J.R.A.S.* 1875, p. 196.
3. Oldenberg, *Vinaya Piṭakaṁ,* II. p. 284f.
4. *Cf.* Strong, Pref. viii. ff., supporting Sobhita, who in the introduction to his edition (1890) discusses the question a authorship in same way.
5. The *Dhatuwansaya* of the Thera Kakusandha, edited by Gintoṭa Dhammakkandha, Dodanduwa, A.B. 2433=A.D. 1890. DeZoysa, *Catal,* p. 17.

12

Who was the Patron of Vasubandhu?

D.R. Bhandarkar, *M.A. Poona*

M. M. Haraprasad Shastri was the first to draw attention to the hemistich occurring in Vāmana's *Kāvyālaṁkāra-sūtra-vṛitti,* which speaks of a son of Chandragupta. In the last June number of this Journal, Prof.K. B. Pathak has brought the same passage to the notice of scholars, apparently not knowing that it had already been done, but his paper is interesting because the view he therein sets forth is different from that of M.M. Haraprasad Shastri. The interest of this subject was increased by the letter of Dr. Hoernle, which has appeared in the last September number. In this number has been published another letter on the same subject, *viz.,* from M.M. Haraprasad Shastri, in which he defends the view originally propounded by him. As the whole discussion has become very interesting, I feel tempted to state here my own view of the matter. In fact, the more I think of the hemistich, the more it appears historically important to me.

In the first place, it is of paramount importance to settle the correct reading of the explanatory note which Vāmana adds to the hemistich quoted by him. According to some MSS. it is आश्रयः कृतधियामित्यस्य वसुबन्धुसाचिव्योपक्षेपपरत्वात्साभिप्रायत्वम्। According to others it is exactly the same, but, instead of *Vasubandhu,*° they have *cha Subandhu.*° And so the question arises: which is the correct reading? In my opinion *Vasubandhu*° is the correct reading. For if we suppose for the moment that *cha Subandhu*° is the correct reading, the word *cha* becomes devoid of any significance. The passage cited above is followed by Vāmana's further note ऐतेन 'रतिविगलितबन्धे केशपाशे सुकेश्याः' इत्यत्र सुकेश्या इत्यस्य च

साभिप्रायत्वं व्याख्यातम्। Here also the word *cha* occurs, but here this word is perfectly appropriate and intelligible, as it obviously joins this sentence to the preceding. But it becomes meaningless in the first passage, if we suppose that *cha Subandhu*° is the correct reading. I have, therefore, no doubt that *Vasubandu*° represents the correct reading. And as Subandhu, being a Brāhmanic poet, was better known to the scribes than the Buddhist monk Vasubandu and as the form of the letter *v* is even to this day found extremely similar to that of *ch* in old MSS., it is perfectly intelligible how *Vasubandhu*° came to be written *cha Subandhu*°. There is another consideration also which supports the reading *Vasubandhu*° and not *cha Subandhu*°. In the tenth of the prefatory verses of the *Vāsavadattā,* Subandhu wails that on the death of Vikramāditya, love or poetry was gone. But he speaks of Vikramāditya in such a way as to clearly show that the former was never a contemporary of the latter but that the latter was so much prior to the former that he had come to be looked upon as the traditional patron of poets. The wail is exactly like that which was given expression to by much later poets. This, on the contrary, is strong evidence, in my opinion, for putting Subandhu not earlier than A.D. 500 *i.e.,* at least a hundred years later than Chandragupta II, if we suppose with Dr. Bhandarkar and others that he was the traditional Vikramāditya. I therefore firmly believe that *Vasubandu*° and not *cha Subandhu*° must be the correct reading. And the objection that "a Buddhist monk would not accept office" can very well be answered by saying with Dr. Hoernle that the term *sāchivya* does not necessarily refer to the ministerial office but may simply mean "companionship" or "friendship".

In this connection it is important to read the following, which has been gleaned by Dr. Takakusu from Paramārtha's *Life of Vasubandhu*—"King Vikramāditya of Ayodhyā, North India, was first a patron of the Sāṁkhya School, but afterwards a patron of the Buddhism on account of Vasubandhu's success in religious activity. He sent his Crown Prince (Bālāditya) to Vasubandhu to learn Buddhism, and the queen too became one of his disciples. When he came to the throne, king Bālāditya, in conjunction with his Queen-mother, invited Vasubandhu to Ayodhyā and favoured him with special patronage."[1] Now, who were this Vikramāditya and his Crown Prince Bālāditya? Dr. Takakusu takes Vikramāditya to refer to Skandagupta, and says simply that Bālāditya was his successor, whosoever he may be. Mr. V.A. Smith identifies them with Skandagupta and his nephew Bālāditya, known as Narasiṁhagupta from the Bhitarī seal, thus setting aside the distinct statement of Paramārtha that Bālāditya was the son and not nephew of Vikramāditya.[2] Prof. Pathak agrees with both Dr. Takakusu and Mr. Smith in taking this Vikramāditya to be Skandagupta but regards Bālāditya whom he, like the latter, identifies with Narasiṁhagupta, as the immediate successor of Skandagupta, setting aside Puragupta, father of Narasiṁhagupta mentioned in the Bhitarī seal. I think it is not justifiable to accept Paramārtha's testimony only partially, or to frame any theory contrary to the evidence of the Bhitarī seal. In my opinion, the Vikramāditya alluded to by Paramārtha can be no other than Chandragupta II. Skandagupta was not the only Gupta prince who bore the title of Vikramāditya. Chandragupta II also was styled Vikramāditya. And that he is the Vikramāditya referred to by Paramārtha is rendered certain by the hemistich quoted by Vāmaṇa and the note appended to it by him. For Vāmana distinctly gives us to understand that the patron of Vasubandhu was a son of Chandragupta. Thus we require a king, who, according to Vāmana, was Chandragupta, and, according to Paramārtha, Vikramāditya. Chandragupta II only can answer to this description, as he is Chandragupta and had, we know, the title Vikramāditya. Any other conclusion would lead us to confusion as Prof. Pathak's, I am afraid, does. For, following Dr. Takakusu in taking Vikramāditya to be Skandagupta, he accepts Vasubandhu's date, *viz.*, A.D. 420-500, proposed by the former and yet says with Vāmana that the son of Chandragupta, who is represented to have just ascended the throne and who according to him is Kumāragupta, was also the patron of Vasubandhu. Kumāragupta, we know from the Bilsaḍ inscription,[3] must have come to the throne not later than G.E. 96=A.D. 414, the date of this inscription, *i.e.*,

Vasubandhu had distinguished himself as a literate six years earlier than A.D. 420, the date of his birth, according to Dr. Takakusu, which Prof. Pathak accepts. The conclusion, in my opinion, is therefore irresistible that the Vikramāditya mentioned by Paramārtha is Chandragupta II, and not Skandagupta. And the question now arises: who was the son of this Chandragupta-Vikramāditya, who has been referred to as Bālāditya by Paramārtha? Can it be Chandraprakāśa? After having seen that he is of the Gupta family it will not be difficult to reject such a supposition. Knowing as we do what the names of the imperial Guptas were like, it is inconceivable that Chandraprakāśa could have been the proper name of any Gupta sovereign. Can it then be Kumāragupta? This question, I am afraid, cannot satisfactorily and with certainty be answered. But I think he was probably not Kumāragupta. For he is already known to us as Mahendrāditya and cannot in all likelihood be Bālāditya. Who can this Bālāditya then be? In this connection it is worth while to turn our attention to certain inscribed clay seals, which the late Dr. Bloch discovered during his excavations at Basarh, the ancient Vaisalī, nearly eleven years ago.[4] The most important of these seals bears the following inscription: –

(1) *Mahārājādhirāja Śrī-Chandragupta-*
(2) *patnī Mahārāja-śrī-Govindagupta-*
(3) *mātā Mahādevī śrī-Dhru-*
(4) *vasvāminī.*

Here the great queen Dhruvasvāminī is mentioned as the wife of the *Mahārājādhirāja* Chandragupta and mother of the *Mahārāja* Govindagupta. The names Chandragupta and Dhruvasvāminī are an unmistakable indication of their being Chandragupta II and his wife Dhruvadevī, whose names we find mentioned in the Gupta inscriptions. As the names of both Chandragupta and his son Govindagupta are mentioned in the seal, both must be supposed to be living at that time if the seal is to be supposed to have any significance. Every queen belonging to a dynasty in power is the wife of one king and mother of another, and there is nothing special in the fact if both did not live and were not kings at one and the same time. I am therefore inclined to believe that Chandragupta and Govindagupta were both living when the seal of Dhruvasvāminī was impressed on the clay piece. Chandragupta, as he is called *Mahārājadhirāja,* was, of course, the paramount sovereign, and Govindagupta was holding some province under him, probably the district about Basarh, as the title *Mahārāja* shows. But let us proceed a step further and ask why, if Kumāragupta was also a son of Chandragupta and Dhruvadevī, his name is omitted and that of Govindagupta alone mentioned. The name of the latter only is specified because I think he was *Yuvarāja.* For in the seal of a queen it is natural to expect the names of her husband the king and her son who is heir-apparent to the throne.

Now, it is worthy of note that none of the seals found at Basarh speak of any place or district except Vaisālī and Tīrabhukhti, the district of which Vaisālī was the headquarters. It is therefore difficult to avoid the conclusion that the seals were not attached to letters come from outside Basarh, whatever Dr. Bloch has said to the contrary. Again, if they had really come from other districts, they would not have been all found together in one room, as was actually the case, but would have come to light in the different parts excavated. I suspect that the place where the seals were found was that of a potter who was, perhaps, the only person entrusted in Vaisālī for preparing seals. When these seals were prepared, he must have naturally caught hold of some stray pieces of clay and impressed them with the seals to test them. This explains, I think, why some clay pieces have more than one seal impressed on them, which are apparently unconnected with one another. That this place belonged to some potter, receives confirmation from the face that "the seals were found mixed up with fragments of pottery." I have, therefore, no doubt that the seals here found all belonged to officials and private individuals connected with and residing in Vaisālī. Some of the seals of the former class have the following one them: *"Śrī-Yuvarāja-bhaṭṭārakapadīya-kumārāmāty-ādhikaraṇasya*—"Of the office of the Kumārāmātya of His Highness the Crown Prince" and (2) *Yuvarāja-bhaṭṭāraka-padīya-bal-ādhikaraṇasya*—"Of the Military office of His Highness of Crown Prince."

This shows that the district of Tīrabhukti with Vaisālī, as its capital, was held by the Crown Prince during the reign of Chandragupta II, to whose time all the seals belong, as Dr. Bloch rightly supposes. This also is quite in keeping with the supposition made above that Govindagupta's name is mentioned in his mother's seal also, because he was the ruler of the province round about Basarh. All things considered, Govindagupta appears to be the *Chandragupta-tanaya* alluded to in the verse quoted by Vāmana and also the Bālādiya, son of Vikramāditya (Chandragupta II), mentioned by Paramārtha.

The latest date for Chandragupta II is G.E. 93=A.D. 411, supplied by a Sānchi inscription, and the earliest date for Kumāragupta is, as stated above, A.D. 414. Govindagupta-Bālāditya has, therefore, to be placed between A.D. 411-14. It is difficult to say why he had such a short reign. He may have been ousted by his brother Kumāragupta or he may have died a natural death and without any heir.

References

1. *Jour.* R. As. Society, for 1905, p. 44.
2. *Early History of India,* pp. 292-3.
3. *Corpus Inscriptionum Indicarum,* Vol. iii, p. 42 ff.
4. *Archæol. Survey of India, Annual Report* for 1903, p. 101 ff.

13
The Ājivikas – A Sect of Buddhist Bhikshus

K.B. Pathak, *B.A., Hubli*

The Buddhist emperor Aśoka and his grandson Daśaratha dedicated certain cave-dwellings to the sect of the Ājīvikas. Mr. V.A. Smith, in his *Early History of India,* p. 156, tells us that the members of this sect went about naked and were noted for ascetic practices of the most rigorous kind. In his opinion the Ājīvikas had little or nothing in common with the Buddhists and were intimately connected with the Jainas. It will, therefore, be very interesting for Sanskrit scholars to know what a distinguished Digambara Jaina author, who lived at a time when Buddhism still prevailed in Southern India, has to say regarding this sect.

The Jaina work entitled *Āchārasāra,* which is in verse, and its Kannaḍa commentary which is in prose, were both composed by Vīranandi on Monday the first of the bright half of Jyêshṭha in the cyclic year Śrīmukha and Śaka 1076, as we learn from the colophon: –

Svasti śrīman-Méghachaṁdra-traividya-dévara-śrīpāda-prasād-āsādit-ātma-prabhāva-samasta-vidyā-prabhāva-sakala-dig-vartti-śrīmad-Vīranaṁ li-siddhāṁta-chakravarttigaḷu Śaka varsha 1076 Śrīmukha-nāma saṁvatsara Jyéshṭa Śukla 1 Sômavārad aṁ lu tāvu māḍid Āchārasārakke Karṇṇāṭaka vṛittiyaṁ māḍiḍaparu|.

There are numerous references to Buddhism in the *Āchārasāra*. This clearly shows that in the Kanarese country there were numerous followers of Buddha in Śaka 1076. We read

ब्रह्मोमापतिगांर्विदशाक्येंदुतपनादिषु।

मोहकादंबरीमत्तेषा (ष्वा)सधीर्देवमूढता॥

Āchārasāra III, 46

बाह्ये विचारचारूणि सौगतादिमतान्यलं।

क्लेशातिमोहदान्येव स्युः किंपाकवदंगिनां॥

Āchārasāra III, 59

The most interesting fact preserved for us by Vīranandi is that in his time there was a very influential sect of Buddhist mendicants called Ājīvakas, who subsisted on *kāṁji,* and whose intensely severe austerities called forth the admiration of their Jaina contemporaries. Though wanting, as Buddhists, in righteousness as defined in the Jaina scriptures and thus incapable of attaining *nirvāṇa* in the Jaina sense, the Ājīvakas were nevertheless considered by the author of the *Āchārasāra* so great as to be able to reach the heaven called *Sahasrāra-kalpa* in Jaina cosmography. Vīranandi says:—

परिव्राड् ब्रह्मकल्पांतं यात्युग्राचारवानपि।

आजीवकः सहस्रारकल्पांतं दर्शनोज्झितः॥

Āchārasāra XI, 127

Commentary

Parivrāṭ | *parivrājakaṁ* | *Brahmakalp-āṁtaṁ* | *Brahmakalpaṁ-baraṁ* | *aty-ugrāchāra-vān api* | *beṭṭitt appa negartteyan vḷḷan ādoḍaṁ* | *Ājīvakaḥ* | *Bauddha-bhédam appa kāṁji Bhikshu* | *Sahasrāra-kalp-āṁtaṁ* | *sahasrāra-kalpaṁ-baraṁ* | *darśan-ôjjhiṭaḥ* | *samyaklvam illadaṁ* | *yāti* | *pékuṁ* || ||

Translation

An ascetic, though practising very severe austerities goes up to the heaven called Brahma-kalpa. An Ājīvaka, a Bhikshu of a Buddhist sect, subsisting upon *kāṁji,* goes up to the heaven called Sahasrāra-kalpa [in Jaina cosmography].

There are two paper manuscripts of the *Āchārasāra.* One belongs to the Lakshmīsêna-Maṭha at Kolhāpur and is dated Śaka 1692; and the other is the property of the Jaina community of Śiroḷ in the Kolhāpur State, and was copied by a famous

Jaina nun named Anantamati in Śaka 1666. Both manuscripts are written in Old Kanarese characters. The form Ājīvaka occurs in both. The correct form should be Ājīvika, a believer in non-existence of the soul, from *a-jīva,* of आस्तिक and दैष्टिक Pāṇinī IV, 460. Anantamati's manuscript reads *kāji* for *kāṁji, Baudda,* for *Bauddha* and *pokkuṁ* for *pôkuṁ.* The reading *kāṁji* is supported by the authority of Mādhavachandra, who in his comments on the 545th *Gāthā* of the *Trilôka-sāra,* says: –

नग्रांडलक्षणाश्चरका एकदंडित्रिदंडिलक्षणाः परिव्राजका ब्रह्मकल्पपर्यंतं गच्छंति। न तत उपरि। कांजिकादिभोजिन आजीवा अच्युतकल्पपर्यंतं यांति। न तत उपरि।

The *Māghanandi-śrācakāchāra,* which belongs to the middle of the 13th century speaks of the Buddhists as meat-eaters who defended their practice by saying that what is dropped in a plate is holy and sanctioned by the *Sūtras*: –

Pātré patitaṁ pavitraṁ sūtr-ôktam id eṁdu Baudd(ddh)ar aḍagaṁ tiṁbaru.

Māgh., Chap. VI, Śiroḷ MS., p. 714b.

As regards the Ājīvakas, we are told that they will be born as inferior gods in the heaven called Achyuta-kalpa.

Māgh., Chap. II, Śiroḷ MS., p. 669.

The *Māghanandi-śrāvakāchāra* is frequently, quoted by Padmaprabha-traividya, who may therefore be assigned to the end to the 13th century. In the last chapter of his *Viṁśatiprarūpaṇi,* Padmaprabha thus explains the first part of the *Gāthā* in the *Trilôka-sāra,* referred to above: –

चरया य परि० बाजा बह्मो०ति अ०चुद पदो०ति आजीवा।

....

Ājīvā | ambila-kūḷan umbaru | Achyuta-pad-otti | Achyuta-kalpa-paryyaṁta [ṁ] puṭṭuvaru.

The Ājīvās, eaters of *kāṁji* food, will be born in the Achyuta-kalpa.

The conclusion, that we can safely draw from the passages cited above, is that the Ājīvakas were well-known to the Jaina authors of the later Chālukya and Yādava periods as a sect of Buddhist Bhikshus who lived solely or chiefly on *kāṁji.*

[All references to Ājīvakas have been culled together in my paper on this sect (*Jour. Bomb. As. Soc.*, Vol. XXI, pp. 403-5). The Jainas have no doubt called them to be a sect of the Buddhist Bhikshus, as Professor Pathak has conclusively shown us. But the Buddhists also appear in their turn to have shown them to be Nirgranthas, for the latter have actually been once called Ājīvakas in the *Divyāvadāna* (Cowel and Neil, p. 427). The truth of the matter is that they were neither Buddhists nor Jainas even in much later times, but formed a distinct sect; and consequently Professor Hultzsch is not correct in taking Ājīvakas mentioned in some of the South Indian Inscriptions to be Jainas (Vol. I, pp. 88, 89, 92 and 108).—D.R.B.].

14

On Buddhamitra, the Teacher of Vasubandhu

K.B. Pathak

Dr. Takakusu says that Vindhyavāsa was successful in a dispute with Buddhamitra, the teacher of Vasubandhu. Vindhyavāsa lived in the middle of the tenth century after the Buddha's Nirvāṇa or about A.D. 450. In A.D. 448-49, corresponding to the Gupta year 129, during the reign of Kumāragupta a Bhikshu Buddhamitra installed an image of Buddha at Mankuwar, and in the inscription on the pedestal of the image tells us that "Buddha was not refuted in respect of his opinions." This shows that this Buddhist Bhikshu was so famous for his learning that no contemporary Brahman scholar, however eminent, could venture to attack Buddhism. I therefore conclude that this Bhikshu Buddhamitra of the Mankuwar inscription was identical with the Buddhamitra who was the teacher of Vasubandhu, the latter being contemporary with Kumāragupta, as I have already shown.

Another inference which I draw from the expression *sva-mat-āviruddhasya* applied to Buddha in this inscription is that the religious controversy, in which Buddhamitra was so signally defeated by Vindhyavāsa that the reigning sovereign Vikramāditya transferred his patronage from Buddhism to Brahminism, could not have taken place in the reign of Chandragupta-Vikramāditya; as in that case the statement that Buddha was not refuted in respect of his opinions, would never have been accepted as true by the people in the time of Kumāragupta. We are, therefore, justified in concluding that this religious controversy took place in the time of Skandagupta-Vikramāditya and that Vasubandhu's patrons mentioned by Paramārtha were Skandagupta-Vikramāditya and Narasiṁhagupta-Bālāditya.

As regards the son of Chandragupta II, whose patronage Vasubandhu enjoyed according to the interesting half-verse which Vāmana has preserved for us, I have already identified this prince with Kumāragupta. It is thus clear that Buddhamitra and his famous pupil Vasubandhu were both living in the reigns of Kumāragupta and Skandagupta; while Vasubandhu was contemporary with Kumāragupta, Skandagupta and Bālāditya, and died at the age of 80, shortly after the accession of the last named prince. The date of Bālāditya's accession is as yet far from being settled. We are, therefore, not able to say how old Vasubandhu was in A.D. 414, the year in which Kumāragupta ascended the throne. Vasubandhu's literary career, nevertheless, nearly coincides with first three quarters of the fifth century; while Dignāga, to whom I-tsing refers as being later than Vasubandhu, must be placed in the last quarter of the fifth and the first quarter of the sixth century (A.D. 475-525). Texts of Dignāga's works on logic were in existence in the year A.D. 539, the date of the Chinese mission, and were carried by Paramārṭha to China in the year 546, and there translated into Chinese.

15

Ajivikas[1]

D.R. Bhandarkar, *M.A.; Poona*

It has been long since recognised that the Ājīvikas of Aśoka's Pillar-edict VII were the same as the Ājīviyas of the Jaina scriptures and the Ājīvakas of the Buddhist canon. And Prof. Kern was the first to contend that they were an ancient ascetic order, worshipping Nārāyaṇa, *i.e.,* a subdivision of the Vaishṇavas. This view he has set forth in *Der Buddhismus und seine Geschichte in Indien,* Vol. II. It was countenanced by Prof. Bühler, who in his paper on "The Barābar and Nāgārjunī hill cave inscriptions of Aśoka and Daśaratha"[2] says as follows: "As Professor Kern's work will not be accessible to the majority of Indian readers, I shall try to give a brief exposition of his arguments, regarding which he has kindly furnished me some fuller information. Assuming, as must be done, that the Ājīvikas of our inscriptions are the same as those named in Aśoka's seventh Pillar-edict, he translates the words 1. 4-5: *hém-éva bābhanésu Ājīvikésu-pi-mé kaṭé imé viyapaṭā hôhaṁti-ti* by 'Likewise I have arranged it that these (*Dharma-mahāmātras*) will be occupied also with the Brāhmaṇical Ājīvikas.' With the information thus elicited from the Pilar-edict, he combines the statements of Utpala regarding the Ājīvikas, who are mentioned in Varāhamihira's *Bṛihat-Jātaka,* XV. 1, together with the Vṛiddhaśrāvakas, the Nirgranthas or Jainas, and other ascetics. Utpala says in his commentary: *ājīvika-grahaṇaṁ cha Nārāyaṇ-āśritānāṁ,* "and the use of (the term) Ājīvika refers to those who have taken refuge with Nārāyaṇa," and in support of this explanation, brings forward two Prākṛit passages, introducing them with the words: *tathā cha vaṁ* [read *tathā ch=aiva*] *Kālakāchāryaḥ*—"and thus (*says*) also Kālakāchārya." In the first of these passages the term *éaḍaṇḍīā, i.e., ékadaṇḍin,* "(*an ascetic*) carrying one staff" (instead of the usual triple staff) is used for *Ājīvika* and in the second a longer explanation is given, which Utpala renders by *Késavamārga-dīkshitaḥ Késavabhaktaḥ Bhāgavata ity=arthaḥ.*" Prof. Bühler further adds that Prof. Kern's "confidence in the statements of Utpala appears justifiable, because the latter are supported by so ancient a writer as Kālakāchārya. The Kālakāchārya, quoted by him, is in all probability the famous Jaina teacher, who is said to have changed the date of the Pajjusan festival in the year 993 after Vīra, or A.D. 466. The identification is suggested by the fact that Utpala's Kālakāchārya is the author of a work on astrology and that the Jainas ascribe to their latest Kālakāchārya an innovation which presupposes the study of astronomy. If thus the author, quoted by Utpala, belongs to the fifth century, his statements deserve to be treated with all due respect."

It will thus be seen that, according to Professors Kern and Bühler, the Ājīvikas are Vaishṇavas. This view rests on two passages from Utpala's commentary on Varāhamihira's *Bṛihajjātaka*. The first passage is: *Ājīvika-grahaṇaṁ cha Nārāyaṇ-āśritānām,* which Prof. Kern renders by "and the use of (the term) Ājīvika refers to those who have taken refuge with Nārāyaṇa". The second passage is a quotation from Kālakāchārya, which Utpala renders by the Sanskrit *Keśava-mārga-dīkshitaḥ Keśava-bhaktaḥ Bhāgavata=ity-arthaḥ* and which, Prof. Kern supposes, shows that the Jaina teacher regards Ājīvikas as Bhāgavatas. Now, in the first place, the translation proposed by Prof. Kern for the first passage is not correct. That this is the case will be seen from the following extract from Utpala's commentary on *Bṛihajjātaka* XV. 1:

एकस्थैश्चतुरादिभिर्बलयुतैर्जाता: पृथग्वीर्यगै:
शाक्याजीविकभिक्षुवृद्धचरका निर्ग्रन्थवन्याशना: ।
माहेयज्ञगुरुक्षपाकरसितप्राभाकरीनै: क्रमात्
प्रव्रज्या बलिभि: समा परिजितैस्तत्स्वामिभि: प्रच्युति: ॥

तत्रादाबेव चतुरादिभिरेकस्थैर्ग्रहैर्जातस्य प्रव्रज्यायोगं शार्दूलविक्रीडितेनाह ॥ एकस्थैरिति । यत्र तत्र राशौ अहाश्चतुरादयश्चत्वार: पञ्च षट् सप्त वा एकस्था यदा भवन्ति । सर्वे बलहीनास्तदा

जातस्य प्रव्रज्या न भवति। तेषां चतुरादीनां एकत्रगाानां मध्याद्यद्येकोऽपि बलवान्भवति तदैव प्रव्रज्याः भवन्ति। यदा बहवो बलिनस्तदा बहवः प्रव्रज्या भवन्ति। एवमेकस्थैश्चतुरादिभिर्बलयुतैर्जाताः प्रव्रज्याभाजो भवन्ति। यस्मादुक्तं॥ प्रव्रज्या बलिभिः समा॥ ताश्च पृथग्वीर्यगैः शाक्यादयो भवन्ति। वीर्यगैर्बलिभिर्ग्रहैः पृथक् समस्ता भवन्ति। शाक्यादीनां माहेयादयो ग्रहा यथोक्तक्रमेण॥ तद्यथा॥ चतुरादीनामेकस्थानां मध्याद्यदा बलवान्माहेयो भवति तदा शाक्यो भवति। शाक्यो रक्तपटः। अथ चतुरादिनां मध्याद्यदा ज्ञो बुधो बलवान्भवति तदा आजीविको भवति। आजीविकश्चैकदण्डी। एवं जीवो बलवान्यदा भवति तदा भिक्षुर्भवति। संन्यासी ज्ञेय[3]। यदा चन्द्रो बलवान् तदा वृद्धश्रावको भवति। वृत्तभंगभयात् श्रावकशब्दो लुप्तो द्रष्टव्यः। वृद्धश्रावकः कपाली। शुक्रे बलवति चरको भवति। चरको चक्रधरः[4]। सौरे बलवति निर्ग्रन्थः निर्ग्रन्थो नग्नः क्षपणकः प्रावरणादिरहितः। आदित्ये बलवति वन्याशनो भवति। वने भवं वन्यं तदआतीति वन्याशनः। तपस्वी मूलफलाशनः। एवं क्रमात्प्रव्रज्यापर्यायः। एते च कालकमताद्व्याख्याताः। तथा च कालकाचार्यः॥ तावसिओ दिणणाहे चंदे कावालिअं तहा भणिअं। रत्तवडो भूमिसुवे सोमसुवे एअदण्डी अ॥ देवगुरु-शुक्क-कोणा कवेण जई-चरअ-खवणाइं॥ अस्यार्थ;। तावसिओ तापसिकः। दिणणाहे दिननाथे। चंदे चन्द्रे। कावालिअं कापालिकः। तहा भणिअं तथा भणितः। रत्तवडो रक्तपटः। भूमिसुवे भूमिसुते। सोमसुवे सोमसुते। एअदण्डी अ एकदण्डी च। देवगुरुर्बृहस्पतिः। शुक्कः शुक्रः। कोणः शनिः। कवेण क्रमेण। जई यतिः। चरअ चरकः। खवणाइं क्षपणकः। अत्र वृद्धश्रावकग्रहणं महेश्वराश्रितानां प्रव्रज्यानामुपलक्षणं। आजीविकग्रहणं च नारायणाश्रितानां। तथा च कालक-संहितायां पठ्यते। जलण-हर-सुगअ-केसव-सुइ-ब्रम्ह-णग्ग-मग्गेसु दिक्काणं। णाअव्वा सुराइ-गहा कमेण नाह गऊं॥ अस्यार्थः जलण ज्वलनः। साग्निक इत्यर्थः। हर ईश्वरभक्तः। भट्टारकः। सुगअ सुगतः। बौद्ध इत्यर्थः। केसव केशवभक्तः। भागवत इत्यर्थः। सुइ श्रुतिमार्गरतः। मीमांसकः। ब्रम्ह ब्रह्मभक्तः। वानप्रस्थः। नग्ग नग्नः। क्षपणकः। मध्गेसु मार्गेषु। दिक्काणं दीक्षानां। णाअव्वा ज्ञातव्याः। सुराइगहा सूर्यादिग्रहाः। कमेण क्रमेण। नाह गऊं नाथ गतः।

Now, with regard to the first passage *Ājīvika-grahaṇaṁ cha Nārāyaṇ-āśritānāṁ,* it is plain that the word *cha* indicates that it is connected with the preceding sentence, and that consequently the words *pravrajyānām=upalakshaṇaṁ* from the latter, require to be understood after *Nārāyaṇāśritānāṁ* in the former passage. Prof. Kern, however, not perceiving the force of *cha* takes *Ājīvika-grahaṇaṁ cha Nārāyaṇ-āśritānāṁ* as a sentence distinct in itself. Evidently, therefore, he cannot be right in translating it by "and the use of (the term) Ājīvika refers to those who have taken refuge with Nārāyaṇa." The true rendering of the passage ought to be: "and (the term) Ājīvika is used as a mark to denote the monastic orders seeking refuge with Nārāyaṇa." Here the most important word is *upalakshaṇa,* which Prof. Kern has entirely lost sight of. *Upalakshaṇa* means a mark indicative of something that the work itself does not actually express. Sanskrit commentators often employ the word *upalakshaṇa,* when they want a certain word or expression in the original to denote things, not, truly speaking, signified by that word or expression. And precisely the same practice is followed here by Utpala. To understand this fully and also the real significance of the two passages, on the misinterpretation of which Prof. Kern's view is based, it is necessary to comprehend the gist of Varāhamihira's stanza and Utpala's commentary thereon, quoted above. According to Varāhamihira, a man turns a recluse when four or more planets are clustered together in one and the same zodiacal division at the time of his birth and at least one of them is powerful. And according as this powerful planet is the Sun, Moon, Mars, Mercury, Jupiter, Venus or Saturn, he becomes a *vanyaśāna,* Vṛiddha [-śrāvaka], Śākya, Ājīvika, *bhikshu,* Charaka or Nirgrantha. Utpala tells us that Varāhamihira has made this enumeration on the authority of Kālakāchārya. The latter's verse *Tāvasio diṇaṇāhe,* etc., is then cited, which tells us that a man becomes a Tāpasika, Kāpālika, *raktapaṭa,* Ekadaṇḍī, *yaṭi,* Charaka or Kshapaṇaka when the predominant planet is Sūrya, Chandra, etc. The Tāpasika, Kāpālika, etc., of this verse are taken by Utpala to correspond to the *vanyāsāna,* Vṛiddha-śrāvaka, etc., of Varāhamihira. How far this procedure of Utpala is justifiable I leave it to scholars to determine. But certain it is that he would have us take Vṛiddha-śrāvaka and Ājīvika to *mean* Kāpālika and Ekadaṇḍī. Now, there is another verse of Kālakāchārya, which also informs us what kind of recluse a man becomes under precisely these astrological conditions. The list of ascetic denominations mentioned in this verse agrees with that previously given except in two points. These exceptions are *Harabhakta* or *Maheśvar-āśrita* and *Keśavabhakta* or *Nārāyaṇ-āśrita,* and, as this second verse of Kālakāchārya says, a man becomes one of these according as the powerful planet is Chandra or Buddha. But is has been just stated about that in the same astrological conditions he becomes a Vṛiddha-śrāvaka (=Kāpālika) or Ājīvika (=Ekadaṇḍī).

Hence arises the necessity, says Utpala, of understanding Vṛiddha-śrāvaka and Ājīvika of the original stanza as marks (*upalakshaṇa*) denoting *Maheśvar-āśrita* and *Nārāyaṇ-āśrita.* Thus, according to Utpala, Ājīvika does not signify *Nārāyaṇ-āśrita, Keśava-bhakta,* or Bhāgavata, as Prof. Kern supposes, but simply indicates it; and it is equally incontrovertible that Kālakāchārya also never held such a view. The theory propounded by Prof. Kern and upheld by Bühler that the Ājīvikas are Vaishṇavas has, therefore, no grounds at all to stand upon.

It will not be our of place, I think, if a short account of these Ājīvikas is given with a view to point out who they were. My work here will be principally that of bringing some of the scattered rays to a focus. The founders of this monastic order were Nanda-Vachchha, Kisa-Saṁkichchha, and Makkhali Gosāla, of whom the last is by far the most famous, as he is one of the six well-known teachers mentioned in Buddhist scriptures. Buddhaghosha tells us that an Ājīvika is *nagga-pabbajito.*[5] Ājīvikas are also described as *achela*[6], *i.e.,* unclothed. And, in confirmation of this, there are at least two stories forthcoming from the *Vinaya-piṭaka.* According to the first, which is in the *Mahāvagga,*[7] while the Buddha and the Bhikshus were once staying in the Anāthapiṇḍikāśrama in Jetavaṇa at Śrāvastī, it began to rain all over the world. The Buddha informed the Bhikshus that was the last mighty storm over the whole world, and consequently asked them to let themselves be rained down upon. The Bhikshus accordingly divested themselves of their robes, and exposed their bodies to rain. On that very day, Visākhā, mother of Migāra, was engaged in preparations for a feast to the Buddha and his Bhikshus. When the preparations were over, she sent her maid servant to the Buddha to intimate that dinner was ready. When the maid-servant approached the Anāthapiṇḍikāśrama, she saw the naked Bhikshus, but concluded from their being naked that they were Ājīvikas. The other story, which is from the *Nissaggiya,*[8] is, that, while a few Bhikshus left Sāketa for Śrāvastī, they were waylaid by robbers, who deprived them of their robes. Being forbidden by the Buddha to ask for another garment, they went naked to Śrāvastī to meet the other Bhikshus there. But the latter instead of recognising them as mendicants of their order, mistook them for Ājīvikas as they were unclothed.

The Ājīvikas covered their bodies with dust, and ate the ordure of a calf.[9] They were noted for ascetic practices of the most rigorous kind. Some of the austerities they practiced are mentioned in one *Jātaka* to have been "painful squatting on heels, swinging in the air like bats, reclining on thorns, and scorching themselves with five fires.[10] Again, as first pointed out by Prof. Bühler, they branded the hands of their novice with a heated ball.[11] Their doctrine has been admirably summed up by the Buddha in the words *n=atthi kammaṁ n=atthi kiriyaṁ n=atthi viriyan=ti.*[12] They were thus complete fatalists.

The Ājīvikas appear to have been in existence long before the rise of Buddhism. The most celebrated exponent of their doctrines in the time of the Buddha was Makkhali Gosāla. But he was only the third of their teachers, the two preceding ones being Nanda Vachchha and Kisa Saṁkichchha. They seem to have been of some consequence during the Maurya period. The Barābar and Nāgārjunī cave inscriptions[13] show that these caves had been excavated and dedicated specially to them by Aśoka and his grandson Daśaratha. The Ājīvikas are also mentioned in Aśoka's Pillar-edict VII, in connection with the religious sects which the *Dharma-mahāmātras* had been instructed by him to concern themselves with.[14] Then we do not hear of the Ājīvikas till the time of Varāhamihira (*circa* A.D. 525) who, as we have seen above, refers to them in his *Bṛihajjātaka*. An allusion to them also occurs in the *Jānakī-haraṇa* of Kumāradāsa (A.D. 725). In chap. X, v. 76, Rāvaṇa is represented to have approached Ṣītā in the guise of an Ājīvika monk. Some inscriptions,[15] found in the Madras, Presidency and belonging to the first half of the thirteenth century, speak of a tax on the Ājīvikas which it appears to have been customary in those days to impose on them. It is not clear why they were so much looked down upon. Prof. Hultzsch, who has edited the inscriptions, considers them to be Jainas, but specifies no grounds in support of his position. He is probably led to hold this view because he thinks that there is no evidence to show that the Ājīvikas were existing so late as the 13th century. But, as has been recently shown by Prof. Pathak,[16] they were well-known to the Digambara Jaina authors of the later Chālukya and Yādava periods and are mentioned as living chiefly on *kāṁji*. They, however, mistook them to be a sect of Buddhist Bhikshus. The Buddhists, in their turn, have mistaken them for Nirgranthas, for the latter have actually been once called Ājīvikas in the *Divyāvadāna*.[17] The truth of the matter appears to be that they were neither Buddhists nor Jainas even in the later times, but formed a distinct sect.

The *Amarakosha*[18] speaks of five kinds of *saṁnyāsins*, among whom Maskarins are mentioned. It is worth nothing that the word *maskarin* occurs also in Pāṇini's *sūtra;* मस्कर-मस्करिणौ वेणुपरिव्राजकयोः (VI. 1. 154). According to Pāṇini, Maskarin was thus a Parivrājaka. Patañjali's gloss on this *sūtra* is as follows: न वै मस्करोऽस्यास्तीति मस्करी परिव्राजकः। किं तर्हि। मा कृत कर्माणि मा कृत कर्माणि शान्तिर्वः श्रेयसीत्याहातो मस्करी परिव्राजकः॥ On the same *sūtra,* the *Kāśikā* has the following: परिव्राजकेऽपि माङ्युपपदे करोतेस्ताच्छील्य इनिर्निपात्यते। माङो ह्रस्वत्वं सुट् च तथैक। माकरणशीलो मस्करी कर्मापवादित्वात्परिव्राजक उज्यते। स त्वेवमाह। मा कुरुत कर्माणि शान्तिर्वः श्रेयसीति॥ Kaiyaṭa's *Pradipa* on Patañjali's *Mahābhāshya* gives the following: मा कृतेति अयं मा कृत अयं, मा कृतेत्युपक्रम्य शान्तितः काम्यकर्नपरिहाणिर्युष्माकं श्रेयसीत्युपदेष्टा मस्करीत्युच्यते। माङ्पूर्वात्करोतेरिनिः सुडागमो माङो ह्रस्वश्च निपात्यते॥ Thus, according to Patañjali, a Maskarin was called Maskarin, because he said मा कृत कर्माणि etc. *i.e.,* "don't perform actions, don't perform actions; quietism (alone) is desirable to you." Now the only sect of ascetics who believed in the inefficacy of action was the Ājīvikas. Their precept: *n=atthi kammaṁ n=atthi kiriyaṁ n=atthi viriyam* has been quoted above. The same doctrine has been set forth at greater length in *Sāmañña-phala sutta* of the *Dīgha-Nikāya,* from which the following may be cited: "The attainment of any given condition, of any character, does not depend either on one's own acts, or on the acts of another, or on human effort. There is no such thing as power or energy, or human strength or human vigour."[19] It will thus be seen that the Maskarins as described by Patañjali can be no other than Ājivakas. This receives confirmation from two sources. First, Gosāla, one of the founders of the Ājīvaka sect, is in the Buddhist texts called Makkhali, which undoubtedly is the Pāli form of Maskarin. Secondly, the verse from the *Jānakī-haraṇa,* to which allusion has been made above, runs thus:

दम्भाजीविकमुत्तुङ्गजटामण्डितमस्तकम्।
कञ्चिन्मस्करिणं सीता ददर्शाश्रममागतम्॥

Here Rāvaṇa who approaches Sītā in a disguised form is called both Ājīvika and Maskarin, which must, therefore, be taken to be synonymous terms. In the *Bhaṭṭi-kāvya*[20] also Rāvaṇa is represented to have come to Sitā in the garb of a Maskarin. Among the various characteristics mentioned, that of his being a *śikhin* is specified. From this the commentator Mallinātha argues that he was a Tridaṇḍin, and not an Ekadaṇḍin, as the latter has no matted hair. But this does not agree with what Utpala says, for, as we have seen above, he gives Ekadaṇḍin as a synonym of Ājīvika. The word *śikhin* of the *Bhaṭṭi-kāvya,* however, agrees with the *uttuṅga-jaṭā*[0] of the *Jānakī-haraṇa,* and as the latter calls an Ājīvikas a Maskariṇ, it appears that an Ājīvika was really a Tridaṇḍin, and not an Ekadaṇḍin as Utpala supposes.

References

1. In June 1902 I communicated a note on the Ājīvikas to the *Jour. Bomb. As. Soc.,* which has been published in its Vol. XXI, p. 399 ff. This paper, though it has attracted the attention of some of the reputed scholars, does not seem to have been largely read. I, therefore, re-edit it here in a slightly recast form and embodying the latest information available to me.
2. Above, Vol. XX, p. 362.
3. Another reading: भिक्षुस्त्रिदण्डी यतिः
4. Another reading: चक्रकरस्त्रिः
5. *Jour. R. As. Soc.* for 1898, p. 197.
6. *Jātaka* I, 390.

7. M. VIII. 15, 2-6.
8. N. VI. 2.
9. *Jāt.* I. 390; the reading *vachchhaka*[0] noticed in the footnote is obviously the correct one,. and not *machchhaka*[0] adopted in the text.
10. *Ibid.*, I. 493; other ascetic practices to which they resorted, have been set forth in the *Majjhima-Nikāya* I. 238, and *Dīgha-Nikāya*. For the translation of this passage, see Rhys Davids' *Dialogues of the Buddha,* I. 227 ff.
11. *Jāt.* III. 542.
12. *Aṅguttara-Nikāya,* Vol. I, p. 286; see also Rhys Davids' *Dialogues of the Buddha,* Vol. I, p. 71 ff, and Höernle's *Uvāsaga-dasāo,* Appendix II.
13. *Ante,* Vol. XX, pp. 169 and 364.
14. *Ep. Ind.* Vol. II, p. 272.
15. *South-Indian Inscriptions,* Vol. I, pp. 88, 89, 92 and 108.
16. *Ante,* Vol. XLI, p. 89.
17. *Divyāvadāna,* by Cowell and Neil, p. 247.
18. Cap. VII. v. 42.
19. Rhys Davids' *Dialogues of the Buddha,* Vol. I, p. 71 ff.
20. Canto V., v.s. 61-63.

16

A Note on Ajivikas

A Govindacharya Svamin, *M.R.A.S., M.R.S.A., M.M.S.*

I read, *ante,* pp. 88 ff, the article on Ājīvikas by K.B. Pathak, who opines that they are a sect of Buddhist Bhikshus. D.R.B.'s bracketed not at the end of this article *(Chapter 28)* that they are neither Buddhist Bhikshus as Mr. Pathak says, nor Jainas as Dr. Hultzsch understands, but they form a distinct sect, seems to be borne out by other evidences. We have one given, *ante,* Vol. XXIII, p. 248, 1894 (which I have quoted in full on page 960, *Jour. R. As. Soc.,* October, 1911), of which the following extract is to the point: –

"The essentials may, however, be stated. They are (1) that the recovery of the Vaikhānasa *Dharma-Sūtra* permits me to fully prove the correctness of Professor Kern's (or rather Kālakāchārya's and Utpala's) identification of the *Ājīvikas* with the *Bhāgavatas,* and (2) that the sacred books of the Buddhists contain passages showing that the origin of the *Bhāgavatas* was traditionally believed to fall in very remote times, and that this tradition is supported by indications contained in Brahmanical works."

One such passage contained in an orthodox Buddhist book, the *Saddharma-Puṇḍarīka*[1] as showing the remoteness of the *Bhāgavata (i.e., Ājīvika)* cult, is that where Mañju-Śrī is compared to Nārāyaṇa. The words run thus: ". . . . . and a body compact as Nārāyaṇa's".

17

A Note on Ajivikas

D. R. Bhandarkar

[Who the Ājīvikas really were was shown by me ten years ago in a note published in the *Jour. Bomb. As. Soc.*, Vol. XXI, p. 399 ff. The same note has been reprinted in a slightly altered form in the is number on p. 286 ff.].

References

1. S.B.E. Series, Vol. XVI, chap. XXIII (Gadgada Svara), translated by H. Kern, see p. 397.

18

A New List of Buddhistic Sanskrit Words

Sylvain Levi and G. K. Nariman

The *St. Petersburg Dictionary,* a monument of Germanic erudition, published at the expense of Russia, contains an almost exhaustive inventory of Vedic and Brahmanic Sanskrit. Buddhism hardly appears in it at all. The authors of the *Dictionary* and their collaborateurs make use of a few meagre texts only. But in the last forty years the material for Saṅskrit Buddhism has vastly increased. The published texts have revealed a perfect treasure of words which classic Sanskrit had ignored or neglected. A Buddhistic Sanskrit Dictionary is one of the tasks to be undertaken in the near future. Meanwhile, it is of importance to elaborate the materials so as to put them on some sort of working basis. Cowell and Neil have given an excellent model in the glossary that they have added to their edition of the *Divyāvadāna.* Mr. G.K. Nariman has been good enough to prepare the list of new words that I have pointed out in my notes on the text and translation of the *Mahāyāna Sūtrālaṅkāra.* It may not perhaps be superfluous to place this list at the disposition of philologists, who are interested either in Sanskrit or Buddhism.

A list compiled by G.K. Nariman of new words unknown in classical Sanskrit and not yet met with in Buddhist Sanskrit except in the *Mahāyāna Sūtrālaṅkāra* of Asaṅga, edited and translated by Prof. Sylvain Levi.[1]

	Page
Abhiprāyika	138
Adhimucyanā	71

Adikālika	159
Adhyavihiṁsaka	31
Akilāsikatva	78
Akilāsitva	86
Anukshudra	55
Antarāyin	3
Anuśāsani	20
Āpāyika	150
Apratiprasrabdha	37
Arihat	127
Atilajjanā	18
Aupalambhikatva	49
Ayoniśatas	132
Balika	143
Bhājanībhāva	116
Citraṇā	40
Daushprajnya	101
Eshikā	50
Hāyin	94
Jugupsin	173
Kaukṛtyāyate	72
Naiyamya	166
Nirabhisaṁskāra	161
Nirjalpa	138
Nirmṛgya	130
Parihānika	111
Parijnātāvin	159
Parinirvāpaṇa	35
Paripantha	51
Pārthagjana	85
Paryeshā	168
Prāhānika	28

Vikopana	114
Vilomayati	4
Vivarṅayati	83
Vyavakiraṇa	181
Vyāvasāyika	142
Vyutthāpana	35

References

1. The spellings of the words in this list are given as they are published in Prof. Sylvain Levi's book.

19

One More Buddhist Hymn

G. K. Nariman, Bombay

The spread of the Mahāyāna religion is due to the appear it makes to the heart, laid on the principle of devotion (*bhakti*), as opposed to the cold intellectuality of the Hīnayāna. We do not find in Pāli any fervid hymns or prayers ever addressed to the Buddha, but we have a large number of them in the later Mahāyāna Buddhism, as witness the *stotra-saṁgraha* published by the *Bibliotheca Indica.*

Some time ago Professor Sylvain Levi reconstructed two hymns, translated in Chinese character from Sanskrit by an Indian monk from the college of Nālanda about the year 1000. They are called *Ashṭama-chaitya-vandānā* and the *Trikāyastava.* The latter is a hymn on the three "bodies" of the Buddha, and consists of sixteen stanzas, of which we find a Tibetan translation under the name of *Sku-gsum-la-dstod-pa.* The Chinese transcription was made by the celebrated traveller Fa-hien. The Sanskrit text of the first twelve stanzas of this ode is also preserved in the beginning of the Tibetan block-print (*Deb-ther-snon-po*) communicated by M. Baradijan to Baron Von Stael-halstein, who expressed his opinion (*Bulletin of Imperial Academy of Science* No. 11, 1911), that the Sanskrit text preserved in the block-print is independent of Chinese tradition and deserves to be published especially, as it sometime deviates from the reconstruction of Professor Levi, and in some cases diverges from the original used by the monk of Nālanda, who attempted about 900 years ago to reproduce the Indian sounds by means of Chinese symbols. The Baron proceeds to give the Sanskrit text and the Tibetan version according to the

Deb-ther-snon-po, as well as the Tibetan text cited from the Tanjur.

All the texts are in the *sragdharā* metre, but whole the Tanjur text represents nineteen syllables, that others have twenty-one.

यो नैको नापि अनेकः स्वपरहितमहासंपदाधारभूतो।

यो नैको नापि अनेकः स्वपरहितमहासंपदाधारभूतो॥

नैवाभावो न भावः स्वमिवसमर॥ विभावः स्वभावः।

नैवाभावो न भावः स्वमिवसमरसो दुर्विभावः स्वभावः।

Note: It seems that even पाह्यान read

निर्लेपं निर्विकारं शिवमसमसमं व्यापिनं प्रपंचम्।

निर्लेपं निर्विकारं शिवमसमसमं व्यापिनं निष्प्रपंचम्।

वंदे प्रत्यात्मवेद्यं तमहमनुपमं धर्मकायं जिनानां।

वंदे प्रत्यात्मवेद्यं तमहमनुपमं धर्मकायं जिनानां॥

लोकापितामर्चित्यां सुकृतसमफलानात्मनो यो विभूतिम्।

लोकापितामर्चित्यां सुकृतशतफलानात्मनो यो विभूतिम्।

Note: पाह्यान must have read also सुकृतसम *see* the French translation of the Chinese para-phrase of त्रिकायस्तर by Sphavannes, R.H.R., 34, 16.

परषन्मत्ते ? विचित्रान् तभयति महतीं मतां प्रीतिहेतुं।

परषमध्ये ? विचित्रान् प्रथयति महतीं धीमतां प्रीतिहेतोः।

For परषमध्यगता see महाव्युत्पत्ति 245, 34.

It may be noted that पाह्यान is not particular about representing the विसर्ग

बुद्धानां सर्वलोकप्रसृतमविरतो दारसद्धर्मकोशं।

बुद्धानां सर्वलोकप्रसृतमविरतो दारसद्धर्मकोशं।

वंदे संभोगकायं तमघनिघ महाधर्मराजां प्रतिष्ठां।

वंदे संभोगकायं तमहमिह महाधर्म राज्य प्रतिष्ठं।

सत्त्वानां भागहेतुः क्वचिदनभ्र इवाभाति यो दीप्यमानः।

सत्त्वानां पाकहेतुः क्वचिदनल इवाभाति यो दीप्यमानः।

संबोधौ धर्मचक्रे क्वचिदपि च पुनर्दृश्यते यः प्रशांतं।

संबोधौ धर्मचक्रे क्वचिदपि च पुनर्दृश्यते यः प्रशांतः।

नैकाकारप्रभृतं त्रिभवभयहरं विश्वरूपिरूपोयः।

नैकाकारप्रवृत्तं त्रिभवभयहरं विश्वरूपिरूपोयः।

वंदे निर्वाणकायं दशदिगनुगतं तं महार्थे मुनीनां।

वंदे निर्वाणकायं दशदिगनुगतं तं महार्थे मुनीनां।

The rest of the text in Baradijun is altogether different from that of पाह्वान, still it may be interesting to compare the last four *ślokas* as given in the Tanjur with the reconstruction of Professor Levi.

सत्त्वार्थैक कृपाणां अपरिमितमहायानपुण्यानयानां

कायानां सौगतानां प्रतिविगतमनोवाक्पथानां प्रयाणां।

कृत्वा भक्त्या प्रणामं कुशलमुपचितं यन्मया बोधिबीजं

त्रिकायस्तेन लब्ध्वा जिगदिदमखिलं बोधिमार्गे नियुंजे।

20

References to Buddhist Authors in Jain Literature

G.K. Nariman, Bombay

Buddhist Sanskrit works of tolerable antiquity in comparison with Pāli texts are so rate that any references to them in other literatures must be welcomed. The Brahmanical Sanskrit literature hardly offers any reference to Buddhist works of antiquity, and, as Vallee Poussin has shown, the *Sarvadarsana-saṁgraha* has no reference to Buddhism that goes back to respectable antiquity. Prof. Mironov in the course of a paper on Devabhadra and his *Nyāyāvatāra-tippaṇa* in the *Bulletin of the Imperial Academy of Sciences. St. Petersburg* (April 15, 1911) points out some Buddhist authors, whose standpoint was familiar to Jaina logicians.

दिग्नागः—

न्यायावतारनिवृत्ति

तदुक्तम् ।

अनुमेयेऽथ तत्तुल्ये सद्भावो नास्तितासति ।

निश्चितानुपलंभात्मा कार्याख्या हेतवस्त्रयः ॥

Devabhadra notes the तदुक्तम् to be दिग्नागेनेति शेषः ॥

न्यायावतारविवृत्ति on the आदिवाक्यः तदुक्तम्

तेनान्यापोहविषयाः प्रोक्ताः सामान्यगोचराः ।

शद्बश्च बुद्धयश्चैव वस्तुन्येषामसंभवात् ॥

The *Ṭippaṇa* sats प्रोक्ता आचार्यदिग्नागेन and एतदर्थश्च विस्तारार्थिना प्रमाणवार्तिके कल्याणचंद्रकृतटीकातोऽवसेयः ।

धर्मकीर्तिः—

The following *śloka* seems to have been borrowed by Devabhadra from *Guṇaratna* with its polemical prefatory remark: –

यदाह रागान्धावस्थायामपि धर्मकीर्तिः।

गच्छतु क्वापि ते स्वान्तकांते कार्ये व्ययैव च।

यदेवार्थः प्रियाकारी तदेव परमार्थसत्॥

धर्मोत्तरः—

The quotation is from his *Pramāṇaviniśchya-ṭīkā* and the comment is on the terms *middha* and *dhaṁdha*.

ज्ञानश्री [मिव]

ननु चार्थक्रिया सामर्थ्यमेव सत्त्वम्। नान्यत्। तथा च ज्ञानश्रीः। यदि नाम प्रतिदर्शनं सत्यभेदस्तथापीहार्थक्रिया सामर्थ्यमेव सत्त्वमभिप्रेतम्॥

He lived at the close of the 10th century as shown by Satishchandra Vidyabhushan and composed three works, *viz., Pramāṇa-viniśchaya-ṭīkā, Kāryākāraṇa-bhāva-siddhi* and *Tarkabhāshā.*

There is also a reference to a *Bauddh-ālaṁkāra*.

These are the allusions to Buddhist authors; the following bear on other schools of philosophy in the same Jain author : –

सांख्यः—

विविक्ते दृक् ? परिणतौ बुद्धौ भोगोस्य कथ्यते।

प्रतिबिबोदयः स्वच्छे यथा चंद्रमर्सोभसि।

Devabhadra thus comments on this : –

विभक्तेत्यादिपाठांतरेण

व्याख्यानान्तरं तु हरिभद्रसूरिकृतं

नेह प्रकाश्यते बहुव्याख्याते व्यामोहप्रसंगात्।

विंध्यावासीः—

पुरुषोऽविकृतात्मैव स्वनिर्भासमचेतनम्।

मनः करोति सांनिध्यादुपाधिः स्फटिकं यथा।

Two *ślokas* from the same Vindhyāvāsī have already been known from Bhoja's commentary on the *Yoga-sūtra,* IV. 22.

वादमहार्णवः—

वादमहार्णवोऽपि अस्मिन् [सांख्य] दर्शने स्थितः प्राह।

बुद्धिदर्पणसंक्रांतसमर्थप्रतिबिंबकं।

द्वितीयदर्पणकल्पे पुंसि अध्यारोहति।

न्यायः—

Of this school only the following authors are referred to, *viz* :—

Akshapāda, Uddyotakara and Kaṁdalīkāra.

वैषेशिकः—

It appears that Vyomaśiva that commentator on *Praśastapāda-bhāshya* ascribes to the *Āchārya* (*Praśastapāda* ?) three *pramāṇas, viz.* :—

प्रत्यक्ष, अनुमान, and शद्ब, as against Kaṁdalīkāra who holds only the first two.

मीमांसा:—

Jaimini is mentioned to show that he taught six *pramāṇas, viz* :—

प्रत्यक्ष, अनुमान, शद्ब, उपमान, अर्थापत्ति, and अभाव। While प्रभाकर understands अभाव as a kind प्रत्यक्ष।

(Jaina) :—जैनः—

As expected the author of the *Nyāyāvatāra-ṭippaṇa* makes mention in several places of his co-religionists. He adduces the three Jaina authors, *viz.*, Bhadrabāhu, Haribhadra and Prabhāchaṁdra. The last who wrote the *Prameya-kamala-mārtaṇḍa* and *Nyāya-kumula-chandra* belonged to the Digaṃbara sect, and lived in the beginning of the 9th century.

His *Nyāya-kumuda-chandra* has a highly important reference to the Buddhist school of the Vaibhāshikas who are defined as :

विभाषासद्धर्मप्रतिपादको ग्रंथविशेषः।

तं विदंत्यधीयते वा वैभाषिकाः॥

Besides the above we may note various other quotations made known by Mironov.

गौडः—

ज्ञानात्मचक्रशकटे पाशकव्यवहारयोः

तुषेकर्षे पुमानक्षं तुच्छे सौवर्चलेंद्रिये ।

This grammarian is cited by Hemachandra and Kshīrasvāmin is their commentaries on the Amarakosha.

The Jaina *Nyāy-āvatāra-ṭippaṇa* also quotes Māgha's *Siśupālavadha, XI. 33.*

21

Some Literary References to the Isipatana Migadaya (Sarnath)

Brindavan C. Bhattacharya

The Isipatana Migadāya[1] derives its importance from the fact that it was here that the Buddha preached his first sermon, the *Dhammachakkappa-vattana Sutta,* advocating abstention from the extremes of luxury and asceticism, setting forth the doctrine of the Four Noble Truths (*Āriya-Sachcha*), and exhorting his auditors the *Pañchavaggiyā* to pursue the *Āriya Aṭṭhaṅgika Magga.*

The locus classicus is in the *Vinaya-Piṭaka* (Ed. Oldenberg) *Mahāvagga* I. 6-10 Seq=*Saṃyutta-Nikāya* (P.T.S.) 5 pp. 420-22.[2]

The place is also the scene of the conversion of Yaśa, son of a merchant of Benares. The interesting story concerning him and his family is given, in detail, in the *Mahāvagga* (*Vinaya* Text 3), p. 15. The Legend of the Burmese Buddha gives the same story with slight alteration in names, *e.g,* there we find Ratna in place of Yaśa. Bārānathī for Bārāṇasī, Migaduvana for Migadāya. [Note the usual phrase—*tatra sutaṃ bhagavā Bārāṇasiyaṃ viharati Isipatane Migadāye.*]

It was in Isipatana that the Buddha recounted the *Udapānadāsaka-Jātaka* (II. 354).

Buddhaghosha in his commentary on the *Mahāpadāna-Sutta* says: *Dhammachakkapparattanaṃ Isipatane Migadāye avijahita ṇ eca hoti.* (It was in the Deer Park of Isipatana that *Dharma-chakrapravartana* was named). In another part of the same commentary, we read: *Kheme Migadāyati—Isipatanaṃ tena samayena khemaṃ nāma uyyānaṃ hoti. Migānaṃ pana abhayavā satthāya dinnattā Migadāyo ti vuchchati. Taṃ Sandhāya vuttaṃ 'Kheme Migudāye' ti. Yathā cha Vipassi Bhagavā evaṃ aññepi Buddhā pathamam Dhammadesana tthāya gachchhatā ākāsena gantvā tattheva otaranti.*[3] (In explaining the expression *Kheme Migadāye* the commentator says: "Isipatana was, at that time, known to be the Khema or the auspicious garden. It was called Migadāya, because it was granted in order that the deer might dwell there in all safety. It was in reference to this very fact that the expression *Kheme Migadāye* was used. Gautama Buddha and the other Buddhas first of all alighted there white going through the air to preach the Sacred Faith).

The scene of the 9th *Vatthu* of the XVIth *Vagga* of the *Dhammapada* (*Nandiya-vatthu*) is laid here. Having heard the teaching of the Buddha, he thought that it would be meritorious to give some dwelling-place to the Order, so he caused to be constructed a *Chatussālā* adorned with four rooms and furnished with chairs and benches, and then handed it over to the Order with the Buddha at its head. This was situated in the *Isipatana-Mahāvihāra*.

The *Mahārasta* tells us that the *Śuddhāvāsa Devas* warned the Pratyeka-Buddhas[4] to vanish; for in twelve years the Bodhisattva would descend upon the earth. At half a *yojana* from Benares were living five hundred Pratyeka-Buddhas; rising in the air, they entered into Nirvāṇa, and their bodies consumed by the elements of fire, which they had in them, fell back upon the earth: *Ṛishayos-tra patitā ishipatanaṃ.*[5] A story resembling the *Nigrodha-miga-jātaka* then follows. Here the king is the ruler of Benares—Brahmadatta by name. From the grant of the boon (*dāya*) made to the dear, the spot was called *Mṛigadāya*. This is the view held by Senart in his notes to which I propose to offer the following emendation. To me it appears that very early the site of Isipataṇa was called *Mṛigadāva* (*dāva* meaning forest) from the fact that it was full of the deer. Afterwards, however, when all places associated with the Buddha's life used to be the favourite scenes of thousands of Buddhistic fables. Isipatana had likewise the story recorded in the *Mahāvastu.* It then came to be known as *Mṛigadāya* instead of *Mṛigadāva.* Since then, very probably the word *dāya* in the original sense of 'forest' has become obsolete and the prākritised word *dāya,* both meaning 'boon' and 'forest' has come into current use in all Pāli works.

References

1. The modern Sārnāth.
2. Compare in this connexion, *Buddhist Birth Stories:* The Pali Introduction p. 112 and Legend of the Burmese Buddha p. 117 Seq.
3. It adds that the Buddha for a special reason went on foot to that place.
4. Cf. *Buddha* by Dr. H. Oldenberg, p. 120 foot note. The great antiquity of the Pratyeka Buddhas is discussed in brief in "Apadāna" folkī of the Phayre MSS.
5. For etymology cf. Senart's view—"En dépit de cette étymologie, les deux orthographes du mot, familières it notre texte, sont, non pas ऋषिपतन mais on ऋषिपत्तन (ci–dessous), p. 366, 1. 8: पट्टन) on ऋषिवदन J' ai don né la préférence ā cette seconde forme" (ordinaire aussi daus les gāthās du Lal. Vist) * * * *—*Le Mahāvastu* Ed. by Senart Vol. I, p. 631.

22

Did Pāṇini know Buddhist Nuns?

K. V. Lakshman Rao, *M.A.; Madras*

While writing an article on *Ashtādhyāyi* for the *Telugu Encyclopaedia,* a *Sūtra* in *Pāṇini* arrested my attention. In the second *Ashṭaka* there is a *Śūtra* कुमारश्रमणादिभि: [II. 1. 70]. All the commentators agree in interpreting this aphorism to mean that the word *'Kumāra'* enters into a *Tatpurusha* compound with the words in the *Śramaṇa*-group. The *Śramaṇā digaṇa* consists of the words श्रमणा, प्रव्रजिता, कुलटा, गर्भिणी, तापसी, दासी, बन्धकी, अध्यापक, अभिरूपक, पण्डित, पटु, मृद, कुशल, चपल, निपुण[1] We find all these words enumerated in *Gaṇaratna-mahô-dadhi* of *Vardhamāna* of the twelfth century and in the *Kāsikā* of the seventh century. *Śākaāya Vyākaraṇa* which may belong to the ninth century and *Jainêndra Vyākarana* which cannot be later than the fifth century A.D. have a Śūtra similar to that of *Pāṇini.* Unfortunately the *Vritti* and the *Mahābhāshya* have not thought it necessary of comment upon this *śūtra* and hence we are not in a position to know *Kātyāyanā's* or *Patānjali's* interpretation of this aphorism.

The illustrations generally given under this aphorism are कुमारी श्रमणा कुमारश्रमणा, (Kāsika), कुमारी चातौ श्रमणा च कुमारश्रमणा, कुमारप्रव्रजिता (*Gaṇaratnamahô-dadhi*).

Though we know that almost all the words we now find in the *Śramaṇādigaṇa* are given in the *Gaṇaratnamahô-dadhi* and *Kāsikā,* it may be said that we cannot be sure that all the fifteen words were included in the group by *Pāṇini* when he wrote the Śūtra. Any how it cannot be doubted that the first three or four words formed part of the group then. Thus the words *Śramaṇā* and *Pravrajitā* cannot but be taken as having been included in the *gaṇa* when *Pāṇini* wrote the *Śūtra.*

The word *Kumārī* means in Sanskrit either an unmarried girl or a very young girl. Hence the compound *Kumāra-Śramaṇā* or *Kumāra-pravrajitā* may either mean a *sanyāsinī* who has joined the order as a *brahmachāriṇī* withour getting married or a *Sanyāsinī* who has joined the order when very young. Hindu girls rarely remained unmarried, and no where was *saṃnyasa* ordained for them. There was therefore no chance for a young Hindu girl to take orders under the Hindu Śāstrās. In the Upanishads we hear of certain *brahmachāriṇīs,* who remained unmarried for a long period, but we do not hear of women who have undergone the ceremony of *pravrajana.*

Now, who were these *Kumāra-Śramaṇās* and *Kumāra-pravrajitās*—the virgin ascetics, the young nuns, the child-*sanyāsinīs,* the girls who were admitted into the sisterhood of *pravrajitās* (Pāli=*Pabbajitās*) when they were very young? Who could they be except the Buddhist nuns? Hinduism does not recognise *Saṃnyāsa* to women and *Śūdrās*. It is *Buddha* who first founded the system of *Saṃnyāsa* for women and consequently references to *bikkhunīs, samanīs, pabbajitās* and nunneries are found in Buddhistic literature from the *Tripiṭ akās* down to the writings of the modern times. We also find these terms applied to nuns in the inscriptions of Nāsik, Kārle and Amarāvati. We find in Buddhistic writings that even boys and girls of seven years, with the consent of their parents, were taken as *Śramanerās;* and *Śramaṇerīes, i.e.,* as young novices to be trained up as a *Sramaṇa* and *Śramaṇī* (*Manual of Buddhism* by H. Kern, p. 77). It is no wonder then that these young female ascetics were called *Kumāra-Śramaṇās* which necessitated a separate rule in *Pāṇini.*

Here I may take into consideration some possible objections to my statement that Hinduism does not recognise female *śramaṇās* and *pravrajitās*. The word *śramaṇa* even in its masculine form has been monopolized by Buddhists and it now practically means a Buddhist monk. But I am aware of its use, though very rarely, in the general sense of a *Saṃnyāsi* in the Hindu religious literature, perhaps prior to Buddha. *Sathapathā Brāhmaṇa Saṃnyāsi* in the Hindu religious literature, perhaps prior to

Buddha. *Sathapathā Brāhmaṇa* (XIV, 6, 122) has चण्डाला: अचण्डाला:, श्रमणा: अश्रमणा:, तापस: अतापस:; *Brihadāraṇyaka* has a similar sentence (IV, 3, 22). *Taittarīyāraṇyaka* also mentions वातरशनाह वा ऋषय: श्रमणा ऊर्ध्वमन्थिनो। Even as to the meaning of the word *Śramaṇa* (in its masculine form) in the above passages, there may be some who may suggest that it refers to the Buddhist *Sraṃanās* before the word was degraded in its significance in the eyes of the Hindus. I may here remind the readers that the late Prof. Goldstucker was of opinion that the Araṇyakās were unknown to *Pāṇini* and came into existence during the period intervening between *Pāṇini* and *Kātyāyana*. But the word *Śramaṇā* or *Śramaṇī* (*i.e.*, in its feminine form) is unknown to the Hindu literature of the pre-Buddhistic period.

We know of a passage in Rāmāyaṇa where a certain *śramaṇī* is mentioned (*Araṇya Kānda, Sarga* 73). There she is called शंसितव्रता, तपोधना, तापसी, सिद्धा, सिद्धसम्मता। She is represented to have come from the low caste of *Śabarās*. Her caste clearly indicates that the word *Śramaṇī* is not used here in the technical sense of a high caste woman entering into an order of *Saṃnyāsinīs*. Even those who may argue that in ancient times Hinduism allowed women to become *Saṃnyāsinīs* or *pravrajitās* cannot go to the extent of asserting that women become *Saṃnyāsinīs* or *pravrajitās* cannot go to the extent of asserting that women who were outside the pale of Hinduism could become *saṃnyāsinīs, śramaṇās, pravrajitās, tāpasīs* in the technical sense, when even men belonging to the Sūdra caste were denied that privilege. I think I need not quote any authorities for this statement; the story of Śambūka from the Rāmāyaṇa itself will illustrate my point. Hence if a woman of a wild tribe is honoured as *śramaṇī* and *tāpasī,* it must be through the influence of Buddhism.

Besides we are not sure about the date of Rāmāyaṇa. The original text may be very old, certainly pre-Buddhistic. But there are many interpolations in it, which we know are certainly post-Buddhistic. The very name of *Buddha*—the *Tathāgata* and the *Nāstika*—is mentioned in it (*Ayôdhya,* 109, 34). There are similar interpolations in the Mahabhārata also.

We find the word *pravrajita* (female ascetic) in *Manu* (VIII, 363) *Vātsyāyanā's Kāmasūtra* (V. p. 69. XXI, p. 234, XXVII, p. 290), *Arthāśastra* of *Kauṭilya* (I, 10; I, 12). But in all these places it is clear, from the contemptuous way in which the female ascetics are referred to, that they are the much hated Buddhist *pravrajitās*.[2] These are generally mentioned along with women of bad character for purposes of espionage and as go-betweens. It is certain that the Hindus began to hate these Buddhists Nuns, as the institutions was unknown to them and as these nuns, at least some of them, must have led a life of doubtful morality. It is natural that they should have hence fallen very low in the estimation of the Hindus. Gradually the word *Śramaṇa* connoted the sense of a beggar-woman, an unchaste woman, a beautiful woman without character. These are some of the meanings given to the word *Śramaṇā* in various Sanskrit lexicons.

I therefore consider the *śramaṇā* and *pravrajitā* mentioned in the *Śūtra* and *Gaṇapātha* of *Pāṇini* as referring to the Buddhist *Śamaṇīs* and *Pabbajitās*.

References

1. Of the fifteen words now found in the *Śramaṇā-digaṇa* the first seven are in the feminine gender and the rest are in the masculine, *Kāsikā* says that the word *Kumāra* enters into compound as a word of feminine gender with those words which have feminine form and as a word of both masculine and feminine gender with those which have a masculine form. "यत्र स्त्रीलिङ्गाः पठ्यन्ते श्रमणा प्रव्रजिता कुलर्टत्येव मादयस्तैः सह स्त्रीलिङ्ग एव कुमारशब्दः समस्यते, येतु पुंलिङ्गा अध्यापको ऽभिरूपकः पण्डितइति, तैरुभयथा, प्रातिपदिकग्रहणे लिङ्गविशिष्टस्यापि ग्रहणमिति।" This means that the compounds कुमारश्रमणः, कुमारप्रव्रजितः, कुमारतापसः cannot be allowed, though both the compounds कुमारपण्डितः, कुमारपण्डिताः कुमाराध्यापकः कुमाराध्यापिका are admissible. *Abāyanandi* commenting upon an analogous sūtra (III. 65) in the *Jainendravyakaraṅa* (Pandit edition) explains in the same way: स्त्रीलिङ्गैरुत्तरपदैः स्त्रीलिङ्गः। अध्यापकादिभिरुभयथा समस्यते। The purpose of the Sūtra is clearly to show that the word कुमार comes always as the first member of the compound in all these cases. *Padamañjari* says कुमार कुमारशब्दस्य पूर्वनिपातनियमार्थे वचनं।

2. *Manu* does not consider the offence of a man who secretly converses with a *parivrajikā* to be very serious. He puts it along with the offence of conversing with a female slave. These offences are to be punished with a small fine. [VIII. 363]. In commenting upon the word *pravarjitā* all the commentators explain it to mean a Buddhist nun. *Vātsyāyana* proposes the use of *pravrajitās* to seduce chaste women. Though Vātsyāyana points them in this ugly light, we know from the *Malati Mādhavam* of *Bhavabhuti* the noble and self-less part which these *Bhikhunts* played in bringing together true, noble and virtuous lovers. *Kautilya* makes use of these Pravajitās as spies for political purposes.

23

Vasubandhu or Subandhu*

A. Rangaswami Saraswati, B.A.

(A Glimpse into the Literary History of the Maurayan Age)

The relation of the life of the famous Buddhist philosopher Vasubandhu to the history of the Gupta Empire forms an important landmark in the literary history of India. Paramārtha, a famous Buddhist author of the sixth century and the author of a biography of Vasubandhu, states that Vikaramaditya of Ajodhya, who at first was a liberal patron of the Sāṅkhya philosophy, was induced by the eloquence of the celebrated Vasubandhu to turn a favourable ear to the teachings of Buddhism and to patronise its professors with equal liberality. His queen and the prince Balāditya, who later on succeeded to the throne, both became disciples of Vasubandhu, and Balāditya after his accession continued his favours to the Buddhist age. The famous Chinese Buddhist pilgrim Hiuen Tsang also gives a variant form of the story, describing the king as Vikramāditya of Srāvasti. This information about the life of Vasubandhu is augmented from an unexpected source. The ancient work on Alaṅkāra, written in the form of aphorisms (*sūtras*) by Vāmana, who also composed a gloss upon it, cites a half-verse wherein Vasubandhu appears to be referred to. This was first brought to the notice of scholars by Prof. Pathak. The half-verse is followed by a short gloss by the author in explanation of the same. The half-verse and the gloss are given below.[2] It occurs under the *sūtra* defining *Ōjas*.

The translation of the hemistich would run thus, "This very son of Chandragupta, the young Chandraprakāśa, the patron of men of letters, fortunate in the success of his efforts, has now (*samprati*) become king." The author explains the passage further in the gloss of the *sūtra,* that the phrase, "Patron of men of letters" is an instance of "allusion," containing a reference to the ministership (*sāchivya*) of Vasubandhu.

This reading of the passage and the comment thereon were first challenged by Mahamahopadhyaya Haraprasada Sastri, who said that the correct reading of the passage should be *cha Subandhu* in the place of Vasubandhu, and maintained that most of the manuscripts of Vāmana's work examined, had the reading Subandhu. He thought that the passage contained a reference to Subandhu, the author of the Sanskrit romance *Vāsavadatta*. He also raised the objection that Vasubandhu, who was a famous orthodox Buddhist Bhikshu, would not have accepted the office of minister under a sovereign. He took Chandraprakāśa in the passage to be the name of Chandragupta's son, and suggested that the emperor Chandragupta II had two sons, Chandraprakāśa and Kumārgupta, and that upon the death of Chandragupta II, a civil war broke out between the two brothers, in which, however, Chandraprakāśa was worsted and Kumāragupta was successful.

This interpretation of the passage was objected to by Dr. Hoernle, who thought that the correct reading was Vasubandhu and not Subandhu. He answered Mah. H.P. Sastri's objection that a Buddhist monk would not accept office, by saying that the word *"sāchivya"* which occurs in the passage may simply mean companionship or friendship. He took the word Chandraprakāśa as the name of Chandragupta's son. But unlike the Sastri, he does not deduce out of the passage a civil war, which broke out on the death of Chandragupta II between his two sons. He says, "Is it not much simpler to suppose that Chandragupta II's son was known as Chandraprakāśa, before he assumed the regnal title Kumāragupta upon his accession to the throne.

Mr. R. Narasimhacharya of Mysore (*ante,* Vol. XL), referring to the same passage, says that his examination of various manuscripts of Vāmana's *sūtras* showed that the correct reading of the disputed portion of the passage was *cha*

Subandhu and not Vasubandhu. He says "in the well known tenth verse of *Vāsavadattā,* Subandhu mourns the death of Vikramāditya, *i.e.,* Chandragupta II, who was apparently his patron. There is nothing unreasonable in supposing that he became the minister of Chandragupta's son, Kumāragupta." It might be urged against this supposition that Subandhu, who mentions Udyôtakāra, and according to some manuscripts, Dharmakīrti's works, could not have been a contemporary of Kumāragupta, who lived in the first half of the fifth century. But according to him, this does not raise any difficulty about the chronology, since the dates of the Udyôtakāra and Dharmakīrti have not been settled. He thought that the half verse occurring in Vāmana's work is a quotation from the introductory portion of some drama, giving the Sūtradhāra's words.

Again Prof. K.B. Pathak wrote in *ante,* Vol. XL, 1911, p. 170. "Kumāragupta, son of Chandragupta II, is alluded to by Vāmana, as a patron of the Buddhist author, Vasubandhu." Vasubandhu was according to him the contemporary of three successive Gupta sovereigns, namely Kumāragupta, Skandagupta and Balāditya, and the interesting half-verse quoted by Vāmana was taken from some lost *Guptavamśamahākāvya,* in which the name of Vasubandhu is directly mentioned, or which was composed by Vasubandhu himself, to congratulate Kumāragupta on his accession to the throne, as the word "*samprati,*" in the verse shows; and he gives expression to the hope that the work may be discovered one of these days and shed fresh light upon Gupta history.

Again Mah. H.P. Sastri (*ante,* Vol. XLI, 1912, p. 15) writes that his study of Subandhu's *Vāsavadattā,* added weight to his belief that the reading Subandhu in Vāmana's hemistich is correct. Subandhu appears, according to him, to mention Chandraprakāśa in his work in the *śliṣṭa* form of the word *Himakarôdyôta* in the fifth verse. (*Himakarôdyôta* and Chandraprakāśa mean the same thing). He reiterates the belief that Chandraprakāśa is a proper name. In the sixth verse Subandhu is very bitter against Khalas, the wicked, who are more wicked than serpents. In the seventh he compares the wicked with owls. In the eighth he is again hard on the wicked. The word *Śaśiruk* in this verse again means Chandraprakāśa, and he complains that the commentator who did not know history does not note the point.

The tenth verse is well known throughout India, and is in the mouth of every Pandit. It says that, "on the death of Vikramāditya, love of art and poetry are gone." "Upstarts are flourishing and everybody's hand is on his neighbour's throat." "What does this mean," he questions, "unless it means a revolution, in which the author did not fare well on the death of Chandragupta Vikramaditya. Read the hemistich with the prefatory verses of *Vāsavadatta*[3] and the inference is irresistible that the changes of the times were ruinous to Subandhu and his party."

Simultaneously with Mah. H.P. Sastri, Dr. D.R. Bhandarkar (*ante,* Vol. XLI, 1912, pp. 1 and 2) gave it as his opinion that Vasubandhu represents the original reading. His conclusion will best be expressed in his own words. "All things considered, Gôvindagupta appears to be the Chandraguptanaya (son of Chandragupta) alluded in the verse quoted by Vāmana, and also the Balāditya, son of Vikramāditya (Chandragupta II), mentioned by Paramārtha." Gôvindagupta Balāditya has to be placed, according to him, between A.D. 411 and 414. He says that Balāditya may have been ousted by his brother Kumāragupta, or he might have died a natural death and without an heir.

The next scholar who took up the subject and dealt with it in a masterly fashion was M. Noel Peri, who wrote in the *Bulletine de l'Ecole française d' Extrême-Orient* and his conclusions were accepted completely by Mr. V.A. Smith, who has given a separate note on the subject in the last edition of his *Early History of India* (pp. 328-334). It would be best to quote his own words on the subject. "If M. Peri is right, as he appears to be, in holding that Vasubandhu lived and died in the fourth century, the Gupta king who patronized him must have been the learned and accomplished Samudragupta, son and successor of Chandragupta I, who might have been actually known as Vikramāditya. It is also possible that the title, even if not actually assumed by Chandragupta I, may have been traditionally assigned to him, as being an ordinary recognised title of any Gupta King. There is no reason whatever to doubt that Samudragupta was actually in possession of both Ajodhya and Śrāvasti, and in all probability his father was so likewise. Assuming the recorded traditions connecting Vasubandhu with a Gupta king to be well-founded, it follows that Samudragupta in his youth must have borne the titles of both Chandraprakāśa (Prabhāva) and Balāditya or Parāditya. There is no difficulty about believing that to be a fact. I therefore conclude, that Samudragupta received Vasubandhu, a Buddhist author and patriarch at Court, either as a minister or as an intimate counsellor with the sanction and approval of his father Chandragupta I, and further that Samudragupta, although officially a Brahmanic Hindu, studied Buddhism in his youth with interest and partiality.

There seem to be many serious difficulties in accepting this conclusion. The initial objection, whether the correct reading of the name in the passage from Vamana is Subandhu or Vasubandhu, is not answered. Manuscript evidence seems to lead to the preference of the reading Subandu, which does not fit in with the theory propounded above. Again, in trying to establish his theory, M. Peri has recourse to too many conjectures. There is nothing whatever either in literature or epigraphy to show that Samundragupta had to titles or other names of Chandraprakāśa (Prabhāva) and Balāditya or Parāditya. Of these we know that the term Balāditya was the title of Narasiṁhagupta, and we do not know any other prince who assumed that title. No attempt is made here to prove that no other king could have had that title. There is nothing to prove that Samudragupta was otherwise known as Balāditya. Again as to Chandaprakāśa or its variant Chandraprabhāva, it does not appear to be either the name or the title of any king. It seems merely to be descriptive of the prince, whose full name ought to have occurred in the latter portion of the verse, which has not come down to us so far.

The next difficulty is about Vikramāditya. The two sources of information about Vasubandhu vary in their accounts of the capital of this Vikramāditya. One says it was Śrāvasti and the other Ajodhya. This discrepancy might not be very material. But to a large section of scholars, Chandragupta I of the Gupta dynasty is too early a sovereign to have had that title; and according to them the first Gupta sovereign to assume that title was Chandragupta II, son of Samudragupta. But there are others who think that there might have been an earlier Vikramāditya, who might have founded the era after his name, or lent his name to an already existing era of Māḷava. Even among these, none seems to favour the view that Chandragupta I of the Gupta dynasty was a Vikramāditya.

Again, it is suggested that the verse may have been taken from a historical work dealing with the Guptas, under some such name as *"Gupta-vaṁśamahākāvya,"* which might have been dedicated to Samudragupta, who is mentioned in it as Chandraprakāśa, and that it should have referred to many historical events; and Mr. Pathak expresses the hope that the work may yet be discovered somewhere in Kashmir, where Vasubandhu spent a considerable portion of his life. But is was Mr. R.A. Narasimhacharya who first thought that the verse might have been taken from the introductory scene of a drama dedicated to the son of Chandragupta, perhaps Kumāragupta, by Subandhu. Subandhu mourns the death of Vikramāditya in the famous tenth verse of the *Vāsavadattā,* and the other verses also are taken to refer to contemporary events. This theory might have proved unassailable, had the knowledge of scholars been limited merely to the above stated data.

Since these discussions began, there have been some very notable discoveries in the field of Sanskrit literature, which promise to throw additional light on the subject and clear the existing mystery. One of the works discovered by the Madras Manuscripts Library, the *Avantisundarīkathā,* which is attributed to the famous poet and rhetorician Daṇḍin in the eighth century, contains at the beginning a number of verses wherein famous authors who lived before his time are referred to in terms of praise. One of them refers to Subandhu, and it runs:–

"सुबन्धुः किल निष्क्रान्तो बिन्दुसारस्यबन्धनात्।
तस्यैव हृदयंजह्रे वत्सराज कथा...... ॥

The verse is incomplete, and the break in the end can be easily filled up. Freely translated, it would mean, "Subandhu came out of his captivity (imprisonment) by order of Bindusāra, and captivated his heart by (composing) the story of Vatsarāja." From this we understand that Subandhu was a contemporary of Bindusāra, and the latter seems to have imprisoned him first and then released him. Subandhu appears also to have written a story of Vāsavadattā. So far we know only of one Bindusāra in the whole range of Indian history. He was the son of Chandragupta Maurya, the first Mauryan Emperor and the uprooter of the Nanda sovereignty. Accordingly to the theory now accepted by Sanskritists, the age of the Mauryas, or that of Chandragupta and Bindusāra, was not the age when *Kāvyas* could have been written. This view, although generally accepted, was opposed by a few scholars, among whom the most famous and the earliest was Goldstücker. These maintained that there ought to have existed many works in what has been called Classical Sanskrit in the Mauryan age and even before. A grammar like that of Paṇini and the commentaries on it, like those of Vararuchi and Patañjali, could not have been written without the existence of *Kāvyas*. Patañjali makes a distinct mention of a *Kāvya* by Vararuchi (*Vārarucham Kāvyam*), and in another place derives a word like *Vāsavadattika,* meaning thereby one who studies a *Kāvya* dealing with the story of Vāsavadattā. Paṇini, the great grammarian, himself is said to have been the author of a poem called *Pātāḷavijaya,* from which several verses have been quoted in all standard anthologies. Orthodox tradition does not known of the existence of two Paṇinis. It is likely that Subandhu wrote a work on Vāsavadattā, and the *Vāsavadattikās* of the time of Patañjali might have been very familiar with the work.

But hitherto, the only work known to scholars as the work of Subandhu was the prose romance *Vāsavadattā*. The introductory verses of this work mention the death of Vikramāditya, who has been thought to be the same as Chandragupta II. So *Vāsavadattā* should have been written after the death of Chandragupta II, and the reference in the *Mahābhāshya* of Patañjali could not have been to this work, if

Patañjali really had been a contemporary of this Sunga sovereign, Pushpamitra, and if he mentions Menander's conquests as contemporary events. Arguing on this line, some scholars thought that Patañjali might have lived later than the Guptas. Even Dr. Peterson, who seems to have had an intuition in dealing with the dates of Sanskrit poets and argued against the view of the late origin of Patañjali, thought that there was sufficient reason to change his view, and one of his reasons was Patañjali's mention of *Vāsavadattā, Subhāsshitāvali of Ballabhadéva,* edited by Dr. Peterson, Introduction.

All this confusion was due to the fact that scholars thought that there was only one Subandhu, and that his only work was the romance *Vāsavadattā,* whose date could be fixed from other data. But we have some more information about Subandhu, to which previous scholars had not access. The commentary of Bharata's *Nāṭyaśāstra* by Abhinavaguptapāda, which has been discovered by the Madras Library, has a passage wherein Subandhu and his work are mentioned.

This occurs in the commentary on the following passage from the *Nāṭyaśāstra* (xxii *Adhyāya*).

(4) नाट्यायितं तूपचारैर्यत्क्रियतेऽभिनयोऽत्र सूचनानाट्ये।
काव्यप्रहर्षहेतोः प्रवेशकैस्सङ्गमो यावत् ॥ 46 ॥
स्थाने ध्रुवास्वभिनयो यत्क्रियते हर्षशोकरोषाद्यैः।
भावरससंप्रयुक्तैर्ज्ञेयं नाट्यायितं तज्ञ ॥ 47 ॥

The commentary on the passage runs thus: –

(5)[4] नाट्यायितमित्याद्यार्यायास्तात्पर्ये पूर्वप्रविष्टेन पात्रेण सह सङ्गमं विधाय पश्चात्प्रविष्टस्य पात्रस्य पूर्वप्रविष्टपात्रपरिक्रमणादिकाले स्थानकेनैवासीनस्य तूष्णीं स्थितौ प्राप्तायामभिनयस्तदपि नाट्यायितमिति। सपरार्यायां तात्पर्यमिति श्रीशङ्कुकाद्याः। तच्चायुक्तं। .... प्रयोगकुशलाएवं विधेर्धर्मिलिखति इति पालयन्नाट्यस्थं यथा पुरापचयं नाटयतीति।

नाट्यस्य सन्धानरूपत्वं च वाक्यसूचादीनामपि सम्भवत्येव वा नाट्येन नाट्या सन्धीयत इति नाट्यायित वाचोयुक्तिरपि कथं तत्स्यादित्येवमेतद्व्याख्यातम्। इह यदा स्वप्नोऽप्येकघनो दृश्यते तन्मध्य एव च किं दृश्यमानं परस्य स्वप्न एव जाग्रद्रूपतामापादिते स्वप्नोऽयं मया दृष्ट इति वर्ण्यते। तदा जाग्रदपेक्षस्वप्नव्यवहारो न तत्र पारमार्थिक इत्यौपचारिकं। तदपेक्षं तस्य स्वप्नत्वमिति। कस्य स्वप्नायितव्यवहारो दृष्ट एवमिहापि नाट्ये एकघनस्वभावेऽपि स्थिते तत्रैवासत्यनाट्यानुप्रवेशान्नाट्यपात्रेषु सामाजिकीभूतेषु तदपेक्षया यदन्यन्नाट्यं तस्य तदपेक्ष

नाट्यरूपत्वं पारमार्थिकमिति नाट्यायितमुच्यते। तच्च द्विविधं नाट्यरूपकनिष्ठमेव वा काव्यं तदनिष्ठापातस्य क्रमेण लक्षणमार्याद्वितयेनोच्यते।

नाट्ये यत्प्रवेशकैर्नाट्यान्तरगतैरिव पात्रैः।

अत एव ततः प्रविशतीत्युक्तैस्सङ्गमः क्रियते॥

तस्मान्नाट्यायितम्। कीदृशैरभिनयद्वारेण यत्सूचनं न तूपचारैः परमार्थतया उपचर्यमाणैर्न तूभयमपि नाट्यं तस्मान्न भवति। न त्वेकघनेत्याशङ्क्याह-कालप्रकर्षलक्षणाद्धेतोरन्योन्यभिन्नकालत्वात् कथं तत्रैकघनतयायुक्तेरिति भावः। यावदिति भूयस्तरं प्रबन्धं व्याप्नोतुं परीतुं वा सर्वे तन्नाट्यायितमित्यर्थः। तथा यावदिति स्वप्ने स्वप्नान्तरं तत्राप्यन्यत्स्वप्नान्तरमित्यादिन्यायेन वा भवेत्वेकस्वप्रायितवत्या वा सर्वथा तन्नाट्यायितं।

तत्रास्य बहुतरव्यापिनो बहुगर्भस्वप्रायिततुल्यस्य नाट्यायितस्योदाहरणं महाकविसुबन्धुनिबद्धो वासवदत्तानाट्यधाराख्यः समस्त एव प्रयोगः।

तत्र हि बिन्दुसारः प्रयोज्यवस्तुक उदयनचरिते सामाजिकीकृतोऽप्युदयनो वासवदत्ताचेष्टिते?। एष चार्थः स्वस्मिसूत्ररूपके दृष्टे सुज्ञानो भवति। अतिवैतत्यभयात्तु न प्रदर्शितः। एकस्तु प्रदेश उदाहियते। तत्र ह्युदयने सामाजिकी कृते सूत्रधारप्रयोगः।

"तब सुचरितैरेव जयति" इति।

उदयनः॥ "कुतो मम सुचरितानि"

इति सास्रं विलपति।

"एह्यम्ब किं कटकपिङ्गलवाचकैस्तैः

भक्तोऽहमप्युदयनः सुललितानायः (?)।

यौगन्धरायण ममानय राजपुत्रीं

हा हर्षरक्षित गतस्त्व [म] पिप्रभावः(?)॥

तत्रैव बिन्दुसारः सामाजिकीभूतः परमार्थतामभि (मन्य) मानो धन्यां खलु प्रलापैश्च (?) सति॥

प्रतीहारी॥—(आत्मगतं)

"अ अणिदपरमात्थकलहिञ्छिइखुदेवो"

इत्यादि परिमितव्यापिनो गर्भस्य नाट्यायितस्योदाहरणम्॥

The passage deals with *nāṭyāyitā,* a term which occurs in the *Nāṭyaśāstra;* but has not hitherto been properly understood. With the help of the commentary, which is unfortunately broken in a few places, and in other places misunderstood on account of the corrupt text, *nāṭyāyiṭa* seems to refer to a device by which the actors in a play are represented, or are supposed to be represented, as conversing with the actors in another play, the scence and time of action of which might be far removed from them. The device seems to have been used in a very masterly way in the work *Vāsavadattā-Nāṭyādhārā* of the great poet (महाकवि) Subandhu. The work is said to have had many *garbhas* in it, meaning many incidents are represented in it, as in a dream, which belong to a time and scene different from that of the action proper. Thus as soon as the stage manager utters something, Bindusāra is introduced and speaks. This speech of Bindusāra is represented as having been heard by Udayana, the hero in the drama proper. Thinking that what Udayana heard had reference to himself, Udayana is represented as exclaiming 'कुतो मम सुचरितानि,' and as reciting the following verse :–

'एह्यम्ब किं कटकपिङ्गलवाचकैस्तैः
भक्तोऽहमप्युदयनः सुललितानीयः(?)।
यौगन्धरायण ममानय राजपुत्रीं
हा हर्षरक्षितगतस्त्वमपिप्रभावः(?)।

Again Bīndusāra seems to have been represented as hearing this verse. After this a herald प्रतीहारी seems to be introduced into the drama with the Prakrit passage:–

"अ अणिदपरमात्थकलहिञ्चिइखुदेवो।"

The *chhāyā* or Sanskrit rendering of this is uncertain. The herald, *Pratihāri,* with this sentence seems to introduce the hero Udayana to the audience. With the appearance of Udayana on the stage the *Pravéśaka* closes and the drama proper begins.

From the verse uttered by Udayana, which is again unfortunately corrupt, we are able to guess that, in the drama *Udayanacharita* or *Vāsavadattā-Nāṭyadhāra,* Kaṭakapingaḷa, Yaugandharāyaṇa and Harisharakshita were the names of some of the characters. Of these Harsharakshita might have been the name of the herald (*pratihāri*) who ushers in Udayana, the Kaṭakapingaḷa might have been the *vidushaka* or the jester, the inevitable companion of the hero in Sanskrit dramas. After this Abhinavaguptapāda gives another example of the *nāṭyāyiṭ a* from *Bālarāmāyaṇa.*[5]

The passage contains information which we have not got anywhere else in the whole range of Sanskrit literature. We do not have any other explanation of this *nāṭyāyita,* nor have we another example of a *nāṭyadhārā.* Leaving aside conjectures about what we cannot know with the limited resources now at our disposal, let us examine how this passage affects our main theme, the date of the poet Subandhu. He becomes a contemporary of the Mauryan emperors, Chandragupta and Bindusāra. He was the author of a work called *Vāsavadattā-Nāṭyadhārā.* His patrons, Chandragupta and Bindusāra, also appear to have been present during the representation of the drama. This throws a flood of light into a region of the history of Sanskrit literature, which has remained quite dark to the present. The epoch of which it formed part, seems to have been not a dull one, and the scholar is led to infer that there ought to have existed quite a large number of dramas in Sanskrit. Most unfortunately we do not possess any other example.

The study of Indian literature and epigraphy so far has not revealed any achievements of this Bindusāra. But the records of the Greek Ambassadors who visited the courts of ancient Indian kings, and the ancient Indian works translated and preserved in the Tibetan language, have some information about him. They represent him as a great conqueror and historians think that the Maurayan Empire may have been extended to South India during his time. In the Greek references his name is given as Amitrochates, which is a corruption of *Amitraghātin,* a title that appears to have been assumed by Bindusāra. The word means 'the destroyer of enemies', and seems to refer to his widespread conquests. The Sanskrit extracts and the whole of the previous discussion show Bindusāra in a new light as a great patron of letters. The extract from Vāmana seems to refer to Subandhu as a minister of Bindusāra and suggests that he was a very clever minister (*kṛitadhī*). He ought to have been a fitting successor to Chāṇakya, *i.e.,* Kauṭilya, the famous minister of Bindusāra's father Chandragupta, and the real founder of the Mauryan Empire. Kautilya was the author of the great ancient work on Polity, the *Arthaśāstra.* Like him, his successor Subandhu, the minister of Bindusāra, was the author of the dramatic work *Vāsavadattā Nāṭyadhārā.* He must also have become famous as a minister, as is evidenced by the epithet *kṛitadhé,* referring to him, and Vāmana's note on the same. Abhinavaguptāpāda, the famous Sanskrit Rhetorician and authority on poetics calls him a great poet (*mahākavi*). Dandin's reference to him in the beginning of is *Avantisundarikathā* throws further light on his life. He is said to have come out (निष्क्रान्तः) from the bondage (बन्धनात्) of Bindusāra, having bound his (Bindusāra's) heart by the story of Vatsaraja. It is a pity that the new information about Subandhu is too scanty compared to the importance of the subject. Rākshasa, the minister of Bindusāra's father Chandragupta, is said to have been first imprisoned by Chandragupta and Chāṇakya and then released to take up the office of a minister. Can it be that Subandhu also, like Rākshasa, was suffering imprisonment, for having taken part in some political revolution, when he was released by the sovereign after writing the *Vāsavadattānāṭyadhārā?*

Again, the famous poet Bāṇa, the author of *Kādambarī,* who lived in the court of the Emperor of Kanauj, Śrī Harsha, refers to a number of previous authors in the beginning of his *Harshacharita.* Among these there is a reference to a work called *Vāsavadattā.* This is in the eleventh verse and follows the reference to the *Mahābhārata* and precedes the references to the poets Bhaṭṭāra-Harichandra, Sātavāhana, Pravarasêna, Bhāsa, Kāḷidāsa and the author of the *Bṛihatkathā* (Guṇāḍhya). The verse runs thus :–

"कवीनामगलद्दर्पो नूनं वासवदत्तया।
शक्तयेव पाण्डुपुत्राणां गतया कर्णगोचरम्" ॥ 11 ॥

The gist of the verse is "The pride of poets vanished before Vāsavadaṭṭā, as the pride of the Pāṇḍavas when the weapon (शक्ति) given by Indra came to the possession of Karṇa." Scholars thought that this verse referred to the romance *Vāsavadattā* and its author. But the position of the verse in the series, coming as it does immediately after the verse referring to Vyāsa and before the verses referring to Sātavāhana, Pravarasêna, Bhāsa, Kāḷidāsa and Guṇāḍhya, preclude such a conclusion. Again Vāsavadattā has not, as a work, such merit as to deserve so high a praise. Scholars will remember that it was the study of the *Vāsavadattā* of this later Subandhu, with "his taste for the pleasures of sensual life, and the zest with which he describes the mere physical side of love, which shows him up to us and seems to prove that he has not passed the stage of a refined voluptuary." Subandhu has used expressions which must adversely affect the reputation of any writer for taste and refinement. It should be remembered that it was this work of Subandhu that brought down the ire of the editor, F.E. Hall, which has expressed itself in the following strong attack against Sanskrit culture itself :—"In short, it is nothing beyond the voucher of the severest verity to rank him (Subandhu) with his fellow Asiatics, be it in their highest taste, as no better, at the very best, than a specious savage." Dr. Peterson has amply replied to this attack in his works, and there is no need for us to reply to the attack so late in the day. It is only mentioned here to show that the references of Bāṇa could never have been to the existing *Vāsavadattā*.

Of the several attempts to extract history from the verse quoted in Vāmana's *Alaṅkārasūtra,* one makes an effort, from the introductory verses of the *Vāsavadattā,* to prove the occurrence of a political revolution in the Gupta Empire, after the death of Chandragupta II, Vikramāditya. In the light of the previous discussion and the new passages that have been quoted therein, it is plain that there is no reference in the verses to any events of the Gupta period. On the strength of the supposed references in the verses and the similarity between the expressions Chandraprakāśa, Himakarôdyôta, and Śaśiruk in the beginning of *Vāsavadattā,* the whole theory of Subandhu's taking part in the revolution and his being detrimentally affected by it was built up. This theory has now to be given up and the verses taken to contain no reference to enemies of Chandraprakāśa, who were tyrannising the whole country and particularly Subandhu's party. They are merely verses containing the *kukavinindā* (censure of bad poets). Now if the hemistitch of Vāmana has no reference to the Buddhist scholar Vasubandhu, his date ought to be determined on other grounds. The discrepancy between the two accounts of Paramārtha and

Hiuen Tsang about the place where Vikramāditya, the patron of Vasubandhu ruled, Ajodhya or Śrāvasti, might not be serious, as both the places belonged to the empire. But the question as to the Vikramāditya who patronised Vasubandhu, and his son Bālāditya, who summoned Vasubandhu to his court after he became emperor, are not so easily solved. If M. Peri is right in holding that Vasubandhu lived and died in the fourth century, the conclusion seems plausible that Chandragupta I may have had the title of Vikramāditya, which is not impossible, since the theory that Chandragupta II was the first sovereign to assume that title is at least not proved. But we do not know if Samudragupta had the title Bālāditya or Parādiya, and until we get independent proof that he had either of the titles, the question regarding the date of Vasubandhu and the identity of his patron are bound to remain unsettled.

The age of Subandhu must have been an age of very great literary and artistic activity. There must have been written at this period works in the *kāvya* and *nāṭaka* styles as well as in the *sūtra* style. But for the existence of many dramas, a work like the *naṭasūtras* referred to by Patanjali, dealing with dramaturgy could not have been written. The dramas of the period must have differed much from those of the later ages, as is evidenced by the *Nāṭyadhārā* and *Nāṭyāyita* of Subandhu. The age in which Subandhu lived was the age in which the ancient Greeks were just coming in contact with India. The Indian drama of the time seems to have already been in a much developed stage, for which there is no parallel even in the literary history of India at any later period. In the light of this, theories of India's borrowing her drama from Greece may have to be give up, and search has to be conducted in India itself for specimens of dramas, composed earlier than the age of Alexander's invasion. The hope of new and epoch-making discoveries in this field appears to be capable of realisation, and the discoveries will surely open to scholars a new epoch in the history of Sanskrit literature.

References

1. This paper was first prepared in the year 1921 and read before the Second Oriental Conference in January, 1922.

2. साभिप्रायत्वं यथा—

   सोऽयं संप्रति चन्द्रगुप्ततनयश्चन्द्रप्रकाशो युवा

   जातोभूपतिराश्रयः कृतधियां दिष्टयाकृतार्थश्रमः ।

   आश्रयः कृतधियामित्यस्य वसुबन्ध साचिव्या पक्षप परत्वात्साभिप्रायत्वं ॥

3. सजयति हिमकर लेखाचकास्ति यस्यो मयोत्कया निहिता ।

   नयनप्रदीपकज्जलनिघृक्षया रजतशुक्तिरिव ॥ 4 ॥

   भवति सुभगत्वमधिकं विस्तारित परगुण सुजनस्य ।

   वहति विकासित कुमुदो द्विगुणरुचिं हिमकरोद्द्योतः ॥ 5 ॥

   विषधरतोप्यति विषयः खल इति न मृषा वदन्ति विद्वांसः ।

   यदयं नकुलद्वेषी सकुलद्वेषी पुनःपिशुनः ॥ 6 ॥

   अतिमलिने कर्तव्ये भवति खलानामतीव निपुणा धीः ।

   तिमिरेहि कौशिकानां भवतिखलानामतीव मलिनत्वं ॥ 7 ॥

   विघ्नस्तपरगुणानां भवतिखलानामतीव मलिनत्वं ।

   अन्तरित शशिरुचामपि सलिलमुचां मलिनियाऽभ्यधिकः ॥ 8 ॥

   हस्तइवभूति मलिनो यथायथालङ्घयति खलस्सुजनम् ।

   दर्पण इवतंकुरुते तथा तथा निर्मलच्छायम् ॥ 9 ॥

   सारसवत्ता विहवा नवका विलसन्ति चरतिनोकङ्कः ।

   सरसीवकीर्तिशेषं गतवति भुवि विक्रमादित्ये ॥ 10 ॥

* This paper was first prepared in the year 1921 and read before the second Oriental Conference in January 1922.

4. The passage is given as found in the palmleaf MSS. which seems to have some mistakes. It is not attempted here to correct them.

5. This is said to be in the *garbhāṅka* of that drama. I have not been able to locate the passage in the published drama *Bāḷarāmāyaṇa* of Rājaśêkhara.

24

Remarks on the Word Śramaṇa

Samuel Beal

General Cunningham (*Bhilsa Topes* p. xii) seems to conclude finally that Śramaṇa is a Buddhist title. But Colebrooke (*Essays.* vol. II. pp. 203, 204) arrives at another conclusion, that the followers of Buddha are clearly distinguished from Brachmanes and Sarmanes (arguing from Justin, whose opinion, however, is not final as the passage is ambiguous). Colebrooke as a general definition extends the term Samanæans to ascetics of various tribes (p. 204).

But to examine Cunningham's argument. He mentions first that Buddha was called Mahā Śramaṇa, but this proves no more than that this term was employed by Buddhists, adopted by them as it was by the Jainas (Colebr. *u.s.* p. 196) and ascetics generally, as is evident from the inscription placed over the remains of the Indian who committed himself to the flames at Athens (Strabo, lib. xv. p. 720 Casaub).

He then concludes that the Śramaṇas or Germanæ of Megasthenes must be the Buddhists, because it is said that women were allowed to join them (*σνμφιλοσοφετυ*) on taking vows of chastity (*ἀπεχομενας ἀφροδισιϖν*), adding that the Buddhists alone had nuns; but here we observe the words in the original do not bear out the assertion that the women were under vows, or became nuns; and we also find the same words used by Nearkhos (Strabo, xv.,§ 66 ed. Siebenkees) in reference to the Brahmans (*σνμφιλοσοφετν ϑἀντοις κἀι γυνατκας*), so that this is no corroboration of the theory.

The division of Klitarkhos of the Pramnæ into (*ορεὶνοι, γνμνηται,πολιτικοι,προσχαριοι*) deserves consideration.

The identification of the first with the Arhans will not, I think, prove satisfactory – first as they used the skins of stags for their clothing – studying the art of healing, &c., which does not apply to the condition of the Rahat; and secondly, as we know that at the time when Buddha became an ascetic, there were in the mountains a class of men clothed as these mountaineers are described, in skins of stages, &c. As to the *γυμνηται*, it is distinctly said "*γυμνους διαζην*," which will apply to no portion of the Buddhist community. The *πολὶτικοι* are described as wearing skins, and having their hair bound up, which is equally foreign to Buddhist custom.

With respect to the division of the Germanæ, described by Megasthenes, into 'Υλοβιοι, ιατρὶκοι, δπàιται – if the Υλοβιοι[1] be Alobhiya[2] in Sanskrit, it does not seem to refer exclusively to the Buddhists, for there were other ascetics who lived in woods and fed on berried; nor is it so applicable to the Buddhist as to others, for the Aranyaka or Buddhist ascetic was allowed to receive food from the householders (*vid.* Pratimoksha). With respect to the *ιατρικοι*, even if this were a corruption of *πρατικοι*, how do we account for the description that they were phy-sicians and concerned themselves with women ? a thing strictly forbidden to the Buddhist.

On the whole we see no reason to argue the antiquity of the Buddhist community from any of these suggestions.

But observe, on the other hand, that the word Śramaṇa (*i.e.*, Germanæ) is distinguished by Buddha himself from the Brahman, and yet does not refer to his followers. (*Lalita Vist.*, pp. 248, 246). "Bhikshus ! there are Brahmaṇs and Śramaṇas who believe that there is a purity resulting from abstinence," &c., and so on, in all which passages the same division between Brahmaṇs and Śramaṇs is observed, which is noticed by the Greek writers above quoted. We argue therefore that this division was one generally accepted, and was equivalent to Brahmaṇs and non-Brahmaṇs.

Observe again that Buddha, when on his tour of inspection from the four gates, is described as meeting a Shaman with a joyful face, &c. So that even before he entered on a religious life we read of this sect of Śramaṇas as existing commonly in India, proving (unless we allow a great solecism) that this appellation was applied to others besides Buddhists. If this were once granted, the argument falls to the ground.

References

1. *Αλλὰcβιοι* of Clemens Alexandrinus, *Strom,* lib. I. 15.—ED.
2. From *alubdha*—content, free from covetousness.

25

Śramaṇas

Nārāyaṇa Aiyengar, *Shimoga*

I have read the Rev. S. Beal's remarks on the word Śramaṇa published in the *Indian Antiquary,* vol. IX, p. 122 for May 1880. In support of the conclusion arrived at by him from a survey of Greek and Buddhist works that Śramaṇas were not exclusively Buddhist priests, I attempt to show here that the ancient Brāhmaṇs themselves have used the word in such a sense as would preclude the idea of a Buddhist being thereby meant. The word occurs in several places in the *Rāmāyaṇa.*

In the *Balakāṇḍa* in describing the feeding at the sacrifice performed by Daśaratha, this śloka occurs: –

Brāhmaṇā bhunjate nityam nāthavantaścha bhunjate.

Tāpasā bhunjate chāpi Śramaṇā bhunjate tathā.

Every day Brāhmaṇs eat, the well-to-do also eat, Tāpasas eat, and Śramaṇās also eat.

The commentator says *Śramaṇāh digambarāḥ yadvā chaturthāśramiṇaḥ.*

In sarga 38 of the *Ayodhyākāṇḍa* Daśaratha plaintively asks Kaikeyī: –

Iyam hi kasyāpakarōti kinchit tapasvinī rājavarasya kanyā.

Yā chīram āsādya janasya madhye sthitā visamjñā Śramaṇīva kāchit.

"What harm this Tapasvinī (Sitā) done, who now stands sadly amidst the people wearing a bark cloth like a Śramaṇī ?"

Commentator : – "*Śramaṇī tapasvinī śramu tapasi khede cheti dhātuḥ.*"

In sarga 73 of the *Araṇyakāṇḍa,* Kabandha tells Rāma and Lakshmaṇa to go to Mataṅgāsrama, "where," he said, "lived pious Ṛishīs, the disciples of Mataṅga, and although they went away (died), their long-lived female servant (*parichārini*), a Śramaṇī named Śabarī, is still seen there. On seeing you, Rāma, who art god like and venerated by all creatures, she will go to Svarga." The brother accordingly went there. She fell at their feet and offered them *pādya* and *āchamana.* Rāma asked her if she fared well in her *tapas.* She said: "By seeing you I have this day secured the fruit of my *tapas–svarga.*" She then shewed them the different parts of the *āsrama,* and having kindled a fire, threw herself into it, went to Svarga, and obtained that happiness which Ṛishīs obtain. Here also the commentator has construed the word *Śramaṇī* to mean *Tāpasī.*

Vālmīki condemns Chārvākas in no measured terms, and if Śramaṇas were Buddhists, who rejected the *Vedas* and ridiculed the Vedic rites, it is improbable that he would have honoured them with a dinner at a Vedic sacrifice, and would have considered a female Buddhist to be worthy of Svarga and of that bliss which Ṛishīs there obtain. Śabarī burns herself to death,–a practice which is often alluded to in the literature of the Brāhmaṇs as having been observed by them. It does not appear that the Buddhists ever observed the practice. Mataṅga, whose disciples Śabarī served, was a great Ṛishi. It is to be noted that Rāma was saluted by Śabarī although she was a Tāpasī; but the reason seems to be that she was a servant and of inferior caste. Amara classes the Śabaras among Mlechchās. It therefore appears that at the time when the *Rāmāyaṇa* was written, other than Brāhmaṇ females were also members of the Śramaṇa form of asceticism.

In sarga 18 of the *Kishkindhā Kāṇḍa,* in which Rāma justifies his killing Vāli, the following śloka is addressed by Rāma to Vāli :–

Āryeṇa mama Māndhātrā vyasanam ghoram īpsitam |
Śrāmaṇena kṛite pāpe yathā pāpam kṛitam tvayā |

"My ancestor Māndhātā has ordained terrible punishment if a Śramaṇa commits sin, as you have done."

Here the commentator makes the Śramaṇa a Kshapaṇaka, *i.e.* a Buddhist; for as an orthodox Brāhmaṇ he cannot see anything improper in his adversary taking the blows, while, when the same name is mentioned in connection with Brāhmaṇs, sacrifices and Svarga, it should mean a different person. It is true that in the *Dharmaśāstras* Brāhmaṇs enjoy immunity from the more rigorous punishments; but if the Śramaṇas were a kind of ascetics other than the Brāhmaṇs, it is not inappropriate in Rāma showing Vāli how even ascetics were liable to punishment for their offences, and how a Vānara king should not grumble at his punishment.

The word occurs in the *Yajurveda Āraṇyaka, Brahmayojna praśna,*[1] 7th anuvāka, and as this old work should command great attention in connection with this subject, I quote it fully :—

वातरशना हवा ऋषय: श्रमणा ऊर्ध्वमंथिनो बभूवुस्तानृषयोऽर्थमायँस्तेऽनिलायमचरँस्तेऽनुप्रविशु: कूष्माण्डानि ताँस्तेष्वन्वविन्दञ्च्छ्रद्धया च तपसा च तानृषयोऽब्रुवन्कया निलायं चरथेतित ऋषीनब्रुवन्नमो वोस्तु भगवन्तोस्मिन्धाम्नि केन व: सपर्यामेति तानृषयोऽब्रुवन्पवित्रभो ब्रूत येनारेपस स्यामेति त एतानि सूक्तायपश्यन् ''यद्देवा देवहेलनं'' ''यदीव्यन् नृणमहं वभूवा'' ''युष्टे विश्वतो दधदि'' त्येतैराज्यं जुहुत ''वैश्वानराय प्रतिवेदयाम'' इत्युपतिष्ठत यदर्वाचीनमेनो भ्रूणहत्यायास्तस्मान्मोक्ष्यध्व इति त एतैरजुहवुस्तेऽ रेपसोऽभवन्कर्मादिष्वेतैर्जुहुयात्पूतो देवलोकांत्समश्नुते[2] ॥

"Now there were Ṛishis (*named*) windgirt, (*being*) Śramaṇas (*and*) celibates. (*Other*) Ṛishis solicited them. They (*the Śramaṇas*) observed *anilāya* (living houseless) and they entered into the *Kūshmāṇḍa* (*mantras*). In these they (*the Ṛishis*) found them by means of devotion and penance. The Ṛishis asked them, 'Why do you observe *anilāya ?*' They said to the Ṛishis—'Salutation to you, O Bhagavats! in this abode wherewith can we honour you ?' The Ṛishis replied to them—'Tell us of some means of purification whereby we may become sinless.' They (*the Śramaṇas*) saw those hymns (*sūktas*) : *Yad dévā . . .*, *Yad adīvyan . . . Āyush te . . .* 'With' these (*mantras*) do ye offer ghī and with the *mantra-Vaiśvānarāya . . .* worship (*the fire*) and free yourselves from all sin short of fœtus-killing !' They (*the Ṛishis*) sacrified with these, and became sinless. In the beginning of sacrificial acts (*karma*) one should sacrifice with these, and, purified, he obtains the worlds of the Dévas."

The mantras quoted are to the present day used in a ceremony called *Kūshmāṇḍa homa,* and the *sankalpa,* or the object of it, is repeated in the following words being the same as set forth in the *Āraṇyaka*:– *Bhrūṇahatyāyā arvānchi yāvanty eṇāmsi mayi sambhavanti tāvatām enasāṁ nivṛittyarthaṁ Kūshmāndair hoshyāmi.* It is not necessary here to quote the mantras themselves in full as they are in praise of Agni and other Vedic deities. It will be seen that in the *Āraṇa* Śṛamaṇas are held in high esteem, and recommend to Ṛishis the performance of a Vedic ceremony. Surely Śramaṇa here cannot mean a Buddhiṣt.

The word also occurs in the *Bhāgavata Purāṇa* 11th skandha 2nd adhyāya and 20th śloka :–

Navābhavan mahābhāgamunayo hy arthaśamsinaḥ | *Śramaṇā vātaraśanā ātmavidyāviśāradāḥ.*

The next śloka names the nine Munis :–Havis, Hari, Antariksha, Prabuddha, Pippalāyana, Āvirhotra, Dramīla, Chamasa, and Karabhājana.

Commentator : *arthaśamsinaḥ paramārthanirūpakāḥ, Śramaṇāh Śramavantaḥ Ārmābhyêse kṛitaśramā ityarthaḥ, vātaraśanāḥ digambarāḥ.*

Although in the 7th act of the *Mṛichchhakaṭika nāṭaka* simply *Śramaṇaka* is mentioned (as an ill omen, if met in the road), still in the 2nd act in which the character is first spoken of, the word *Śākyaśramaṇaka* occurs,–*aham etena dyūtakarāvamānena śāhyaśramaṇako bhavishyāmi.* The qualifying word *Śākya* is rather noteworthy, and would be superfluous if Śramaṇa was exclusively Buddhist.

From the uncertainty about the date of the *Rāmāyaṇa,* it cannot of course be presumed that Śākyaśramaṇas did not then exist. But the *primā facie* antiquity of the *Yajurveda Āraṇyaka* and the circumstances noticed by the Rev. Mr. Beal, render it almost certain that long before Buddhism, the religious zeal of the miscellaneous classes of ancient India had developed itself into Śramaṇism, if I may use the expression, and it is natural that the name of this form of asceticism was found appropriate to be adopted by or applied to Buddhist Bhikshus, and in course of time, exclusively,—the other classes probably discarding it owing to the notoriety it had in the palmy days of Buddhism. Perhaps the present Bairāgis, who are half naked and wander from place to place from the Himālayas to Cape Kumārī, are the survivals of the pre-Buddhist Śramaṇas.

Since writing the above, I have read Prof. H. Jacobi's article on "Mahāvīra and his Predecessors" (*Ind. Ant.*, vol. IX, p. 158) and also that portion of the *Bhāgavata Purāṇa* (V. 4) in which the story of Ṛishabha is narrated. In the *Vishṇu Purāṇa,* Ṛishabha is not mentioned as the incarnation of Vishṇu, but is said to have been a great king, who performed various sacrifices, installed his eldest son Bharata, went to the Āsrama of Pulaha, performed *tapas* and sacrifices according to the *Vānaprastha Vidhāna,* and went the *Mahāprasthāna* journey, naked, gagging his mouth with *vīṭā*-stone (*Kandukasadṛiśamaśmakabalam,* commentator) *Tapasākarshito'tyarthaṁ kṛiśo dhamanisantataḥ* | *Nagno vīṭ ām mukhe kṛitvā vīrādhvānam ito gataḥ* | *Vishṇu Purāṇa,* II, 1, 32.

The *Bhāgavata* says that king Arhan and other fell into bad ways, by presuming to imitate Ṛishabha, an incarnation of Vishṇu. The word Arhan is evidently Jaina, and it is evident, as observed by Prof. Jacobi, that Jainas are meant. But it is said in the latter part of *Bhāgavata* V. 3, that Ṛishabha was born to teach duties to *vātaraśanānām Śramaṇānām ṛishīṇām ūrdhvamanthinām;* the very named by which Śramaṇas are called in the *Āraṇyaka.* And the nine Śramaṇas named in *Bhāgavata* X. 2, 20, are stated in V. 4 of the same, to have been nine of the one hundred sons of Ṛishabha, and also thus: 'These are the nine mahābhāgavatas, the expounders of the *Bhāgavata dharma,* whose history (*charitam*) illustrative of the greatness of god and occurring in the dialogue between Vasudeva and Nārada will be described by us by and bye.'—The *charita* occurs as far down as the 10th skandha, which is in poetry, while the story of Ṛishabha is in prose, and it may perhaps be suspected that the story was added afterwards, but no conclusive inference can be drawn that its author was different from that of the other portions of the *Purāṇa*. We have therefore in this work the Jainas denounced as heretics, and the Śramaṇas spoken of as holy men. The different ślokas which Nārada puts into the mouth of each of the nine Śramaṇas in the 10th skandha teach *bhakti*. On the theory that Śramaṇism gradually developed itself into Jainism and Buddhism, it is not improbable that before the development took place, it was not decidedly antagonistic to the *Vedas;* that on account of the pious life it taught, even Brāhmaṇs counted its leaders as great men and accepted their teachings, and that the author of the *Bhāgavata* had a tradition of that period, though the particular *bhakti* doctrines attributed to the nine Śramaṇas may have been the work of imagination.

The word Śramaṇa occurs also in the *Arjunavanarāsaparva* of the *Mahābhārata* (ādiparva, adhyāya 214). The following classes of men followed Arjuna: *Brāhmaṇā vedapāragāḥ* (1) *Vedavedāngavidvāṁas tathaivādhyātmachintakāḥ* | *Bhaikshāś cha bhagavadbhaktāḥ sūtaḥ paurāṇikāś cha ye* (2) *Kathakāś chāpare, Rājan, Śramaṇās cha vanaukasaḥ* | *Divyākhyānāni ye chāpi paṭ hanti madhurṁ dvijāḥ* (3). Here Śramaṇas are made to honour a Brāhmaṇical hero with their company in his journey to holy places, along with Brāhmaṇs. It is also to be noted that they, the Śramaṇas, are stated to be dwellers of forests, *vanaukasah*.

References

1. *Taittiīya Āranyaka,* 2nd prap. 7th Anuv. *Bibloth. Indica,* vol. I, p. 228.—ED.
2. The above is copied from a manuscript here. It is recited by the Yajurvedius.

26

Buddhist Legends

G. De Vasconcellos Abreu.[1]

From "Fragmentos d'uma Tentativa de Estudo Scoliastico da Epopeia Portugueza,"

Translated with Additional Notes by Donald Ferguson, Ceylon

Origin of the King of the Lions and of the Name of Ceylon

Vestiges of a Buddhist Legend in the "Lusiads."[2]

There are legends of peoples descended from the unnatural connection of a wild beast with a human being, the mythological value of which may serve as a guide for the historical knowledge of the origin of those peoples.

In this case the legend which explains the name of Ceylon given to the ancient isle of Tāmra, Tāmra-dvīpa, or Tāmra-parṇa, is related by the Buddhist authors in their sacred language, the Pāli, or in Sanskṛit or Chinese.

In the oldest classical texts in Sanskṛit, the *Mahābhārata* and the *Rāmāyaṇa,* we find the word Laṅkā, as the name of the capital of the island, and—by an extension—the whole island of the savage Rākshasas, whose king was, according to the Hindu epic, the terrible Rāvaṇa. Another name equally ancient is that met with in a *Harivaṁśa,* Ratna-dvīpa, "isle of precious things," which the Chinese translated by the word *Pao-chu.*[3]

Hiuen-Tsiang, in the 7th century, however, employs the name of Ling-kia, from the Sanskṛit Laṅkā, but to designate simply a high mountain inhabited by evil spirits in the south-east corner of the kingdom of Seng-kia-lo, in Sanskṛit Siṁhala "country of lions."[4]

In the 6th century, Cosmos Indicopleustes, the Egyptian navigator of the Indian seas, in his *Topographia Christiana,* calls the island of Ceylon, Selediva; and one of the names best known by the navigators and merchants was, in effect, that of Serendivus,[5] Singaldib,[6] or Sirindib.[7]

These names are derived from the Pāli word *sīhala-dīpo,*[8] the Sanskṛit form of which is *siṁhala-dvīpa,* "isle of the Siṁhalas," the island of Ceylon, as is seen from the collection of Hindu fables and apologues, the *Hitôpadéśa.* The word *dvīpa,* isle, *dīpo* in Pāli, is transformed in the language of the Arabs into *dyvah, aldybah,* as is seen from a Portuguese document of the 16th century, though Fr. João de Sousa transcribes *adiba,*[9]

Previous to this the word *siṁhala-dvīpa* had been brought by the Arabs to Europe, for Ptolemy uses the adjective *salike* to designate all the inhabitants of Sālai. Lassen[10] identifies this name, given by the Greek geographer, with an abbreviated form in Pāli, Sīhala, signifyiṅg "dwelling of the Siṁhas," not of actual lions, but of the warriors who emigrated thither with Vijaya, the Hindu conqueror, to whom is attributed the Buddhist civilization of Ceylon.

But a confirmation of the legend we have mentioned, that the island was formerly called Tāmra-parṇa, or in Pāli Tamba-paṇṇi,[11] is found in the fact that this designation was brought to the knowledge of Onesikritos before that of Sālai, and had thus been in the west since Alexander–

"A nobre ilha tambem de Taprobana,

Jā pelo nome antigo tam famoza."–

Lus. x. fol. 169[12]

From the name of the Siṁhalas the island takes in Pāli that of Sīhalaṁ, the popular form of which, Sīlaṁ,[13] gives origin to the forms Sailān, used by the Persian Rashidu'd-din, a contemporary of Marco Polo, and that used by this same Polo, Seilan, as well as our Ceylāo [Ceylon].

It is noteworthy that Camoens has identified[14] the two names, Ceylon and Taprobana, because in 1537, from ambiguity arising from a false interpretation of the geography of Ptolemy by the school of Behaim,[15] Taprobana is explained as the island of Sumatra.

In 1559, Jomard again confounds the two names of Sumatra and Taprobana, which are distinguished both in the maps of this geographer of Henry II, and in the magnificent portulane of Charles VI,[16] from this supposed Taprobana, the island of Ceylon, whose position is accurately marked.

The name of Taprobana, or in Sanskṛit Tāmra-parṇa, is, as we have seen, the oldest known Hindu name given to the island of Ceylon.[17] The name Laṅkā appears to have been that by which it was known to the first Aryans who went thither from India.

The name of Ceylon or island of the Siṁhalas is, however, of such remote origin that even the *Mahābhārata* speaks of the Siṁhalas as inhabitants of the island at the south of India.[18]

Childers[19] says that the Siṁhalas, or as we now call them the Siṁhalese, are "only the Aryan inhabitants of Ceylon, descendants of a people who emigrated from Lāla, in Magadha, in India, and came thither many centuries before our era." The capital of Lāla, the Larikê of the Greeks, was Siṁhapura, "the city of Lions."[20]

These historical questions having been settled, we give some Buddhist legends regarding the origin of the Aryan civilization of Ceylon. The mythological elements which are found in them are common to other European legends, and a comparison of them is therefore interesting.

Conquest of the Island of Laṅkā, and Founding of the Siṁhalese or Lion Dynasty

From *Chap. IX of the Pāli Chronicle, Dīpavaṁsā.*[21]

1. This island of Laṅkā was formerly called Sīhala from the name Lion (*Sīha*). Listen, therefore, ye, to the narration of its origin, which I shall relate to you.
2. The daughter of the king of Vaṅga cohabited in the forest with a wild lion, in consequence of which two children were born.

3. Sīhabāhu and Sīvalī[22] were two lovely children; the mother was named Susimā,[23] and the father was called (the Lion) Sīha.
4. On the expiration of sixteen rainy seasons the son of Sīha departed from the cave, and founded the most noble city of Sihapura.
5. The son of Sīha (the Lion), a powerful king in the country of Lāla, ruled the great kingdom in the most noble city of Sīhapura.
6. Thirty-two brothers were the progeny of the son of Sīha (Lion), and of these the eldest were Vijaya and Sumitta, both of extra-ordinary beauty.
7. The young prince Vijaya was audacious and without instruction, and committed acts of the greatest wickedness and unparalleled extotions.
8. The merchants and all the other men of the country assembled, and went to complain to the king of the crimes of Vijaya.
9. On hearing their clamorous voices, the king, full of anger, gave order to his ministers, "Expel this young man;
10. and all these slaves, wives, and children and relatives, and servants of both sexes, and workmen, expel all these people."
11. Then they expelled him, separating him from all his relatives, and they put them on broad a ship, and the ship sailed away upon the sea.
12. "Let them go wherever they please, and they shall not be seen any more, nor shall they return to our kingdom to dwell amongst this people."
13. The ship with the children went on shore on an uninhabited island, whence it got the name of Naggadīpa.[24]
14. And the ship with the women went on shore on an uninhabited island, and hence they called it Mahilāraṭṭha (Kingdom of Women).
15. The ship with the men, sailing over the sea without a destination, futilely and without a course, arrived at the port of Suppāra.[25]

16. And when seven hundred disembarked at Suppāra, the Suppārakas received them with much welcome and many honours.
17. Whilst they were being thus received, Vijaya and his company, all these strangers, practised cruel deeds,
18. Giving themselves to drunkness, theft, adultery, treachery, murder, and the most vile, immoral, and horrible modes of procedure.
19. The Suppārakas were irritated at these horrors of unsurpassable cruetly and barbarous savagery, and agreed: "Let us quickly kill these wicked ones."
20. There was formerly Ojadīpa, Varadīpa, or Maṇḍadīpa, also called Laṅkādīpa, and which is known as Tambapaṇṇi.
21. At the time when Sambuddha, the best of men, attained *parinibbāna,*[26] this son of Sihābāhu, the Khattiya (*Kshatriya,* warrior prince), Vijaya.
22. Arrived at Laṅkādīpa, after having departed from the land of Jambudīpa (*one of the names of India);* The excellent Buddha had prophesied: "The prince will be the king (*of Laṅkā*)."
23. At that time the Master (*Gautama, the Buddha*), said to Sakka,[27] the chief of the gods, "Do not neglect thy care, Kosiya,[28] of Laṅkādīpa."
24. Sujampati, the king of the gods, after hearing this warning of Sambuddha, charged Uppalavaṇṇa,[29] to protect the island.
25. Hearing the order of Sakka, the powerful Devaputta,[30] with the Parisas,[31] protected the island of Laṅkā.
26. After staying at Bhārukachchha and exasperating the inhabitants, Vijaya returned to his ship.
27. Having with his company gone on board, they put to sea, and soon a furious wind made them lose sight of the coast.
28. They arrived at Laṅkādīpa, where they disembarked, and went on shore. But on *terra firma* they felt exhausted with hunger, thirst, and fatigue; they could scarcely walk.
29. They went on their hands and feet, and afterwards rose and stood on their feet, and saw their hands (*pāṃ*) shining.

30. The very red dust of that earth covered their arms and hands; and from this cause that place was called Tambapaṇṇi.

31. The first city in the renowned Laṅkādīpa was Tambapaṇṇi, and dwelling there Vijaya ruled his kingdom.

32. Vijaya and Vijita and with them Achchutagāmi and Upatissa, were the first who landed there and took possession (?)[32] of territory.

33. A great multitude of men and women came together, and one Khattiya (*prince*) built cities here, another there, in all the country.

34. Vijaya built the city of Tambapaṇṇi, with its suburbs, on the south bank of the river in the most charming place.

35. Vijita built the city to which he gave his name, and then that of Uruvela; and the minister, who got his name from the asterism Anurādha, founded the city of Anurādha.

36. He whose name was Achchutagāmi founded Ujjeni, and Upatissa, Upatissa—the city of beautiful markets, rich, vast, of great prosperity, and delightful.

37. The first king of famous Laṅkādīpa was king Vijaya in Tambanpaṇṇi.

38. When seven years of his reign had passed, many people had come thither. His reign was thirty-eight years.

39. In the ninth month of Sambuddha,[33] the Yakkas were destroyed; in the fifth year of Sambuddha the Jina conquered the Nāgas;[34] in the eighth year of Sambuddha the *Samāpatti*[35] was completed.

40. On all these three occasions Tathāgata[36] came hither. In the last year of Sambuddha, Vijaya came hither.

41. Sambuddha, the best of men, made the island of Laṅkā fit for the habitation of men; and by the *anupādisesā*[37] extinguished himself in all his *upadhis* (*upadhi*).[38]

42. The Khattiya reigned thirty-eight years after the *partinibbāṅa* of Sambuddha, the shining lord of truth,

43. And sent to Sīhapura a messenger to Sumitta: "Come shortly to us to this magnificent Laṅkādīpa.

44. There is no one to succeed me in the rule after my death; I yield in your favour this island which I conquered by my valour."

Prince Simhala saved by The Magic Horse

A Buddhist Legend[39] on the Origin of the Name of Ceylon[40]

"Siṁhala, son of the merchant Siṁha, having embarked to go in search of precious stones in a distant island, is assailed, on approaching Tāmradvīpa (the same as Tāmraparṇa, the Taprobane of the ancients), by a tempest raised by the Rākshasīs, wicked divinities, which inhabit that island. He is shipwrecked with his companions, and by swimming reaches the shore, where the Rākshasīs appear, and under the guise of beautiful women entice the merchants to yield themselves to pleasures with them. Siṁhala, after passing the night in the arms of one of these women, discovers by the lamp which lightens them that he has fallen into the hands of an ogress, whose pleasure he serves and who will devour him. He learns that other merchants, shipwrecked like himself, have been since their arrival thrown into a prison whence the Rākshasīs take them daily to feed on their flesh. Taught by the revelations of the lamp, he goes with his companions to the shore, where there appears to him a miraculous horse which is to transport him from the island. But he has to take care not to turn his head back; any one allowing himself to be moved by the tears of the Rākshasīs and casting a single look towards the shore is condemned to fall into the ocean, where the ogresses wait to put him to death. The companions of Siṁhala consent gladly to leave the island with him; but faithless to their promises they give an ear to the lamentations of the women whom they are leaving, and disappear one after another, devoured by the Rākshasīs. Siṁhala alone escapes; and, in spite of the endeavours of the women he has left in the island, the marvellous horse transports him to India.

"The Rākshasī from whose hands Siṁhala had escaped seduced the king Siṁhakèśarin, and entered his inner apartments. Assisted by the other demons whom she summoned form the island of Tāṃradvīpa, she devoured the king and his family. Siṁhala, who alone was able to explain this disaster, was proclaimed king;

and he formed the resolution of going to destroy the Rākshasīs of the island, in order to spread there the doctrine of the Three Precious Objects. The demons retired into a forest; and from that event the country formerly called Tāmradvīpa took the name of Siṁhaladvīpa."

This legend is completed by the following, of what we know of the origin of the Siṁhalas :–

Origin of the Kingdom of Simha (Lion)

According to the "Mahāvaṁsa".[41]

"There was once a king who ruled in Baṅganagara in the land of the Baṅgas, and whose spouse was a daughter of the king of Kāliṅga. They had a very beautiful daughter, who, one day, going for a walk by herself, met a caravan, going to Magadha, and accompanied it without making herself known. On reaching the land of Lāla, they were separated from each other by a lion.

"The daughter of the king, remembering that it had been prophesied that she would cohabit with a king of animals, caressed the lion, and the latter carried her to his cave, and there were born to them a son with lion's feet and hands, and a daughter.[42] The mother then gave them the names of Siṁhabāhn (lion's arms) and Siṁhāvalī (lion's offspring).

"When the son had completed sixteen years his mother discovered to him his origin; taking advantage of the lion's absence, he took his mother and sister on his back and carried them to a neighbouring village, where Anura, son of a maternal uncle of his, the commander-in-chief of the armies of Baṅga, was commissioned to direct the labours of the villagers.

"The latter received them into his house, and clothed them, and gave them food on tree-leaves. The clothes then become of the richest textures, and the leaves were changed in to golden vessels. Astonished at such marvels, he asked his guests about their origin, which the mother then related to him. He thereupon conveyed them to the capital of Baṅga, and took the daughter[43] for his wife.

"When the lion returned to his cave, which was deserted, he searched for his children, and not finding them he entered the villages, putting to flight the inhabitants. These hastended to complain to the king, showing him the danger they were running. As the king could find no one able to capture the lion he twice offered still larger rewards to whoever would give chase. Twice the mother of Siṁhabāhu forbade him to accept the offer; but the third time Siṁhabāhu offered himself, without first asking the consent of his mother, and the king promised to give him the kingdom if he succeeded in capturing the lion.

"Siṁhabāhu then sought out the lion in his cave, pierced him with an arrow, and fled back to the capital of the kingdom like a wild beast. The king had died without a successor seven days previously. The ministers, being informed of the fact that he was the grandson of the king and his mother the daughter, and astonished at this, assembled in council, and unanimously invited him to be king. Siṁhabāhu assumed the rule but resigned the kingdom to him who had married his mother, and returned with his sister to his native country. There he founded in the kingdom of Lāla the city of Siṁhapura and villages in the forests, and married his sister. The latter had twin sons sixteen times, the eldest of whom was Vijaya, and the second Sumitra, the first of whom his father at a suitable age nominated *Uparāja* (chief heir)."

In these legends we have to separate the historical portion from the mythological.

The historical portion is evidently the Aryan conquest of the island of Laṅkā, and its conversion to Buddhism.

But before this Buddhist conquest the island had already been conquered by the Āryans, as is sung in the epic of Rāma; in these legends we see only the legendary series of which the *Rāmāyaṇa* is the most beautiful expression.[44]

The Pāli chronicle attributes to the same invaders the two names, Tambapaṇṇi, in Sanskṛit Tāmraparṇa, or Tambadīpa, in Sanskṛit Tamradvīpa, and Sīhaladīpa, in Sanskṛit Siṁhaladīpa, in Sanskṛit Siṁhaladvīpa. Here, in my opinion, there is confusion.

The chronicler explains the etymology of Tambapaṇṇi in a quite erroneous way, as we hear people ignorant of etymological processes explaining local names, for example, Ribeira's of 'Coselhas,' 'Odemira,' 'Miragaya.'

It is sufficient for us to note the two *ṇ*'s in *paṇṇi* to trace to word to the Sanskṛit *parṇi,* which we refer to *parṇa,* 'left,' with the feminine termination in composition. The word *pāṇi,* 'hand,' corresponds identifically with the Sanskṛit. The word *tamba,* 'copper-coloured, vermilion,' corresponds in Sanskṛit with the word *tāmra,* 'copper-coloured, vermillion,' but is also the name of several plants, and among them the *Rubia munjista* of Roxburgh, which name in Sanskṛit is also given to *mañjishṭ hā* (Pāli *mañjiṭṭhā*), the madder of the dyers, and a kind of sandal, the vermilion of which Garcia da Orta (*Colloquio,* xlix) speaks, but which must not be confounded with the actual *Pterocarpus santalinus,* better known by the name of *Lignum santalinum rubrum* [red sanders wood].

According to the statement of Flückiger and Daniel Hanbury,[45] we are led to believe that in the time of the physician of D. João III, the wood known by the name of red sandal in commerce was not that of a variety of sandal, an article of trade even than very different from that which nowadays has that name in Europe. Garcia da Orta himself confesses that he did not know the tree, but was informed that the natives of India used a portion for fevers, and considered the wood good for working, and suitable from its size for pagodas and idols.

The true region of the sandal in India is from Malabar to Coromandel, especially the mountains of Malaya.[46] Hiyen-Tsiang,[47] describing these mountains, says : – "There rise the mountains Mo-la-ye (Malaya) with their scarped sides and their frowning summits, their gloomy valleys and their deep ravines. On these mountains grow the white sandal, and the tree called Chen-t'an-ni-p'o (*Chandanéva,* 'like sandal')."

And in the region of the Malaya mountains, which in ancient India exactly formed one of the nine divisions[48] of the country of Bhārata (India), the division of *khaṇḍa* of Tāmraparṇa is the river of the same name.[49]

The trade in sandal was of the greatest importance in Ceylon in the first centuries of our era. However, the larger merchants who had the opportunity procured supplies from abroad. Ceylon imported it to export it, because she was the emporium of the

Asiatic world, as being the central point of all the maritime commerce.[50]

On the other hand, it is certain that previous to the Aryan expedition attributed to Vijaya, and with which Buddhism was introduced into Ceylon, the Aryan expedition attributed to Rāma took place. Of the expedition of Vijaya there is a tradition on the eastern coast, of the expedition of Rāma there is living tradition on the western coast, in Malabar. Among the Malabars exist even now families with the ancient names of the race of the Ikshvākus, ancestors of Rāma.[51]

It is possible, therefore, that the name of Tāmraparṇa, anterior to that of Siṁhaladvīpa, originated from the region of Malabar.[52]

In the mythological portion we distinguish, as having historical value, the death of the lion.

The speaking lamp, the magic or flying horse, and the misfortune of any one looking back from it, are mythological elements of another order.

These assassinations, nearly always fratricides, but also parricides and filiicides, are connected with the building of a city raised over the hole into which has been cast the head, or the phallus, of the individual sacrificed, and whose name is sometimes given to the city.[53]

The lion killed by Siṁhabāhu has in Greece its mythological representative in the lion of Herakles, which some mythologists explain as the cloud, dark and thundering, conquered by the solar god.[54] In Hellenic tradition is known the monstrous and terrible lion, the devastating lion of the country of the king of Megara, whose daughter is to marry the hero who slays it; and yet the lion has not its habitat in the Peloponnesus, nor in any part of the Doric region, to which the cities of Megara and Nemea belonged.

The tradition is common to the mythology of the Aryan races. And to further confirm it there is the circumstance of the hero of India and the hero of Greece being a great traveller by sea.[55]

In the middle ages the lion and the virgin of the Buddhist legend are the monoceros and the maiden, who embraces him round the neck, attracting him by the enchantments of her beauty or by the delicious perfume with she exhales.[56]

Before examining the other mythological elements, it may be as well not to forget that in the classical literature of Europe mention is made of female beings similar to the cruel Rākshasīs, such are, in the African island, always populated, the fanciful beings, exclusively of the female sex, whom Pomponius Mela (III, 9) notices. And Athenæus (V, 64), tells us the Marius brought from Afrcia the skins of marvellous animals, which he offered to the temple of Herakles.

The origin is well known of the name of *gorilla,* given in the *Periplus* of Hanno by the Carthaginian navigator to certain animals of the tropical zone encountered by him on the western coasts of Africa. The animals which, from among these, he brought and consecrated to the temple of Tanit (Juno) were three females.

So, then, if there are identical traditions of an island of fierce female beings, both in India and in Europe, there is also a historical fact by the resemblance of which we can explain the Hindu tradition. In fact, tradition in Europe supplies the lack of antiquity, in anatomy and mythology, of the centuries which elapsed between the Punic navigator and the geographer of the time of Claudius.

The inhabitants of the female sex, the fierce Rākshasīs of the island conquered by Vijaya, must not, however, be set down as fabulous. We have every reason rather to consider them as the savage women of Henno, who, according to Pomponius Mela, were fanciful beings.

Besides the tradition common to the whole Aryan race, there exist in Europe traditional vestiges which mythographers prove to be of Buddhist origin. They had easy access into Italy, where we find them in abundance, and from thence they spread to the west.

We do not know that there is among us any popular story in which speaking lamps are mentioned. In Italy many are known, and the reader can see them in the magnificent, collection of Pitré, *Fiabe, Norvells e Racconti Popolari Siciliani,* for example, in the story of "La soru di lu Conti."[57]

In Italy we also meet with the tradition of the magic horse. But in this case there enter in common Aryan elements and elements of tradition, which is the daughter of importation through Buddhist influence.

Before the winged horse described by Ariosto, Greece knew Arion, the horse of Adrastus, and Pegasus, another marvellous horse.[58]

In fact, a patrimony of Aryan legends must be assigned to the myth of the horse of the hero, which saves him from difficulties, like the horses of the two Aśvins and the horse of Indra, which warns him or at least foretells to him, like the horse of Rāvaṇa, weeping, of future disgrace, or neighing predicts, as to Darius, glory and triumph; the myth of the horse which identifies itself with the hero, on whose strength depends the strength of the hero, and whose rider bears a name given to him from the horse he rides and from the strength of that horse, like Aśvatthāman (*aśvasthāman,* strength of a horse), the son of Drôṇa, in the *Mahābhārata.*

The later transformations of the myth of the magic horse, the horse of the hero, indicate to us, however, an importation of Buddhist traditions. Thus transformed, the magic horse is in Lisbon the pair of cork boots; and in literary productions, who does not recognize it in the mantle of the lame devil and the cane of M. de Balzac ?

In popular stories their parallels are found in the carpet on which the hero ascends, and on which he is transported through the air, the boots of swiftness which the three brothers procure,[59] and the show of Cinderella.

An example these of transformations in the east before those known to be European is the *Avadāna* No. lxxiv, of the Indian stories and apologues, translated from the Chinese by Stanislas Julien.[60]

The Dispute of the two Demons

"There were formerly two Piśāchas, who had each a box, a stick, and a shoe. These two demons disputed with each other, each washing to have these six objects at once. They passed whole days quarrelling without being able to come to an agreement. A man, being witness of this obstinate discussion, questioned them and said: 'What then is there so wonderful in a box, a stick, and a shoe, that you dispute with such hotness ?'

"'From this box,' replied the two demons, 'We can obtain clothes, drink, food, bed-coverings, and, in fact, everything necessary for life and comfort. When we hold this stick our enemies submit humbly, and no one dares dispute with us. When we have put on this shoe, by its power we can go flying without meeting any obstacle.'

"On hearing these words, the man said to them: 'Go a little way from me; I am going to make a fair division.'

"At these words the two demons retired apart. The man took the two boxes and the two sticks, put on the two shoes, and flew off. The two demons were stupified on seeing that nothing was left to them.

"The man then spoke to the demons, and said to them: 'I have taken away what was the object of your quarrel, I have taken away what was the object of your quarrel, I have placed you both in the same condition, and have relieved you of all subject of jealousy and dispute."

Our leading mythographer, Sr. Adolpho Coelho, knows a Portuguese popular story, of which, however, he cannot obtain a complete version, in which there are three brothers, one of whom has an eye with which he sees at great distances, another has a carpet which carries one far away, the other has an apple or a water which cures every disease. Professor Adolpho Coelho sees in this story, to which, he says, there are many European parallels, a Buddhist origin; and traces it to the story which we have given from the *Avadānas*.

The parallel story in India is No. 24 of vol. II of the collection *Tuti Nāme,* edited by Georg Rosen, Leipzig, 1858, quoted by De Gubernatis, *Mythologie Zoologique,* vol. I, p. 135.[61]

In the collection of Hindu fables, in Sanskṛit, the *Pañchatantra,* the reader may find an interesting variant of the episode, in the story of "The Weaver who passed himself off as Vishṇu." Benfey in his valuable study on these Hindu stories and apologues comments on some peculiarities of this story.[62]

The horse, which we thus see substituted by the mantle, the carpet, the boots, the shoe, is in the Buddhist religion one of the necessary requisites of the *Chakravartin.*[63]

A *Chakravartin* is he who possesses all that exists in the limits of the world. Buddha is a *Chakravartin.* His horse is white as the light of day, and has hair like the golden rays of the sun; he lives by drinking in the winds, and flies, traversing the whole of space.[64]

According to the *Raya-Tch'er-Rol-Pa,* the horse belonging to the Buddha *Chakravartin* is grey,[65] has a black head, its hair plaited, is covered with a net of gold, and traverses all the heavens. The *Chakravartin* mounts it at break of day, any traverses, from one side to another, as far as the oceanic confines, the entire world, not before the keeper, who has the courser in his charge, first ceases to ask it to neigh.

From the Vedic hymns we see that the sun is designated as a god who sees and knows all, to whom nothing is hidden, and, who rises, drawn by his rays, by his horses,[66] and this conception reveals a great development of anthropomorphism, because to the sun is given in the hymn VII, 77, 3, the double qualification of "eye of the gods," and "shining white horse." On the other hand, the sun is compared to the fire of the altar, and the fire of the alter is compared to the sun, because in mythology, as in all the Vedic cult, to celestial phenomena correspond like terrestrial phenomena, what takes place on earth has equally a place in heaven. The fire, *agni,* in Latin *ignis,* is also compared to a horse.[67] It is he who goes from earth to heaven bearing the sacrifice to the gods,[68] neighing from the first moment, *i.e.* crackling on the altar of sacrifice, roaring, flashing in the midst of the cloud-like lightning which pierces space.

It is he who draws the gods to the altar,[69] it is he who gives the victory, it is he who leaps from abysses, he is the victor who saves the hero.[70] It is he who feeds on the winds, who is the friend of the wind;[71] he is the horse of which we can say with Ariosto: —[72]

"Questo è il destrier . . . . . .

Che di fiamma e di vento era concetto;

E senza fieno e biada, si nutria

Dell'aria pura. . . . . .

Secure when attached to the hair of the magic horse, the companions of Siṁhabāhu can save themselves from the voracious Rākshasīs, but under the condition imposed on Orpheus, of not looking back. They suffer themselves, however, to be enticed by the sirens of Ceylon, and die by their hands, as Orpheus by the hands of the Bacchantes of Thracia; they are lost through the motive which robbed Orpheus, the morning star rising over the earth, of the beautiful Eurydice, the aurora, his beloved.[73]

In the Semitic mythology the same myth is met with. Goldziher[74] explains by the solar theory the myth of the daughters and wife of Lot. Like so many other traces of ancient legends, so also this, Sr. Adolpho Coelho tells me, is reproduced in modern popular stories, for example, in different European versions of "The Two Envious Brothers."[75]

In some popular versions of the story, which Sr. Adolpho Coelho possesses, and which he kindly showed me, two of the three brothers of the story, when they go in search of certain marvellous objects, are converted into statues of stone for looking back on hearing various voices.

The legends of individuals converted into stones are not peculiar to the Aryan race, as we see by the example of Lot. But still further, they are not peculiar to the white race. They are met with in North America, as is seen from the *Popol Vuh,*[76] and from the studies of Müller on the primitive religions of the American Indians.[77] The manner in which these legends are there described is a confirmation of the solar theory, which in itself is not false, but only defective, when exclusive in mythological explanations, as some mythologists have in an exaggerated manner used it :– "A giant guarded the carverns where were the men whom the mother earth had produced; one night this giant left the caverns, and after the break of day the sun surprised him and transformed him into the rock Kauta."

We cannot fail to see in this legend the resemblance of the legend of Atlas, the giant of the west, transformed into a mountain.

And from the relation in which Atlas, Perseus of the *pès alados,* and the Gorgons (to whom may be compared the wild women of Hanno) stand, and also the horse Pegasus, born from the blood of Medusa, it would be impossible to deny that throughout these transformations into stone are legends whose explanation is found in the passage of night to day, and the entry into or falling upon the earth of darkness, in the subterranean world called Tartarus by the Greeks, Talātala by the Hindu Aryans,[78] invisible as the region Amenti of the Egyptians,[79] for which the solar theory satisfactorily accounts; nor would it be possible to deny the intimate connection between the mythological elements of the Oriental legends which we have given, and the identical features of the legends of classical antiquity.

With these legends, also, are connected superstitions which we meet with in our day in Europe, so that in Portugal the people say that "to go backwards is to call on the demon," that go backwards is to call on the demon," that "to go backwards is to fall into hell," and the Norwegians say that "he who goes backwards drags his father and mother with him to hell," as they also say that "to beat the mother is to beat the earth," and "to beat the father is to bear a stone,"[80] superstitions which are also met with on the other side of the ocean in America, according to Müller.[81]

Thus, as the Aryan conception of the white horse of the hero furnishes a solar myth, so its explanation in like manner is the belief in traces of the visits of a divinity to the earth, and chiefly the belief in divine footprints on the summit of mountains.

In the Buddhist religion the horse and the feet of Buddha are objects of the greatest veneration in his temples. And as such we see them represented on bas-reliefs, on sculptures; and

> ".....em Ceylão que o monte se alevanta,
> Tanto, que as nuvens passa, ou a vista engana,
> Os naturaes o tem por cousa sancta
> Pela pedra onde estã a pegada humana."[82]
>
> *Lusiada, X, fol. 183*

Camoens, and before him Duarte Barboza, were acquainted with this trace of Buddhist legend; but it seems that they heard it from the Arabs.[83]

Commencing with low lands, the island of Ceylon runs down to 7^0 51' south latitude, rising, little by little, and appearing to attain to the highest ranges, which fall suddenly from the clouds to the other shore of the sea. Of the mountains which form the crown of this "jockey's cap," a remarkable one is the Samanella, "rock of the divine assembly in the mountain,"[84] which the Europeans, following the Arabs, call Adam's Peak, and which the Buddhists had previously named Siripāda in Pāli, in Sanskṛit Śrīpāda, "foot-mark of the Fortunate One," because they believe that there the footprint of Buddha is still visible.

The true Pāli name of this mountain is Sumanakūṭo, so-called because the divinity (*dêva*) Sumana dwelt there, says Childers (Pāli Dict., s. v.), "mountain of the happy," or, as Lassen[85] says, "mountain of the gods." Another name of this mountain is Sumbhakūṭa, "the shining mount," the last from which, in the south, the sun disappears.[86]

Hardy (*Manual of Buddhism,* p. 211-12) gives the following Ceylonese legend :– "The dewa (*the divinity*) of Sumanakūṭa (*another name* of Samanella), Samana, having heard of the arrival of Budha, went to the place where he was, and after, he had worshipped him, he presented a request that he would leave an impression of his foot upon the mountain of which he was the guardian, that it might be worshipped during the five thousand years his religion would continue among men. . . . . . . Budha went to it (*the mountain*) through the air, attended by 500 rahats (*saints*). At the right hand of the sage was Sumana, in beautiful garments and rich ornaments, attended by all his inferior dewas, with their queens, who made music and carried flags and banners, and scattered around gold and gems. Sekra,[87] Maha Brahma,[88] and Iśwara,[89] were all there with their attendant retinues; and like the rolling of the great ocean upon Maha Méru or the Yugandhara rocks, was their arrival at the mountain. The sun remained in the midst of the sky, but his rays were cold as those of the moon; there was a slight falling of rain-like the water that is sprinkled around a throne to allay the dust; and the breeze, charged with sweet perfume, came from all sides to refresh the illustrious visitant. At his approach, all the trees of the mountain were as though they danced in gladness at the anointing of a king. In the midst of the assembled dewas, Budha, looking towards the east, made the impression of his foot, in length three inches less than the cubit of the carpenter; and the impression remained as a seal to show that Lankā is the inheritance of Budha, and that his religion will here flourish."

Hardy says in a note, that the print of the foot of Buddha is an "indentation upon the summit of Adam's Peak." Ibn Batutah describes the foot of Adam in the island of Serendib (Ceylon), saying : – "The mark of the noble foot, that of our father Adam, is seen in a black and high rock, and in an open place. The foot is impressed in the stone, so that its site is quite depressed; its length is eleven spans. The inhabitants of China came there formerly; they cut from the stone the place of the big toe and of that adjoining it, and deposited the fragment in a temple of the town of Zeitun (Tseu-thung), whither they go from the remotest provinces."

Dr. Davy[90] says that the footprint of Buddha is "a superficial hollow five feet three inches and three quarters long, and between two feet seven inches and two feet five inches wide."

The plain fact, then, is a depression on the summit of the mountain. Of the legends which explain this fact the Buddhist alone has scientific and historical importance. We shall therefore leave on one side what the Muḥammadan Māsūdi and our chronicler, Osorio, tells us of the race of Cain and of the tombs of Adam and Eve in this island; and let us see how the origin of the legend is explained in mythology.

The myth of the horse of the hero and that of the divine footprints are myths that are related. But the horse of the hero, which defends him, counsels him, even bears down and conquers the enemies of the hero, represents force, rapidity, energy, light in a word life; the divine footprints are the trances of mysterious feet which are not known, which no one sees, and which scarcely leave impressed the testimony of his visit after the disappearance of the divinity. Among the Gnostics the soles of feet engraved in stone represented *death.*[91]

The last rays of the sun, traversing space, and as if lighting with the force which draws the luminous god the pyre which devours him, the last *pādas,* that is, the last "rays," gilding the summits of the mountains, and as if emerging from the abyss, are the *pādas,* that is, the "feet" of this god, whose tunic is the twilight, which is put off when he is about to die. And in the midst of these *pādas,* "feet and rays," of these *pādas* of light, is seen even in the last moments of solar disc, through the impression which the retina retains. His vermilion-hued heart is like the bleeding wound of a cruel torment. These feet converge one towards the other, are superimposed, and the god of the large footprints, the god of the three footprints, becomes the god of one single footprint, and the god of one single foot, whose ankle is not seen, or, as the Siamese explain it, whose ankle is in the middle of his foot, and whose toes are united like those a *śālapāda,* those of a palmipede.

This conception, so singular, of the foot of the god, is of great value, if we compare it with the conception by which the Chakravartin has his neck immovable, independently of his body, and looks always forward, always in the same position, and has to turn his whole body when he turns his face.

It is undoubtedly the anthropomorphic conception of the sun.[92]

The complication of myths, says my teacher in Paris, M. Bergaigne, any of rites which are their image, results from the combination of natural observations with the idea of the cult in it simplest form. The Vedic ritual is the reproduction of the Vedic mythology; and the domain of Vedic mythology includes earth and heaven. The mythologist, consequently, cannot explain the Vedic mythology either by the heaven alone or by the earth alone.

And, in fact, the ritual represents the phenomena of the celestial world, and the celestial world only preserves its order by the order of sacrifice. The liturgical order and the cosmogonic order are interdependent.

Adolpho Coelho told me, some time ago :–

"The mythologist must never forget that the heaven, the earth, and sea are confounded when the uncultivated man explains the phenomena of nature;' what is on the earth is in the sea and what is in the sea is on the earth, and what is in the heaven is on the earth and in the sea."

Starting from this principle, of which I have already made use in this essay, I shall attempt to give another explanation of the divine footprints on the summit of mountains.

On the mound of earth, the altar raised in the place of Vedic sacrifice, and to the east, was called *vêdi*. The *uttara-vêdi*[93] is the superior, culminating *vêdi,* the *vêdi* of fire. In the middle was a cavity which was called *nābhi,* that is, "navel," where were thrown the pieces of flesh and the *sôma,* the drink of the gods and of the sacrificers, fermented, combustible, on the flames of the sacrificial fire.

This extinguished, Agni dead, there were scarcely the traces in the place where he reposed, there was the *nābhi,* the hole opened on the top of the highest mound, like a single footprint of this god, who there became extinct.

Thus hymn 164 of Maṇḍala I of the *Ṛīgvéda* says in *Ṛich* 34 :—"I ask thee for the farthest extremity of the earth; I ask thee where is the navel of the world; I ask thee for the seed of the horse; I ask thee for the highest heaven of the voice." And in *Ṛich* 35 it is answered :—"This *vedi* is the farthest end of the earth; this sacrifice is the navel of the world;[94] this *sôma* is the seed of the horse; this Brāhmaṇ is the highest heaven of speech."

My professor in Munich, the late Dr. Martin Haug, the Orientalist who has best explained this hymn, so beset with thorny difficulties and mysterious problems, does not say, in the study devoted to the hymn and published by him shortly before his death under the title of *Vedische Rāthselfragen und Rāthselsprüche,*[95] what is the horse. But this is no loss. It is the cloud which by its rains brings fertility to the earth, and hence the horse of Agni or Agṇi himself, the celestial messenger fire of the sacrifice or conductor of the gods over the altar of sacrifice.

It is prolific, because to the celestial fire the ray succeeds the *seed,* that is, the rain which makes the earth suitable for production, and which raises the fire, as is mentioned in different passages of the *Vêdas,* in the bosoms of the plants.

The highest heaven of the voice is the Brāhmaṇ, says *Ṛich* 35. And Dr. Martin Hang explains :—"The Brāhmaṇ treated of here is probably the Brāhmaṇ presiding at the sacrifice; in him are combined all the sacred sacrifice, all the hymns, sentences, &c., which only he with his voice can chant and cause to be heard."

I may, however, add to this explanation that the Brāhmaṇ presiding at the sacrifice was the highest heaven of the voice only as representative on the earth of the god who made his voice heard on the earth. This voice is the *vāgāmbhṛini,* the "voice of the cloud," sung in hymn 125 of the Maṇḍala X of the *Ṛīgvêda,* and in hymn 30 of the *Kāṇḍa* IV of the *Atharvavéda.*[96] It is the voice which announces the will of the gods, it is the messenger of heaven, the inspirer by whom is revealed the sacred word, the divine messenger of whom the Ṛīshis, the Vedic poets, speak, and also Homer; it is the one who proclaims the law of universal order, both cosmogonic and liturgic.[97] It is like the voice from the burning bush, terrible and threatening; but yet soft and magic as the sound of the flute of the Maruts and of Yama. It is that which makes itself heard, descending to the earth, from the height there, from the *dêva-sadanam,* the "abode of the gods," to which ascended the mortals who had become immortal, and where *sôma* runs in floods, and where echo the songs and melodies of the divine flute of Yama, where is the tree of shining leaves.[98]

And if we record finally that in mythology (Aryan, at least), tree, mountain, and altar are synonyms and expressions almost identical, the connection will then be plainly seen of the horse of the hero and of the footprints of the god on the top of mountains, symbols almost inseparable in the Buddhist religion.

Notes by the Translator

I. The Cloud-horse Jātaka[99]

"Those who will not carry out the advice." Thus spake the Teacher, while dwelling in Jetavana, concerning a certain unhappy monk. This monk having been asked by the Teacher: "Is it true that you are unhappy?" replied: "It is true!" When asked, "Wherefore ?" he said: "On account of having looked with desire upon a beautiful woman." Then the Teacher said to him: "O monk, these women who allure men by their form, voice, odour, taste, and touch,[100] and also by the charm of female fascination,[101] getting them into their power, and knowing that they have attained their wish, through loss of (men's) purity and wealth, are, on account of their sinfulness, called Yakkhinīs, for in former days also Yakkhinīs approached a company of men by means of female artifice, and having fascinated the merchants and got them into their power, seeing other men also, brought about the destruction of them all and devoured them, crunching[102] them, with the blood flowing from both sides of their jaws." He then related the story:–

In former times there was in the island of Laṅkā a Yakkha city Sirīsavatthu. Therein dwelt Yakkhinīs. These, when a shipwreck took place, were accustomed to go to meet the merchants in splendid clothing, surrounded by slaves, carrying children on their hips, and offering food and drink. That they might think, "We have come to an abode of men," they would show here and there men ploughing and tending cattle, and so forth, herds of cattle, dogs, &c., and approaching the merchants they would say: "Drink this rice gruel, partake of this rice, eat this food." The merchants unawares enjoy the things given by them. Thus having eaten and enjoyed, while resting they exchange friendly greetings. They ask : "Of what place are you inhabitants, whence do you come, whither are you going, on what business have you come hither ?" And they answer : "We have come hither having been shipwrecked." Responding :"Well, sirs, our husbands also, three years ago, went on boardship and went away; they must be dead; you are also merchants, we will be your wives," they enticed those merchants with female blandishments, and leading them to the Yakkha city, the first men being captured, having bound them as it were with supernatural chains,[103] they hurry them into the abode of destruction. If they do not obtain shipwrecked men near their own place of abode they wander along the seashore, as far as Kalyāṇī on the further side and Nāgadīpa on this side, and this is their custom. But one day five hundred merchants crossed over to their city. The females, approaching them, enticed them, and bringing them to the Yakkha city, binding the men whom they first captured as with supernatural chains, they hurried them into the abode of destruction, and made them their husbands, the chief Yakkhinīs, the chief merchants, the others, the remainder, and so the five hundred Yakkhinīs, the five hundred merchants. But that chief Yakkhinī in the night time, when the merchants had gone to sleep, rising, goes to the abode of destruction, and killing men, eats their flesh, and returns. The others also do likewise. When the chief Yakkhinī had eaten the human flesh, on returning her body was cold.[104] The chief merchant having embraced her knew that she was a Yakkhini, and thought: "These must be five hundred Yakkhinīs; we must escape." On the morrow, in the early morning, on going to wash his mouth, he told the other merchants: "These are Yakkhinīs, not human beings; they will devour us after making us their husbands, as they have done in times past to other shipwrecked men; let us now flee." But two hundred and fifty[105] said: "We are unable to leave them; you go; we shall not flee." The chief merchant, having persuaded the two hundred and fifty by his advice, fled, terrified at the females. Now at that very time Bôdhisatta was born from the womb of a mare; he was pure white, black-headed,[106] muñja-haired,[107] possessed of supernatural power, being able to go through the air. Rising through the air from the Himavanta, he went to the isle of Tambapaṇṇi, and having eaten paddy produced spontaneously in the lakes and ponds of Tambapaṇṇi he went on, and thus proceeding said compassionately three times in a well-modulated human voice: "Does any person wish to go ? Does any person wish to go ?" They hearing the speech came near with folded hands, and said: "Sir, we folk wish to go." "Then get upon my back," said he. Then some got on his back, some seized his tail, but some stood with folded hands. Bôdhisatta by his own supernatural power conveying all the two hundred and fifty merchants, even those standing with folded hands, placing each in his own place, returned to his own abode. But the Yakkhinīs, when the time of the others had come, killed the remaining two hundred and fifty men and ate them.[108]

The Teacher, addressing the monks, said: "O monks, as those merchants went to the dwelling of the Yakkhinīs and met with their death, while those who obeyed the word of the cloud-horse king were placed every one in his own place, even so monks and nuns, laymen and laywomen, not fulfilling the advice of Buddhas, experience great sorrow, through hundreds of misfortunes, by means of the five sorts of bonds, deed, action, condition, and so forth; but those who fulfil the advice obtain the three noble sampattis, the six Kāma heavens, the hundred Brahma worlds, and suchlike conditions, and experiencing the great nibbāna of immortality enjoy great happiness." The Perfectly Enlightened then, having said this, spoke these verses :–

1. "Those men who will not carry out the advice preached by the Buddha will obtain misfortune as the merchants by the Rākshasīs.
2. "And those men who will carry out the advice preached by the Buddha will reach the shore safely as the merchants by means of the horse."

The Teacher, having thus set forth this discourse, illustrating the doctrines, connected the *Jātaka* (at the end of the teaching the unhappy monk was established in the fruit of *sotāpatti,* and many of the rest obtained the fruits of *sotāpatti, sakadāgami, anāgāmi,* and arahatship):– "Those two hundred and fifty merchants who followed the advice of the cloud-horse king were the followers of the Buddha, and I was that cloud-horse king."

II. The mythical horse (ante, p. 41a and note 65)

The Portuguese word is *pigarço,* which I cannot find in the dictionaries, but Lacerda gives *picarso,* which he translates, "having the colour of salt and pepper mixed together." The word used by Foucaux (*Rgya-Tch'er-Rol-Pa,* p. 17) is *gris,* grey, and he says in a note "literally 'bluish, of a black-blue.'" In the *Foé Koué Ki,* p. 133, the horse is thus described :–"The *purple horse,* also called the *stong and rapid, wind.* This horse is of a tint between red and blue. The blessed king of the wheel having come early in the morning to his palace, there suddenly appears to his sight a horse of a violent colour. His hairs are threaded with pearls, which fall when he is washed and combed, and are instantaneously reproduced fresher and more brilliant than before. When he neighs, it is heard at the distance of a *yôjana.* He has strength sufficient to fly. When the king mounts him to traverse the world he departs in the morning and returns in the evening without experiencing any fatigue. All the atoms of dust that touch the feet of this horse are converted into grains of gold." With regard to the solar myth explanation of the horse, I translate what Sénart says (*Essai sur la Légende du Buddha,* 2nd ed., pp. 19-22): – "The Mahābhārata (I, 1095) calls Uchchhaiḥśravas '*mathyamānê' mritôjāṭam aśvaratnaṁ anuttamaṁ;'* thus the Brāhmaṇ mythology speaks expressly of an *'aśvaratna,'* which is no other than the solar steed Uchchhaiḥśravas.[109] On the other hand, the *Lalita Vistara* gives the horse the name of Valāhaka, which means *cloud*[110] and is the designation of one of the steeds of Vishṇu. He receives the same epithets as the Elephant; whilst Uchchhaiḥśravas is of a dazzling whiteness, he is of a dark-blue (*nīlakṛishṇa*), and the Chinese enumeration calls him the 'puple horse,' or the 'strong and rapid wind;' he thus resembles in the curious manner those horses of Indra whose hair has 'the bluish reflections of a peacock's plumage,'[111] and still more those steeds of the wind (*vātasya aśvā*), red (*ṛijra, Ṛ.V.* I, 174.5; *aruṇa, rôhita,* I, 134, 3), who also draw Indra.[112] (*Ṛ.V.* X, 22, 4-6), considered (X, 168, 2) as 'the king of all this universe.' Like the horses of the Walkyries which shake from their hair the rain and the dew, our steed has 'its hairs threaded with pearls (*lightning*), which fall when he is washed (*the rain*) and combed, and are instantaneously reproduced fresher and more brilliant then before';[113] 'when he neighs, it is heard at the distance of a *yôjana,*' for his neighing is nothing but the thunder;[114] if, finally, 'all the atoms of dust that touch his feet are changed into grains of gold,' we recognize there the old image of the thunderbolt conceived as the shoe of the cloud-steed. We do not see why we should be surprised to find in the horse of our legend this symbolic meaning; for it is that which he usually has in the Indian mythology.[115] He appears with this meaning on several occasions as the direct expression of the sun, and in the case of Uchchaiḥśravas, the white horse, which can be seen at the dawn of day,[116] and in the that verse (*R.V.* VII, 77, 3) which describes to us 'the good Ushas bringing the eye of the gods, leading the beautiful white steed . . .,' in many legends, also, from among which I will refer only to those which relate to the Digvijaya and the Aśvamêdha; I shall speak further on of this. This is no reason for separating widely the aśvaratna Uchchaiḥśravas and the *aśvaratna* Valāhaka;[117] the former himself, in the voice of thunder[118] from which he derives his name, and in that black tail which the Serpents, sons of Kadrū,[119] treacherously form for him, has preserved traces of another meaning. This fusion of different symbolisms in a single type might easily suggest various explanations. However, if we consider that in the narrations where the solar god appears actually in the form of the horse,[120] as in the case of Purusha,[121] as in the myth of Vivasvat and of Saraṇyū, it is chiefly with the international signification of a disguise, of a metamorphosis; if we remember that the elephant, the primitive symbolism of which should not be doubtful, has nevertheless come in certain narrations to be identified with the solar hero, we shall, I think, be inclined to consider that the office of horse as representing the cloud answers closely to its probably oldest meaning. Its luminous signification would be only the secondary, as well as ancient, development; it is natural to confound the star with the vapours which conceal it or appear to carry it.[122] The horse may, in like manner, very well represent the lightning which bursts from the cloud. From its central signification a sort of double radiation would be produced; the fact is sufficiently well expressed by the acts which make of the sun, the eye, and of the lightning, the foot of the atmospheric steed. This will explain how the horse properly solar has left in cognate mythologies so few evident traces; how, even in Indian mythology, it only appears mixed with other elements. As to our Buddhist *aśvaratna* in particular, it is certain that if, in the picture which is drawn of it, the primary signification is evidently manifest, its office of carrying the Chakravartin, whom it takes round the earth, the Chakravartin, whom it takes round the earth, leaving in the morning, and returning in the evening, is a very clear expression of the second."

References

1. Published in Lisbon, 1880, in commemoration of the Camoens Tercentenary; pp. 39 ff.
2. It will be seen that the "vestiges" of the Buddhist legend in the *Lusiads* are contained simply in the mention by Camoens of the name of Taprobana for Ceylon, and his reference to the footprint on Adam's Peak–D.F.
3. Stanislas Julien, *Voyages des Pélerins Bouddhiques,* tome III, p. 125. Cunningham's *Ancient Geography of India,* p. 557.
4. St. Julien, *op. cit.,* tome III, p. 144.
5. Amm. Marcell. lib. lxxii, cap. 7.
6. Abu Rihān, *apud* Cunningham, *op. cit.,* p. 558.
7. *Chaines des Chroniques,* p. 5, No. 7, and *passim,* in *Relations des Voyages faites par les Arabes et les Persans dans l'Inde et ā la Chine dans le IXe Siècle,* translated by Renaud, 1845.
8. Childers, *Pali Dict.* s.v.
9. *Documentos Arabicos para a Historia Portugueza,* Lisboa, 1790, p. 107f.
10. *Indiache Alterthumskunde,* 2nd ed., vol. I, p. 241, n.
11. *Dīpavaṁsa,* IX, 20, ed. H. Oldenberg.
12. This verse is thus translated (rather paraphrased) by Capt. Burton in his edition of the *Lusiads* (1880), vol. II p. 389:–

    "And, eke, the noble Island Tabroban,
    whose ancient name ne'er failed to give her note,
    as still she reigns superb and sovereign
    by boon of fragrant tree-bark, biting-hot:
    Toll of her treasure to the Lusitan
    ensign shall pay, when proud and high shall float
    your breezy banners from the loftly tower,
    and all Columbo fear your castled power."–D.F.

13. Childers, *op. cit.* s.v.
14. Camoens says positively: –
    ". . . . . . .Taprobana
    (Que ora he Ceylão) . . . . . "–lib. X. stanza 107.
15. Richthofen, *China,* vol. I, p. 640ff.
16. In the possession of M. Frederic Spitzer, in Paris.–Richthofen.
17. The first to show that Taprobanê was the Greek form of Tāmraparṇa was Eugêne Burnouf in 1834. The monograph read by him in that year before the Acad. des Inscr. et B. Lettres of Paris was published in the *Journal Asiatique* of January 1851. I have not been able to utillize it, as the *Journal* for this year is missing from the library of the A.R.S. [the separate reprint is dated 1857–D.F.]
18. *Sanskṛit Wôrterbuch,* s.v.
19. *Pāli Dict.* s.v.
20. Lassen., *Ind. Alterthumsk.* vol. I, p. 105; cf. *infra* the legend which we translate from the *Dīpavaṁsa,* IX, ed. Oldenberg.
21. This translation differs somewhat from that of Prof. Oldenberg. I will here mention the chief points : –

    Ver. 2. For "children" the Portuguese has "irmãos," corresponding to the Pāli *bhātaro*=brother and sister.

    Ver. 13-14. Instead of "went on shore on an *uninhabited* island," Oldenberg has, "was *helplessly* driven to an island." The Pāli has "*dīpaṁ avassakaṁ,*" and the latter translation seems the correct one.

    Ver. 17. Instead of "strangers" Oldenberg has "unnoticed (?)." The Pāli text is uncertain.

    Ver. 18. Instead of "murder" Oldenberg has "slander."

    The Pāli word is *pesuṇaṁ,* which does not occur in Childers' *Dict.*, though *pesuññaṁ* and *pesuṇeyyaṁ* are given, with the latter meaning. Why Sr. Abren has "murder," I cannot understand.

    Ver. 28. Instead of "could scarcely walk," Oldenberg has "were unable (?) to walk on foot." The Pāli is uncertain.

    Ver. 29. "They went on their hands and feet." The Portuguese is "Foram de gatinhas com pés e mãos," literaturally "They acted like little she-cats with feet and hands." Oldenberg has : –"They crawled about on the ground with both hands and knees," which is more literal.

Ver. 32. Instead of "landed there and took possession of territory" Oldenberg has "came first to this country." The Pāli is uncertain, Oldenberg reading *Anurādhanakkhatlena* instead of *nāvaṁ anūrakkhena,* and therefore adding the name of Anurādhanakkhatta to those given above—D.F.

22. See further on, p. 37 b.
23. The beautiful wanderer.
24. Nagnadvīpa in Sanskṛit ? "Island of the Naked."
25. See *Ind. Ant.* vol. XI, pp. 236, 247, 293, 294. It is evident from the mention of Bharukachchha (Bharuch) (v. 26) along with Suppāra, that the *Dipavaṁsa,* places Lāla on the *west* coast of India or in Gujarat, and the Siṁhapura stated to be the capital may be Sīhor in Kāṭhiāwāḍ, about 18 miles south of the site of Valabhī, and the traditional capital of the Siṁha dynasty—ED. *I.A.*
26. In Skr. *parinirvāṇa.* This term is used to designate the death of the sage, the Buddha, or of an Arhat, "a Buddhist ascetic and saint." The Buddhist era counts from the death of the sage, Gautama, the Buddha. According to some writers, among them Childers, it occurred in the year 543 before Christ. Now, since the latest works of Cunningham, although even before that the great Burnouf had cited the passage which served as a basis for the discovery of the English archæologist,—it is reckoned from about 482 or 472 A.C.
27. In Sanskṛit Śakra, powerful, an epithet of Indra.
28. Kauśika in Sanskṛit is an epithet of Indra.
29. See the following note.
30. *Dêvaputra* in Skr. To the inhabitants of the *dêvaloka* (paradise) are attributed male and female sexes. Dêvaputra is celestial being of the male sex. Such is Uppalavaṇṇa, *i.e.* Vishṇu, a god in the Brahmanical religion, an archangel in the Buddhist. There is an archangel of the female sex (*dêradhitô*), whose name may easily be confounded with Uppalavaṇṇa, and Uppalavaṇṇā, "name of an eminent nun who was of Gautama's *aggasdvīlais* (*Dh.* 213)," says Childers, citing the *Dhammdpadam* of Fausbôll. We may also refer to the chronicle which we are translating, *Dīpavaṁsa* XXVIII, 9, and *Vinaypitakaṁ, Challavagga,* X, 8. *Aggasāvikā,* in Skr. *Agraśrāvikā,* "principal female disciple," follower of Buddha. Gautama's two were Khemā and Uppalavaṇṇā, besides other lesser ones.
31. Angels under the command of an archangel.

32. Cf. Oldenberg, p. 58, with p. 162.
33. See note 26, *ante*, p. 35.
34. *i.e.*, consolidated Buddhism.
35. This Buddhist term is translated by "attainments, endowments," which are eight successive states induced by ecstatic meditation (Childers, *Pāli Dict.*, s.v.). The explanation of Burnouf (*Lotus de la Bonne Loi*, pp. 348-9) appears to me to be exact: *Samāpattī* is the moral state, which is reached by *samâdhi; samôdhi* is one of the conditions for becoming a perfect ascetic and one of the perfections of the ascetic; and these perfections are—*jhāna*, "profound meditation," *vimokha*, "freedom destruction of passion," *samādhi*, "perfect tranquillity," *samāpatti*, "sweet joy, tranquil delight, the calm and holy happiness resulting from the superior perfections." And the annihilation of all suffering and of all enjoyment of every physical sensation is the ecstatic feeling of delight in the indifferent contemplation of the exterior world. The eight successive states are like bridges, degrees of progressive acquisition of each of these perfections. See Burnouf, *Lotus*, p. 789.
36. "Gautama Buddha in the *Suttas* frequently speaks of himself as the Tathāgaṭa, and the epithet is analogous to that of Son of Man applied to himself by Jesus Christ." (Childers, *Pāli Dict.*, s.v.) But it appears to me that this name of Tathāgata, composed of *tathā-āgata*, "coming thus (like the other Buddhas)," signifies "a redeemer."
37. Complete annihilation by the destruction of the five elements of being.
38. *Substrata corporis*, *i.e.*, entered into complete *nibbāna* (*nirvāṇa* in Skr.) or *parinibbāna*.
39. According to Burnouf, "*Introd. d l'Hist. du Bouddhisme,*" (1st ed.), p. 223 ff. With this legend compare that given by Hiuen Tsiang apud St. Julien, *Mémoires*, tome II, p. 131 ff.
40. In the *Academy* of Aug, 13 and 27, 1881 (reprinted in the *Indian Antiquary* for Oct. 1881, pp. 291-3), are two interesting communications on the subject of "The Myth of the Sirens," one from Mr. W.E.A. Axon, who drew attention to the "Story of the Five Hundred Merchants," given by Beal in his *Romantic Legend of śākya Buddha*, p. 339 ff.; the other by Dr. R. Morris, who showed that the story is a veritable *jātaka* tale, the Pāli text of which is given in Fausbôll's edition of the *Jātaka*, vol. II, p. 127

ff, under the title of *Valāhassajātaka,* "Cloudhorse *Jātaka.*" As no translation of the *Valāhassajātaka* has yet appeared, I give one below, p. 45 *f.* The explanation of several doubtful passages I owe to the kindness of Mr. L. C. Wijesinha, Mudaliyār, the coadjutor of the late Prof. Childers in his Pāli Dictionary. I have added a few notes – D.F.

41. Lassen, *Ind. Alterthumsk.* (2nd ed.), vol. II, p. 103 ff. Compare this legend with that recounted by Hiuen-Tsiang. (St. Julien, *Mémoires,* tome II, p. 125 ff.)

    I have translated Sr. Abreu's Portuguese translation of Lassen's German translation, which will be found to differ slightly from Turnour's version – D.F.

42. Turnour says: – "They partook of the nature of the lion in the formation of their hands and feet," but the version here given corresponds with the Pāli – D.F.

43. Rather, "the daughter of his father's sister," *i.e.* the mother of Siṁhabāhu and Siṁhāvall – D.F.

44. See Sénart, *Essai sur la Légende du Buddha,* pp. 272-8.

45. French translation of Lanesson, *Histoire des Drogues d' Origine Végétale* (Paris, 1878, 2 vols.), tome II, p. 372-3.

46. *Mahābhārata* and *Rāmāyaṇa* apud *Sanskrit Wōrterbuch.*

47. Apud St. Julien, *Mémoires,* tome II, p. 122.

48. *Siddhānta-śirômaṇi,* III, 41.

49. *Sanskrit Wōrterbuch,* s. voc. *Tāmraparṇa.*

50. Richthofen, *China,* vol. I, pp. 521, 524, note 2.

51. Turnour's *Epitome of Ceylon History.* Conf. also *ante,* vol. XI, p. 257 – ED. I.A.

52. On this subject of the name of Tambapaṇṇi and the landing of Vijaya, I would refer to Dr. Caldwell's *Political and General History of the District of Tinnevelly,* 1881, pp. 9-10, 13-14, where the connection between the river Tāmrapaṛṇī and the name for Ceylon is shown to be exceedingly probable, though it is left doubtful which was borrowed from the other; also Dr. E. Müller's *Ancient Inscription of Ceylon,* 1883, pp. 21-24, where the theory is advanced that the Vijayan invaders came to Ceylon through Southern India. We have not yet sufficient evidence, however, to show that the invaders did land on the west coast of Ceylon – D.F.

53. See Fr. Lenormant, *Les Origines de V Histoirs d'après la Bible et les Traditions des Peuples Orientauz,* 1880, chap. IV; *cf.* V, Abreu,

Investigações sobre o Caracter da Civilização Ārya-Hindū, 1878, p. 38-9.

54. Cf. the explanation of the death of Abel by Cain given by Goldziher, *Der Mythos bei den Hebrāera,* Goldziher-Martinean, pp. 113, 114, 126, et passim.
55. See Decharma, *Mythologie de la Grèce Antiquè,* B. IV, c. 2.
56. Brunetto Latini, *Trésor de Toutes Choses,* Jordanus, *Mirabilia.*
57. Vol. I, p. 60 ff. This story was pointed out to me by my friend and colleague, Professor Adolpho Coelho.
58. The Arab legend of the horse Hizan, which goes over to Moses, protected by the archangel Gabriel, on the other side of the Nile, after his leaving the palace of Pharaoh, is modern.
59. F. Adolphe Coelho, *Contos Populares Portuguezes,* Conto XVI. To this friend and colleague of mine I owe the following communication: – "On an episode in which, in place of boots, figure by turns a mantle and a sadle, which transport through the air, and which are met with in a great number of European and Oriental stories, see Gebr. Grimn, *Kinder-und Haus-mārchen,* vol. III, p. 166 (note to No. 92); R. Kōhler in the *Jahrbuch f. rom. und engl. Literatur,* vol. VII, p. 148 (note to the Venetian story from the collection of Widter Wolf, No. 10, published in the same periodical); J. Grimm, *Deutsche Mythologie,* 3rd ed., p. xxx; F. Liebrecht in *Orient und Occident,* vol. I, p. 132, where the author refers to an article of his in the *Germania* of Pfeiffer, vol. II, p. 244. To the stories mentioned by these writers we may add the following in which the episode reappears: –J.G. von Hahn, *Griechische und albanische Mārchen,* No. 114 (Leipzig, 1864), in which it is the striking of the earth three times with a magic stick which transports the possessor wherever he wishes; Kreutzwald-Lōwe, *Esthnische Mærchen,* No. 11 (cork boots which carry one far); G. Pitré, *Fiabe, Novelle e Racconti Popolari Siciliance,* No. 31 (boots which carry like the wind).
60. Vol. II, p. 8. *Avadāna* means, according to the *Sanskṛit Wōrterbuch,* primarily "frank, honest, upright dealing," later "heroic deed," and finally "legend, story," and thus the title of a collection of stories, such as the *Avadāna-śataka,* "the hundred *avadānas*" (Burnouf, *Intr. ā V Hist. du Buddhisme indien,* 1st ed., p. 115), *Avadāna-Kalpalatā, Dvāviṁśati-Avadāna*. On the great importance of the *Avadānas* and of the Buddhist *Jātakas,* see principally vol. I of the *Pañchatantra* of Benfey; and Liebrecht, *Zur Volkunde,* 109-

21, or in *Orient und Occident* of Benfey, vol. I, p. 129 ff, and Léon Feer, *Etudes bouddhiques,* in *J. Asiat.*, ser. VII, vols. XI, XIV.

61. Cf. Liebrecht, *Volkskunde,* p. 118.
62. *Pantschatantra,* vol. I, p. 159-63.
63. Benfey, l. c.; Spence Hardy, *Manual of Buddhism,* p. 127; Foucaux, *Raya-Tch'er-Rol-Pa,* chap. III.
64. Cf. Sénart; *Essai sur la Légende du Buddha,* passim.
65. See Note II below, pp. 47 f.
66. *Ṛigvêda,* I, 50, I; cf. with *Ṛīgv.* IV, 45, 6 &c.
67. I, 58, 2; 149, 3; III, 1, 4; 2, 7; VI, 2, 8; 12, 6,; &c.
68. III, 27, 14.
69. I, 14, 12.
70. Cf. VIII, 91, 12, with IV, 2, 8.
71. Cf. *Ṛigv.* V, 19, 5; X, 91, 7; I, 94, 10; &c.
72. *Orlando Furioso,* Canto XV, 41. Cf. Custodio Jesam Barata, *Recreaçam Proveytosa,* Part I, Colloquio IV. And also *Dissertações* of Padre Antonio Pereira de Figueiredo, Dis. IV, *Das Egoas da Lusitania,* p. 100-6 of Book IX of the *Hist. e Memorias da Acad. Real das Sciencias de Lisboa.*
73. See Decharme, *Mythologie de la Grèce antique,* p. 571 ff.
74. *Op. cit.*, pp. 189-97.
75. See the list of versions given by out colleague in his collection, *Contos Populares Portuguezes,* pp. xix, xx.
76. *Le Livre Sacré et les Mythes de l'Antiquité Américaine, avec les Livres Héroïques et Historiques des Quichés.* Original and translation by Abbé Brasseur de Bourbourg, p. 243-5.
77. J.G. Müller, *Geschichte der Amerikanischen Urreligionen,* Basel, 1855, p. 179; cf. 110.
78. Benfey, *Hermes, Minos, Tartaros.*
79. We would remark, in this place, of Amenti, that it is not a chance illustration nor a common-place and unnecessary comparison. The motive is correct, and the comparison apt. Chapter XV of the *Book of the Dead* says : – "In the afternoon the sun turns his face to Amenti." Pierret, in the *Vocabulaire Hiéroglyphique,* p. 29, says: – "Ament, Amenti, hell, region where the sun *hides* himself, abode of souls after death." And further on: "Ament, the west, the occidental region." Cf. the same author's *Dict. d'Archéologis*

Egyptienne, s.v. To this definition of Amenti is also to be added that given by P. Guieyesse and E. Lefébure in *Le Papyrus Funéraire de Sontimés,* p. iv: – "It even seems that the myths of Egypt, less diversified by legends and plays on words than those of the Indo-European race, should be more easily penetrated. The hieroglyphic texts show us without possible dispute that from the first centuries to the last most of the divinities have kept their original significations, which their names indicate, and of which the priests did not lose sight. For them as for us, Ra is the sun, Nu the heaven, Hapi the Nile, Amenti the west," &c.

80. Liebrecht, *Norwegischer Aberglaubs in Volkskunde,* p. 310 ff, No. 174 a, b.

81. Op. cit., p. 110. Cf. Grimm, *Deutsche Mythologie,* 2nd ed., 538, apud L.

82. Capt. Burton's translation runs: –

"See in Ceylon that Peak so stark, so gaunt,
shooting high o'er the clouds or mocking sight;
The native peoples hold it sacrosanota
for the famed Stone where print of foot is pight."

83. It is not the only instance of an Indian name being replaced by another of Arab origin, this of "Adam's footprint," in place of "Buddha's footprint," given to the depression on the summit of Samanells. So the Arabs give the name "Adam's Bridge" to the "Bridge of Rāma," the line of rocks which reaches from the Asiatic continent to the island of Ceylon, like enormous stepping-stones, thrown by Hanumat, from the end of the coast of Coromandel to the island of the terrible Rāvaṇa, for the passage of the troops of the heroic Rāma, and called *Sêtubandha* (*Rāmāyaṇa,* ed. of Gorresio, v. 95; trans. vol. 4, ch. 95. In the magnificent summary of H. Fauche, which is, so to speak, the popular *Rāmāyaṇa* in the west of Europe, this chapter, where the work of the allied soldiers constructing the "Bridge of Rāma," is described, is on pp. 163-5 of vol. II).

84. "It is 7420 feet above the level of the sea, and was considered as the highest mountain in the island; but it has been discovered, since the English came into possession of the interior, that there are at least three others that are higher, Pidurutalagala having an elevation of 8280 feet. It will, however, always be the most remarkable, from the many legends connected with it, and the conspicuousness of its appearance, especially from the sea; it is an

insulated cone, rising boldly into the sky, and generally cloud-capped. It is supposed by the Chinese (Davis's Chinese), that at its base is a temple, in which the real body of Buddha reposes on its side, and that near it are his teeth and other relics." Spence Hardy, *Manual of Buddhism,* 1st ed., p. 211.

85. Lassen, *Ind. Alterthumsk.,* 2nd ed., vol. I, pp. 233-4.
86. On the hypothesis, in the idea, that this was the highest. Cf. however, note 45.
87. The lord of Tavutisā (paradise). He is the same as Śakra (powerful), in Sanskṛīt, a name given to Indra.
88. Not to be confounded with the Brahma of the Puranic religion. In that of the *Piṭakas* (Buddhist sacred books) Maha Brahma "is simply the ruler of a brahma-loka" (H., p. 41), of a superior celestial world. See Childers, *Pāli Dict.,* s.v. *Sakko.*
89. Not to be confounded with Iśvara, "supreme lord," in Sanskṛīt. In the Buddhist religion some of the principal Brahmanic divinities are met with as archangels. See Childers, *ut supra.*
90. Apud Sp. Hardy, *op. cit.,* p. 212.
91. C.W. King, *The Gnostics and their Remains.* London, 1864.
92. Cf. with the whole of this explanation Sénart, *Essai sur la Légende du Buddha.*
93. *Kauśika-sūtram,* 137, apud *Sanskṛit Wōrterbuch.*
94. Compare the Greek conception by which the temple of Delphos was the centre of the world. The Buddhists thought, however, that the centre of the world was strictly marked by the sacred tree of the temple near Buddha Gaya.
95. It is a *Separatabdruck* of the *Sitzungsberihten der philosophischen und historischen Klasse der Kōṅiglich baierischen Akademie der Wissenschaften su München,* and has the subsequent title of "*Übersetzung und Erklārung des Dirghatomās Liedes, Ṛīgv.* I. 164—München, 1876."
96. See the magnificent translation of Whitney in the *Essays of Colebrooke,* vol. I, p. 113.
97. *Ṛīgvêda,* I, 151, 4, 6, with 1, 3, 3.
98. Cf. *Ṛīgvêda,* X, 14, with X, 135.
99. Ante p. 36*b* and 40. "Cloud-horse" :—Pāli *valāhassa,* a compound of *valāha* and *assa,* but *valāha* is not recorded by Childers, though he gives *valāhaka,* cloud. Dr. Morris says *valāha* means "horse," and it occurs, with the meaning of "Mare" apparently, further on

in this *Jātaka;* but in the title of the *Jātaka valāha* seems to stand for *valāhaka,* cloud.

100. "Women who allure men by their men by their form," &c. See *Aṅguttara Nikāya, Ekanipāta Vagga,* I, ed. by Morris for the Pāli Text Society, 1883, pp. 1-2 and 86-91.

101. "Female fascination." The Pāli is *itthikuttaṁ,* the latter part of which is not given in Childers' *Dictionary.* It occurs three times in this *Jātaka,* and is also found, as L.C. Wijesinha Mudaliyar kindly points our to me, in the *Takkajātaka,* p. 296, vol. I, of Fausbōll's edition. As to this word, which Dr. Morris does not explain, Mr. Wijesinha writes that he does not recollect meeting with it in any other Pāli books but the *Jātaka,* where it is almost synonymous with *līlhaṁ.* He points out the resemblance to the Tamil *kūttu,* dance, and suggests that it is of Dravidian origin, which is not improbable.

102. "Crunching." The Pāli is *murumurāpetvā,* from *murumurāpeti,* an apparent causative of *murumurāyati,* an imitative word, not found in Childers' *Dictionary.* Dr. Morris, however, considers the word not a causative but a "denominative verb of onomatopoetic origiņ, like our words *munch, chump, crunch,* &c." The verb *murumuru,* to murmur, is given in Winslow's *Tamil Dictionary*—The Sans. verb *maḍamaḍa* in a similar sense occurs in the beginning of the IVth Act of *Uttararāmacharita.*

103. "Supernatural chains": Pāli *devasaṅkhalikāya,* where, as Mr. Wijesinha points out, *deva* can hardly be translated, divine; he suggests a corrupt reading for *tadaheva*, but as the word occurs twice, and Fausbôll gives no alternative reading, I have let it stand.

104. "Her body was cold." I have not elsewhere met with this characteristic of Yakkhinīs.

105. "Two hundred and fifty": Pāli *addhateyyasatā,* literally two-and-a-half hundred.

106. "Black-headed." "Pali *kākasīso,* i.e., "crow-headed."

107. "Muñja-haired": *muñja,* according to Childers, is "a sort of grass, *saccharum munja*, from the fibre of which the Brahmanical string *munja,* from the fibre of fish." No doubt the first meaning applies here. According to the *Rgya-Tch'er-Rol-Pa,* quoted further on, the horse's hair is plaited.

108. On Ceylon as the island of demons, see Sénart's *Essai sur la Légende du Buddha,* p. 231 et. seq.

109. So also the *Rāmāyaṇa,* ed. Gorresio, I, 46, 29.

110. Especially the stormy cloud. Cf. *Mahābhārata,* I, 1289, where Indra is thus invoked; *Tvaṁ vajram atulaṁ-ghoraṁ ghôshavāṁs tvaṁ Valāhakaḥ,* Cf. also *Lal. Vist.* 341, 6 &c.

111. For the quotations of Muir, *Sanskṛit Texts,* V. 85.

112. Elsewhere, X, 49, 7, Indra traverses the sky, drawn by the horses of the sun, which proves the essential identity of both.

113. Grimm, *Deutsche Mythol.,* quoted by Kühn, *Herabkdes Feuers,* p. 132. Other traces of the same mythological idea, preserved in the Brahmanic cult, and to which we shall return, fully warrant such a clear agreement. Cf. also *Ṛ.V.* V, 83, 6, where the Maruts are prayed to make abundant the waters of the fecund horse (*vṛishnôaśvasya*).

114. Cf. Agni, that is, the Agni of the atmosphere, the thunder, compared to a neighing horse, for example, *Ṛ.V.* I, 36, 8. Likewise, when they neigh, the steeds of Indra are streaming with ambrosia, *Ṛ.V.* II, 11, 7, quoted by Gubernatis, vol. I, p. 286.

115. Cf. especially the struggle of Kṛishṇa with the horse Kêśin in the *Vishṇu Purāṇa,* ed. Hall, vol. IV, p. 339f.

116. *Mahābhārata* I, 1205.

117. All the less that *Ṛ.V.* VIII, 1, 11, makes a close agreement between Etaśa, the steed of the sun, and the winged and rapid horses of Vāta.

118. Kuhn, *Herab. des Feuers,* p. 251.

119. *Mahābhārata* I, 1223 and fol. Cf. *Ṛ.V.* I, 32, 12, Indra transformed into a horse's tail to deliver the imprisoned waters.

120. I see nothing in the passage (*Ṛ.V.* I, 132, 6) quoted by M. Kuhn, *Zeitschr, für vergl, Sprachl.* IV, 119) to prove precisely that we must understand thereby a *horse's* head.

121. If, as M. de Gubernatis asserts (*Zool. Myth.* I. 302), *baḍavāmukha* (*Rām.* ed. Gorresio, IV, 40, 50), applies to Vishṇu, which, considering the state of the text, is very doubtful, this passage would furnish another argument for the ideas expressed here; and this horse's head would recall very forcibly the very clear meaning of the head of Dadhyañc, on which Cf. Schwartz, *Sonnw, Mond und Sterne,* p. 126ff.

122. So Tārkshya, the solar bird, gets the epithet of *arishṭanāmi* (*Ṛ.V.* I, 89, 6; X, 178, 1); it is then, in fact, distinguished form solar *wheel,* exactly as Etaśa, the steed of the sun, always represented as *bearing the wheel.* (Cf., for example, Kuhn, *Herabk, des Feuers,*

p. 62 and fol.) Mr. Kuhn (*Zeitschrift,* vol. I, p. 528 and fol.), formerly gave expression to observations which seem to me very similar to these, but his idea was not explicit enough for me to shield myself with his authority.

27

Bulletin of the Religions of India

A. Barth *of the Institut De France*

Translated from the French by Dr. James Morison

Buddhism

Putting aside two or three events which the Greeks have recorded, the dated history of India begins with the inscriptions, and the oldest of these inscriptions, the celebrated edicts of King Piyadasi Aśoka (in the middle of the third century before our era), are, at the same time, the first Buddhist documents of indisputable authenticity we possess. It is very probable that, among the materials incorporated in the *Tripiṭaka,* there is an element which goes further back than this, for it is certain that the Buddhism, which we see in the inscriptions to be in a manner elevated into the position of the state religion of the most powerful empire of India, had a literature even then. But several reasons justify us in doubting whether it was in possession of a canon so early as that.[1] In any case, there is not a single fragment of the canon in its present form, either in Pāḷi or Sanskrit, which we can affirm with any degree of confidence to belong to so remote an age. Further, every discovery which adds a fragment to his precious series is a king of event, and happily recent years have enriched us with several. The English translation of M. Senart's brilliant labours on these inscriptions was not yet completed.[2] Professor Bühler was in the middle of the painstaking revision which he was devoting to them, partly with the help of better copies,[3] when new versions of the edicts were found near the Afghan frontier.[4] Then came the fuller versions of the edicts of Sahasrām and Rūpnāth, found by Mr. Rice in Mysore. The monuments have suffered a great deal, and the first facsimiles were very imperfect, at least M. Senart was unable to make out a coherent text.[5] At the same time he brought out well the importance of the discovery of inscriptions by the great northern king so far to the south, so far from the coast, far within the central plain in countries which have sometimes been represented as hardly our a state of barbarism seven or eight centuries later.[6] Professor Bühler has contributed his share of elucidations of these inscriptions, and has promised others. Meanwhile he has called attention to the hitherto unnoticed fact that the signature of the writer of these inscriptions is in the southern variety of the alphabets named after Aśôka.[7] Many points in these texts are still obscure; and conspicuously the principal difficulty which those of Sahasrām and of Rūpnāth still present has been found more complicated than simplified. Better copies are necessary before greater success can be obtained. Professor Bühler has pointed out a new variety of the southern alphabet on an unedited monument from the valley of the Kṛishṇā,[8] and he has recovered a variant of the Kôsambi edict of Aśôka among General Cunningham's facsimiles of the Sāñchī inscriptions.[9] His latest communication on this subject, made after examining the better copies sent by Prof. Führer, shews that the surname of the king *devānāṁpriya,* restored on Cunningham's facsimile, is not found on the original. The connection which have been pointed out and the place of origin of the fragment are quite consistent, and it seems likely that, even before this epoch, a Buddhistic sanctuary existed in these parts. Last of all, a short time ago, Dr. Burgess announced the discovery, in the Teraī of Nêpāl,[10] of a new column covered with Aśôka inscription, and exhibiting two hitherto unknown, besides the seven, edicts commonly found on such monuments.

More or less closely connected with these first inscriptions are others in a character either identical or very slightly modified, whose date must for the time remain undermined within a century or more, according as we assume this southern alphabet, or alphabet of the *lāṭs* or pillars to have changed more or less rapidly and specially more or less uniformly and more or less definitely. Of this class must be mentioned in the first place, because of the amount of information which they give as to primitive Buddhism, the curt but varied inscriptions of the *stūpa* of Bharhut (or Bharaut, according to Mr. Fleet) of which we owe a new and carefully revised edition to Dr. Hultzsch,[11] and the analogous inscriptions of the *stūpas* of Śānchī which had been published by General Cunningham, and of which Prof. Bühler has undertaken a critical and much more complete edition, after the excavations made by Dr. Führer and with the help of new facsimiles furnished by that explorer. In place of the 241 numbers contained in the *Bhilsa Topes* of Cunningham, the collection placed at the disposal of Prof. Bühler contains nearly 500, of which 486 are legible.[12] The commentary on what he has published is such as we might expect from Prof. Bühler and abounds in interesting remarks. Among other details he draws attention to the great number of religious men and women, that is persons who can have had no private property, whose names are inscribed on these monuments as donors, and he explains this fact (which is observable elsewhere) by supposing that their gifts were the result of begging. This is, of course, very possible, but the texts do not say this, and the conjecture is perhaps also possible that side by side with rule of poverty there were then relaxations. Strictly speaking, the communities, as well as their members, were debarred from possessing property, and yet everything indicates that from a very early time they were wealthy. Besides the ancient inscriptions, which are by far the most numerous, there are found at Sāñchī inscriptions of a modern date. We have seen above that Prof. Bühler has tried to prove the existence in these parts of Buddhist worship before the age of Aśôka. This worship kept its ground long, and, even in the tenth or eleventh century of our era, statues were there erected to Buddha. There is similarly at Sahêt Mahêt, the ancient Śrāsvastī, one of the cradles of Buddhism and Jainism, a long Buddhist inscription of the 13th, century discovered by Dr. Fühler, among remains of various dates.[13] So at Buddha-Gayā, the sanctuary of the tree of wisdom, where the Master attained the perfection of a Buddha, and whose long continued history has lately been recounted by the veteran of Indian archæology, in a magnificent volume.[14] Here again the inscriptions date from the earliest times down to the twelfth century. The long series of excavations executed under his direction[15] have enabled General Cunningham to determine the successive additions which made the actual building, and to reconstruct the plan and chief arrangement of the original sanctuary. In agreement with tradition, he attributes this sanctuary to Aśôka, and this conclusion is not impugned by epigraphy; for, though the name of the king has not been met with, the characters of the inscriptions, those at least of oldest date, are the same as those of his edicts.[16] At the extreme north-west of the Pañjāb and of India, where the alphabet called northern, Bactropāli, Indo-Bactrian, or as Prof. Bühler prefers to call it, the Kharôshṭhī, prevails, we are face to face with a similar problem. There also we have on a series of monuments, a form of writing, which beginning with Aśôka, remained with hardly any change for several centuries. A considerable number of these inscriptions is dated; but, in certain cases, when we have not to do with the epoch established by Kanishka, which scholars are almost all agreed in fixing at A.D. 71, there is anything but agreement as to the era or eras to which these dates refer. In a carefully written essay.[17] M. Senart has tried to let some light into this darkness. Founding on a recently published inscription,[18] which he was the first to decipher correctly,[19] and, bringing it into connection with several other monuments of the same class, he gave it as his opinion that the dates of these texts have reference to an era the beginning of which would fall between 90 and 80 B.C., and the establishement of which must be attributed to those Parthian dynasties, which come between the Greek kings and the great Indo-Scythic empire, and which held sway in the basin of the Indus at the commencement of the Christian era. These results, especially if we take into account the cautious reserves with the author has taken pains to guard them, ought always to be taken into serious consideration, although it is certain, after the publication of the new facsimile by Mr. Smith, that the date of the inscription of Hastnagar contains signs for hundreds, and that the most likely reading is 284[1] and not 84. Along with the era proposed by M. Senart, this would bring us, in fact, to about 200 A.D. and, though it is hard to see how this local Parthian era should, in this region, have survived not only these Arsacide dynasties, but even the establishment of the era of Kanishka; it is still more difficult to reckon here according to that latter era, and, with Mr. Smith, bring down this inscription and the alphabet in which it is written as low as 362 A.D. As, on the other hand, we cannot think of the era of the western Arsacides, an era which the Parthian dynasties themselves such as Gondophares, did not employ for their inscriptions, the hypothesis of M. Senart remains the most probable, unless we will fall back on the era of the Seleucides, or content ourselves with a simple confession of ignorance. In any case, to judge by the facsimile, this date of 200 A.D. is not contradicted by the scene depicted on the pedestal. Its pilasters with their broken Corinthian capitals, its foreign garments, its heads with nothing Indian about them but the mode of dressing the hair, its prettiness, which is slightly vulgar and quite secular though the subject is a religious act, very likely an offering to Buddha: all we can say of this sculpture is, that it is derived from western workmanship, and is connected with some period of Græco-Roman art.

(To be continued)

References

1. The word *paṁchanêkāyika,* found in the inscriptions at Bharhut and Sāñchī, which Prof. Bühlet and Dr. Hultzsch agree in translating by "knower of the Five Nikāyas" (in any case the compound would be hardly regular), would cause us to admit a codification for an epoch which is not, perhaps, much later than that of Aśoka. But to assume from this phrase the existence of the Five Nikāyas of the Pāḷi Canon is rash. This division, like many others is unknown in the sacred literature of the north.
2. *The Inscription of Piyadasi* in the *Indian Antiquary,* Vol. IX (1880), Vol. X (1881), Vol. XVII (1888), and Vol. XXI (1892); this last series has additions in which the author expresses himself more exactly on several of the results of his previous work.
3. *Beitrāge zur Erklārung der Aśoka-Inschriften* in the *Zeitschrift de. deutsch. Morgenl. Gesellschaft,* Vol. XXXVII (1883). Vol. XXXIX

(1885), Vol. XL (1886), Vol. XLI (1887) p. 1, Vol. XLV (1891) p. 144, Vol. XLVI (1892) pp. 54, 539; *Arch. Survey of Sothern India,* Vol. I (1887) p. 144 (the edicts of Dhauli and Jaugada; *Ind. Ant.* Vol. XIX (1890) p. 122 (the pillar edicts); Vol. XX (1891) p. 361 (the cave inscriptions of Barabar and Nagarjuni). Professor Bühler calls attention to the fact that some of these caves were designed for the use of Brāhmaṇ and Jain ascetics, and that we must be careful not to assign a Buddhist origin to all these excavations indiscriminately; *Epigraphia Indica,* Vol. II. 1893, p. 245, the pillar edicts.

4. In the preceding Bulletin (Vol. XIX. p. 267). I reported on the interpretations given of them by M. Senart and Prof. Bühler; by the latter we have further, *Die Mansehra Version der Felsenedicte Aśoka's* in the *Zeitsch. d. deutsch. Morgeul. Gesellschaft,* Vol. XLIII (1889) p. 273, and Vol. XLIV (1890), p. 702.
5. *Noted d' Epigraphie Indienne,* Vol. IV. *Trois Nouvelles Inscriptions d' Aśoka--Piyadasi* (*Jourm. Asiat.* May-June, 1892).
6. As by the late Dr. Burnell, Rev. Thomas Foulkes (*The Dekhan in the Time of Gautama Buddha, Ind. Ant.* Vol. XVI (1887) p. 49) had attempted to prove the contrary; but all the evidence collected by him does not outweigh the simple fact of the presence of these three inscriptions in Mysore.
7. *The Aśoka Edicts from Mysore (Wiener Zeitsch. f. d. k. d. Morgenl.* Vol. VII (1893), p. 29).
8. *A New Variety of the Southern Mauraya Alphabet (Wiener Zeitsch. f. d. k. d. Morgent.* Vol. VI (1892) p. 148).
9. *Ind. Ant.* Vol. XIX (1890), p. 124; *Epigraphia Indica,* Vol. II (1892), p. 87; *Wiener Zeitsch. f. d. k. d. Morgenl.* Vol. VII (1893), p. 292.
10. *The Academy,* October 14th, 1893, p. 324.
11. *Bharaut Inscriptions (Ind. Ant.* Vol. XXI (1892), p. 225. These inscriptions, published besides by General Cunningham, in his large monograph on the monument (1879) had been already revised in part by Prof. Hoernle (*Ind. Ant.* Vols. X and XI 1881 and 1882, and Dr. Hultzsch had given an excellent edition of the whole collection in the *Zeitssch. d. d. Morgenl. Gesellsch.* Vol. XL (1886). The new edition contains a list, with the reference to the collection of Prof. Fausbö, of all the *Jātakas* mentioned expressly or merely represented on the mounment; the number of those thus identified is twenty-four.

12. *Votive Inscriptions from the Sānchi Stūpas (Epigraphia Indica,* Vol. II (1892) p. 87); *The Inscriptions on the Sānchi Stūpas (Wiener Zeitsch. f. d. k. d. Morgenl.* Vol. VII (1893), p. 291).
13. *Archæological Survey of India, New Series,* Vol. I. *The Sharqi Architecture of Jaunpur; with notes on Zafarabad, Sahet Mahet and other places in the North-Western Provinces and Oudh. By A. Führer, with Drawings and Architectural Descriptions by Ed. W. Smith. Edited by Jas. Burgess,* Calcutta (and London): 1889. On the other hand one result of the researches of Dr. Fühler is that the identification of Bhuīla Tāl with the lost Kapilavastu, the place of Buddha's birth, which was proposed by Mr. Carlleyle so confidently, is entirely imaginary—In the following volume of the *Archæological Survey of India (The Monumental Antiquities and Inscriptions in the North-Western Provinces and Oudh, described and arragned,* Allahabad (and London 1891), Dr. Führer has condensed an enormous mass of information on the archæology of that district, which he is exploring with such intelligence and zeal. On Sahet Mahet, the ancient Śrāvastī, see further the essay of Mr. W. Hoey, in the *Journal of the Asiatic Society of Bengal,* Vol. LXI. *Part I, extra number,* 1892. In the preceding Bulletin (to. XIX. p. 267) I have mentioned the discovery of Mr. Cockburn, near the junction of the Ganges and the Jumnā, of the cave where, in the time of Hiouen-Thsang, the shade of Buddha appeared. Mr. Cockburn also recovered there an ancient inscription and took an imperfect copy of it, of which Prof. Hoernle (*Proceedings of the As Soc. of Bengal,* 1887, p. 103) was not able to make much. This inscription, as well as another in the interior of the cave, has since been published by Prof. Führer in the *Epigraphia Indica,* Vol. II (1893) p. 240. It is indeed very old, of the first or second century before our era, but possibly Jaina. In the seventh century the cave had been taken possession of again by Buddhism; at the present time, the nearest inhabitants are Jainas.
14. *Mahābodhi, or the Great Buddhist Temple under the Bodhi-Tree at Buddha Gaya.* London, 1892. I regret to have to record the death of General Cunningham on the 28th November 1893. What a wonderful scientific career came to an end in the death of this bold and tireless worker in his eighty-fourth year, and with his pen still in his hand? His first essay bears the date of 1834, when he was the companion and fellow-worker of James Prinsep, and only the other day the *Transactions of the Oriental Congress* held in London, and the *Numismatic Chronicle* (Part III. 1893) brought us his last labours on the coins of the Indo-Scythic Kings.

15. These excavations have unfortunately ended in restorations for which General Cunningham is not answerable and which are too like an act of vandalism. The temple, which for centuries had become Hindu, has been made brand new by means of countless square yards of stone facing and has been claimed again for the community of Buddhists in all quarters of the globe by agitators in Calcutta and Madras.

16. I bring together in this note some other discoveries and identifications of the sacred places of ancient Hindu Buddhism: – I.E. Abbott, *Recently discovered Buddhist Caves at Nādsūr and Nenavalī in the Bhor-State, Bombay Presidency (Ind. Ant.* Vol. XX (1891), p. 121 – Henry Cousens, *The Caves at Nāḍsūr and Karsambla (Archæolog. Survey of West. Ind.* No. 12, Bombay, 1891) – T.W. Rhys Davids, *Fa-Hien's "Fire Limit" (Journ. Roy. As. Soc. of Gr. Brit. and Ireland,* 1891, p. 337) – T.W. Rhys Davids, *The Buddha's Residences (Ibid.* p. 339) – A Macaulay Markham, *Report on Archæological Excavations in Bijnor, North-Western Provinces (Journ. As. Soc. of Bengal,* Vol. LX (189), p. 1) – Henry Cousens, *Report on Archæological Excavations in Bijnor, North-Western Provinces (Journ. As. Soc. of Bengal,* Vol. LX (189), p. 1) – Henry Cousens, *Report on the Borid Lakha Medi Stūpa near Junagaḍh* (in Kaṭhiāwār) (*Ibid.* p. 17) – L.A. Waddell, *Discovery of Buddhist Remains at Mount Uren in Mongir District, and Identification of the site of a celebrated Hermitage of Buddha* (the hill in Hiraṇyaparvata, where, according to Hiouen-Thsang, the Buddha had conquered a certain Yaksha Bakula) (*Ibid.* Vol. LXI (1892) p. 1 – L.A. Waddell, *The "Tsam-cchô-ḍung" of the Lamas, and their very erroneous identification of the site of Buddha's death* (the Lamas situate it in Assam) (*Ibid.* p. 33) – Lastly I shall mention the very careful translation of the voyages of Fa-Hien by Prof. James Legge, though it has appeared some time ago; *A Record of Buddhist Kingdoms, being an Account by the Chinese Monk Fā-Hien of his Travels in India an Ceylon* (*A.D.* 399-414) *in search of the Buddhist Books of Discipline. Translated and annotated with a Corean Recension of the Chinese Text.* Oxford, 1886.

17. *Notes d'Epigraphie Indienne,* Vol. III. *De quelques monuments indo-bactriens (Journ. Asiat. février-mars* 1890).

18. This inscription, cut on the base of a statue of Buddha and coming from Hashtnagar, in the north of Peshāwar, had been published, with a not very good facsimile. the only one which M. Senart has at his disposal, by Mr. V.A. Smith, in the *Ind. Ant.* Vol. XVIII

(1889) p. 257. A better and more complete reproduction, giving also the bas-relief of which the inscription forms a part (the statue which was erected on this base has not been recovered) has been supplied by the same scholar (*Journ. of the As. Soc. of Beng*. Vol. LVIII (1889) p. 144.

19. The same corrections had been made independently, but after the publication of the second facsimile, by Prof. Bühler, in the *Ind. Ant.* Vol. XX (1891) p. 394. Mr. Smith's reply to M. Senart and Prof. Bühler, *ibid,* Vol. XXI (1892), p. 166; he gave an extended analysis of M. Senart's essay in the *Journ. of the As. Soc. of Bengal,* Vol. LXI (1892), p. 52.

28

Some Notes on Buddhism

G. K. Nariman

Among the problems regarding the origin and history of Buddhism, the most interesting refer to the original language of Buddhism and to the prime original tradition upon which the various schools into which Buddhism was early divided have drawn. In the year 1909 a little work of the highest importance on the question of the formation of the Pāli canon was published by Professor Sylvain Levi (*Les Saintes Ecritures du Bouddhisme*) which has been translated into English by me. Professor Herman Oldenberg has recently brought out *Studien Zur Geschichte des Buddhistischen Kanon* in which he fully recognises the value and indispensable importance of the Chinese versions upon which Prof. Sylvain Levi has relied. Prof. Oldenberg brings out a few fresh points which will be studied with interest by the schools of Ceylon, Siam and Burama. He produces a number of parallels from the Pāli text to the *Divyāvadāna*. He shows that the Pāli school is mentioned by the *Divyāvadāna*. He admits that the Pāli is not the original language of Buddhism and that the Pāli canon is translated from the Māgadhī. He examines carefully the Pischel fragment of the Sanskrit *Aṅguttara Nikāya,* and, with the help of the Chinese rendering furnished by Prof. Sylvain Levi, is enabled to correct the Pāli text; and interprets the whole differently from the construing of the passage by Pischel. Both the scholars emphasise the capital nature of the critical study of Prof. Anesaki on the four Buddhistic *Agamas* in Chinese. Prof. Oldenberg devotes some pages to the literary history of the *Jātaka* and examines finally the history of the canon as constructed by Prof. Sylvain Levi. He is of opinion that the artists of the Bharhut and the Sanchi Topes were acquainted with a later version of the life of the Buddha than that preserved in the Pāli texts. He is of the same opinion as Prof. Lüders that the original language of Buddhism was the old Ardha-Māgadhī. A very interesting fact is the prohibition of image worship by the Buddha as hinted at by Prof. Oldenberg. It would be highly interesting to gather together from the oldest portions of the *Tipiṭaka* direct interdiction of idol worship.

Another contribution of high value from the same distinguished Professor at Göttingen is the *Studien Zum Mahāvastu* which explores the Sanskrit work and takes up the search for parallels, where it was left by Prof. M. Senart and Prof. Windisch. Though generally the Professor is enabled to prove the superiority of the Pāli texts, he himself is the first to bring into prominence such passages in Pāli as have been emended with the help of Sanskrit. A striking instance of the *Mahāvastu* supplying a gap in the Pāli text, as published both in London and Siam, is given at p.. 131. Prof. Oldenberg gives ample instances where the Sanskrit text is more brief than Pāli, and asserts that these are so many exceptions which prove the rule. At times he himself is in doubt to decide which is the older, the Pāli or Sanskrit (p. 135). Here and there Prof. Oldenberg finds traces of the prime canon on which both the Pāli and the Sanskrit are based (p. 150). Prof. Oldenberg objects, in the light of Central Asian discoveries, to the assertion of Prof. Rhys Davids that the old *vinaya* had never been translated into Sanskrit.

In the *Journal Asiatique,* Sept. and Oct. 1912, Prof. Sylvain Levi gives an exhaustive study of the *apramāda-varga* and the Sanskrit *Dharmapada* discovered by the Pilliot mission. A very interesting fact deduced by Prof. Sylvain Levi from the Chinese authorities is that a portion of the *Dharmapada* was translated from Sanskrit into Chinese by a fire-worshipper converted to Buddhism and that the *Mahāvastu* mentions the *Dharmapada.*

Perhaps of still greater value and interest is the Professor's dissertation on the pre-canonic language of Buddhism in the *Journal Asiatique,* Novem. and Decem. 1912. The conclusion of his most fascinating study seems to be that the Aśoka edict of

Bairat mentions portions of the Budhhistic scriptures in the language in which they were first given out, that is to say, the prime language of Buddhism. I hope to give a more detailed notice shortly of Prof. Sylvain Levi's studies, which, if accepted, must greatly modify our views of Ur-Buddhism and its language.

* * *

Theories des douze causes by Prof. L. de la Valle Poussin is his further study of the Buddhist theory of the *pratītyasamutpāda*. The Professor uses, besides the Pāli canon, the Tibetan *Shatistambasūtra,* and Sanskrit works among them the invaluable *Abhidharmakosha* of Vasubandhu. Sanskritists interested in Buddhist philosophy will be glad to learn that the Belgian Academy will soon bring out the third *kosha* and that Prof. Sylvain Levi is engaged on the first dealing with *vijñaña* and *shaḍayatana*.

29

"Dharani", or Indian Buddhist Protective Spells

L.A. Waddell, *C.B., L.L. D.*

Translated from the Tibetan

The cult of protective spells, in the form of magical texts, has been shown by me elsewhere to be widely prevalent throughout Buddhism in all its sects, and to have played an important practical part in that religion from its commencement.[1] Such text under the name of *Parittā* or *Dhāraṇī* are in universal use by all sections of Buddhist, – "Southern" as well as "Northern," – and I there adduced evidence, almost unimpeachable, to show that some of these spells were used by Buddha himself.

I also described the early widespread use of these spells amongst the amulet-loving people, not only of India but of the adjoining lands, that embraced Buddhism. It is also attested by the fact that the great bulk of the ancient Sanskritic manuscripts recovered from Central Asia by Sir Aurel Stein and others consist mainly of fragments of these protective texts, the originals of several of which are as yet unknown.

The interest and historical importance of these spells is not merely Buddhistic. Most of the charms and their associated rituals (*sādhana*) exhibit elements which, like those of the *Atharvavéda,* are manifestly pre-Buddhist and even pre-Vedic, and afford some insight into the religion of pre-Aryan India. Especially interesting in this regard are the vestiges thus preserved of the animal-gods; *e.g.*, the Garuḍa, dating manifestly to the earliest nomadic and pre-historic 'hunting'-stage of primitive society, and the references to the early anthropomorphic 'mother-fiends, (Rākṣinī), also pre-Vedic , and dating to the matriarchal and more settled stage of early civilization; as well as the light that is shed upon the evolution of many of Brahmanical gods of the Vedic and later periods. Thus several of the gods of the Hindu Pantheon are disclosed by these contemporary texts in early or transitional forms, and in the process of being clothed by the hands of the Brahmans with the functions and attributes of popular aboriginal gods and genii, in regard to which prototypes Brahmanical literature is more or less silent.

As little of this Dhāraṇī Literature has hitherto been published for Western readers,[2] and a great mass of it exists in Tibetan texts translated with remarkable fidelity from the Sanskrit, it has been suggested to me that translations of some of these Tibetan versions into English would be acceptable to students of Oriental religion and mythology. I accordingly offer here an instalment of these texts and their translations.

The Tibetan material now available in Europe for this purpose is immense. The British collections in the national libraries are especially full, as they have been greatly increased by the large accessions collected by me during the Lhasa Expedition of 1904,[3] which included several sets of the "*Dhāraṇī Piṭaka*"[4] as well as the series contained in three sets of the great Mahāyāna Canon (*Ka-gyur*), in the Encyclopedic Commentaries (*Tan-gyur*), and in numerous separate texts, mostly in duplicate or triplicate.

The texts which I have selected at present are with one exception (No. 6)[5] now published and translated for the first time and relate especially to the Garuda, which is characterised in the title by its 'beak'. That monstrous bird, which incorporates a sun-myth as well as a thunderstorm-myth, from its widespread prominence amongst primitive people in remote antiquity, presumably was regarded as the supreme spirit in prehistoric times. It is the Phoenix or *Feng* of the Chinese in its combat with the dragon-spirits (the *nāgas* of India) who withhold the rain; it is the *gryps* of the Greeks and the *roc* or *rukh* or *simurgh* of the Persians. In the ancient Indian Buddhist sculptures at Sāñchī and elsewhere it figures prominently in antipathy to the *nāgas,* and in process of being absorbed into Buddhist mysticism. Whilst into later Brahmanism it has been incorporated to form the car of Vishṇu and as the symbol of victory to surmount the standards and banners dedicated to that god by the Imperial Guptas and other would-be Chakravarta emperors. In No. 2 the appearance and functions of the bird are described.[6]

By No. 6 important light is thrown upon the genesis and evolution of the Buddhist goddess Tārā, the so-called 'Queen of Heaven' and 'Mother of the (celestial) Buddhas'. The identity of Tārā with the goddess Uṣṇīṣa-Vijayā was pointed out by me long ago.[7] Now, in this *Dhāraṇī* Tārā is identified with Durgā (who also bears the title of Vijayā) and Kālī and most of those other 'Mother' she-devils of pre-Vedic times, who have in later days been imported into and incorporated with Brahmanism. She is moreover especially identified with the Garuḍa under the title of the "Female Thunderbolt-Beak," Vajratuṇḍi.

In form, these *Dhāraṇīs* or spells are generally given the shape of the orthodox Buddhist *sūtra.* They purport to have been recited in the usual way by Ānanda at the 'First Council,' the place and circumstances where they were 'delivered' is usually mentioned; and the words of the spell are often put into the mouth of Buddha himself. The incantatory formulas, constituting *mantras* or spells-proper, are in crude style of Sanskrit, with recurring cabalistic ejaculatory words, such as are also found in Brahmanical *mantras.*

1. The Iron Thunderbolt-Beak

Vajra-loha-tuṇḍa Dhāraṇī

[India Office Tibetan texts (Waddell Collection) No. 17 Vol. Z. (19). No. 261 in my list n 'Tib. MS. *loc. cit.*].

Oṁ! In the Indian speech [this] is called *Ārya vajra loha-tuṇḍa nāma dhāraṇī:* in the Tibetan speech Phags-pa rdorje gnam-lchags kyi mch'u [or "The noble Iron-Thunderbolt-Beak of the Sky."].

Salutation to Buddha and all the Boddhisattvas ! Thus have I heard. The Blessed One having gone into the country of Magadha passed through 'the mango-grove'. Leaving the mango-grove he sat down in the rock-cave of the Indra hill.[8] Then Śakra the most powerful of the gods together with the [gods of the] directions, came to the outside of the place where The Blessed One was and saluted the feet of The Blessed One. Then Brahmā and Vishṇu and Indra (Śakra) and the four great kings [of the Quarters] thrice circles around The Blessed One and besought him saying :—O Bhagvān we, all assembled, beseech you to capture the heart[9] of the Nāgas to disperse their thunderbolts so that the malignant Nāgas may be destroy the harvest, with manifold despoilation. Turn them aside, the wind and hail of the clouds, that they do not destroy everything, that the flowers and fruits and the harvests be preserved from injury. We beseech you to utter the spell called "The Iron Thunderbolt-Beak of the Sky." We Blesses One for the welfare of all beings to bestow upon us this gift !

The Blessed One [then] spoke thus to Brahmā, Vishṇu and Indra, and the Four Great Kings [of the Quarters], Honourable Sirs ! for the welfare of all beings I shall utter it as a blessing [like one ?] of the noble truths. Then Brahmā, Vishṇu, and Indra and the four great kings heard the *mantras* of the *dhāraṇī* [as follows]:

Salutation to the Three Holy Ones !

Salutation to Buddha Śākya-muni, to all the completely perfect Tathāgata Arhants.

Salutation to all the great Magical powers[10] for compelling the calm of the glorious hereafter. 11

Salutation to the highest in the three worlds.

Matha matha pramathā (twice). *jvalita bhikrita vajra jvaya jvaya; Mahāvaya viryaparakrama. koṭara jaya, pramabhavavuma, pramasare ! Bho bho nāga dipa dipa ! Bhiswaramadha pramadhane namur bhanan sphotayana huṁ huṁ phaṭ phaṭ ! . . . &c. &c. Hantu sarvadushtana bhasvodāya hridaya mahyeśare jiladitri śudaradura hanahana hūṁ phaṭ . . . &c.*

This what you have just now heard is "The glowing[12] Iron Thunderbolt-Beak of the Sky." It will break all the malignant Nāgas, and convert evil things into sweet perfumes. It will madden and destroy [evil] . . . &c.

At the same time, he called forth by name [the following spirits to receive his commands: The *Nāga*-king of the ocean Mātaṅga, the *Nāga*-king [known as] the 'Hooded One' (*Ch'atra*), the great 'Enchanter.'[13] Ten billions, one thousand millions and one hundred thousand saluted the feet of the Bhagavān who, after those Nāgas had formed an outer assembly [said unto them] "Guard ye all the beings of the world (Jambudvīpa) the flowers and fruit and harvests, the trees, leaves and branches ! Free them from wind, hail and excessive drought ! Make timely rain to fall ! By your own vow, by the vow to your tutelaries and to the Tathāgata, guard these for ever henceforth ! Each of you becoming entirely perfect in mind to no injury to man." . . .&c., &c.

2. The Red-copper Beak

[India Office. Tibetan text (Waddell Colln). No. K. 17. Vol. Z. (18): No. 265 in my List].

In the Indian speech [this] is called *Ārya ghadsa pratañ bhanda-ghātākada britachakhadhayā;* in the Tibetan speech *'p'ags-pa-zaṅs-gi moh'u dmar-pos gdug-paī phyogs t'ams-chad gnon par byed-pa śes-bya-baī gzuṅs* [i.e. "The Dhāraṇī of the noble Red Beak of Copper, who expels the mischief in all the directions."]

Salutation to the Buddhas and Bodhisattvas ! Sạlutation to all the noble ones (*āryas*) ! Salutation to all the Buddhas of the directions, to all the Bodhisattvas and hearers ! Salutation to the Blessed One. Tathāgatha Arhanta, the completely perfect Buddha, Sugata the fearless one whose words discipline humanity, the most high one, the leader of gods and men ! Salutation to the faces of the thousand Buddhas ! Salutation to the illustrious Bearer of the Thunderbolt (*Vajrapāṃ*).

This speech was thus heard by me :—The blessed One was seated at the hermitage of the reed-grove[14] by the sheet[15] of lotuses on the bank of the river Ganges,[16] in company with a great retinue of monks and novices.

At that time all the people were overpowered by disease caused by the *nāga* (dragons)[17] and prayed [to Buddha] for the terrific supernatural power of the noble Red-copper Beak, so that the eight plagues of the hot countries should not increase their fury,[18] carry off, upset, suck up the blood and flesh (of the people); that the angry flood of consuming fiery waves might not descend [further]. [Here part of the Shāman's operation in exorcising the Nāgas is indicated].

By throwing the iron-nail[19] the paralysed limbs will despatch their accumulated stupefaction to the cemeteries. By throwing up the seed[20] the diseases of the eight great Nāgas will be ejected and the stupefying wounds over the earth be purified.

He ['the Beak'] has the head of the *Garuḍa* bird with a body of copper.[21] He feeds overhead. He has a beak of copper 900 fathoms long. He devours anyone of the four races of Nāgas. He craves for blood and hail[22] and water. He stares fiercely with red eyes. He crunches [even] the gods. He laps up the marrow of things. He sends suddenly[23] ulcerous diseases. He subdues the foundations of the three worlds. He scatters the poison of fearsome diseases. Below, he strikes widespread panic into the lower hells; above, he sinks down the highest of beings. He splits down in six thousand kinds of plague. He lays low the thousand kinds of Nāgas of the interior [of the earth]. For these reasons there is [amongst the disease-causing Nāgas] fear of his appearance and re-appearance.

Then Vajrapāṇī besought the Blessed One, the beneficent ascetic, [saying] "O Sugata, pray have compassion on the six classes of beings, pray set them free from their disease and distress ! Pray set them free from the disease of passion, pray kill the fire of anger, pulverize the rock of arrogance, clear away the darkness of ignorance, the poison of disease, deliver from the thousands of disease-demons !"

Thus having supplicated, [the Buddha], in compassion seeing [the distress], acted at heart.[24] [Seeing] Vajrapāṇi miserable and the torments of the fierce disease, the state of the bodies of all, the [disease-spirits] breaking [their] promises and vows had tormented by sickness and enfettered with the thread of passion [Buddha-exclaimed], "Come all [diseases spirits] ! swiftly come near here ! I shall explain. Be advised." Thus he commanded.

Then through Vajrapāṇi's [request ?] there arrived near, distressed at the commands of the Victorious One, to attend the presence of the Victorious one, the eight classes of the Rāksa-mother fiends [25] [also ? he or they] called "The swift-goer of the depths, the middle and top," the race of the Brahman Nāga Vasuta.[26] Thus spoke Vajrapāṇi to the [whole] race of the Brahman vasuta Nāga. "Who am I to . . . make useless speech? I am alone ! You do not hear even me ! You do not attend me, the mighty one . . possessed of swift energy." Thus he said. Then Vajrapāṇi reflecting in heart [what he should do] said "You who are the lords of the earth, what should I say to you?" [Then the Nāga replied:] "I am the king of the Nāgas, and am called 'Vasuta' the gem of the Brahmans.[27] To me belongs all poison . . . [here follows five leaves describing the various diseases &c. caused by *Nāgas,* and the spell appears to be disclosed by the Nāga king himself in these words:] These were the words commanded :—*Oṁ Hṛuṁ Hṛī Hṛī Ah Tathāgatā nāga-hridaya, tathāgata namah dhamaya. tathāgate raja srī lhanana, budya budhya, raja iśala pari parilira, nagahu yarbada povamdha svaha ! Guha rāja-la svāhū ! hṛuṁ hṛī ! . . (&c. &c.)*

By this fortunate talisman[28] of the noble one, the sharp Red Copper Beak, may the [evil] power of the six classes of 'Vasuta' be swept away ! ..Then straightway the vanquished race of the Brahman [Nāga] is turned aside.

This *Dhāraṇī* of the 'Red Beak of Copper' is translated by the Indian abbot Jñāna Deva and the Tibetan *Bande* Cho's-'grub, and the translator (-interpreter) sKa-ba Bha-po.[29]

3. The Thunderbolt-Beak

Vajra-tuṇḍa Dhāraṇī

[From *Ka-gyur-rGyud,* Cale. edn. (also India Office ?), Vol. M. fols. 426-466: Csoma, *Analysis* p. 540-7 St. Petersburg ed. 754 W., fol. 27-50: Schmidt, *Index* p. 167, also in *gZuā* (*Dhāraṇī Section*) of latter, 937 W., fols. 38-79].

Oṁ ! In the Indian speech [this is called] *Vajra duṇḷa*[30] *nama nāga samaya;* in the Tibetan speeh *rDo-rjeī mch'u zês-bya-ba kluī-dam tśig-go*—[that is The Nāga's vow called 'The Thunder-bolt Beak.'].

Salutation to the Omniscient One ! At that time The Blessed One[31] was staying at the great city of 'The Striding Servant (?)'[32]

Amongst the great retinue [there] assembled [were] Takshaka [king of the Nāga Serpent-dragons] and the rest of the Nāga retinue, also gods and a great retinue of men assembled for the welfare of living beings. Seeing these, he [The Blessed One] thought that he would completely fulfil the hope of all by explaining the religious means of doing virtuous acts. At this time in that city was a Brahman named Viṣṇu a rich man enjoying great wealth. Proud in the possession of fine clothes and many good and chattels [yet] was he not blessed. The sacred *Vedas* and the Brahmans were [his] means of crossing to the other shore [of existence]. These began and ended merely with *mantras* (spells). By respecting these spells the Nāgas were summoned; by burnt offerings [was summoned] the Fire [? god]. When the harvest of this Brahman ripened it began to be destroyed by exasperating rain. He said I forgot for obtaining victory over this to utter the excellent spell and therefore the rain has begun to fall; so remembering the astrological formula he summoned the *Nāga* [and] performed the burnt offering of fire—mixing together sessamum and fruits, and the mustard grain, butter, salt, he made the burnt offering. Thereupon the *Nāgas* merely appeared [but] were not subjected. He praised the bolt [of Indra][33] and struck the head of the Nāga, and splitting it he enjoyed the pleasure of weakening the downpour. Thereupon the *Nāga* quivering with great rage and fury, instantly by the swift power of a *Nāga* forsook his [former] body and changed temporarily in a vapour of dazzling light to destroy [his assailant]. When this great spirit was descending like a shroud to destroy the body of the Brahman, the latter unassisted by his men was unable to make the burnt offering of fire. Helpless, in order to escape, he besought The Blessed One as a protecting mother to save him. Falling at the feet of the Blessed One he prayed saying: 'O Bhagavān, save my life I beseech you from destruction by the enraged *Nāga* ! Will you not save ! Save, O Bhagavan, Save, O Tathāgata !' Then The Blessed One spake unto that great breathless Brahmin: 'Feat not great Brahmin, I shall be your protector, and saviour and friend,' and having thus spoken and saying no more, he sat down.

Then Vajrapāṇi, the great general of the Yakṣas besought The blessed One, saying :– 'Grant this prayer O Bhagavān, so that the harvest be not destroyed by wild[34] *Nāgas,* also for the sake of [our] complete happiness,[35] in the future. Your instructions are necessary for all living beings. In what way should we act in such an alarming emergency? O Bhagavān what is to be done to benefit the harvests, to protect them perfectly, to increase them to the utmost, for the complete protection of the fields against the hostile *Nāgas*—we beseech you tell us !'

Then, the Bhagavān answered Vajrapāṇi the lord of esoterism and said:–"Vajrapāṇi, the angry heart of the *Nāga* causes it to do angry deeds. The *Dhāraṇī* called the 'Thunderbolt Beak', the heart of the Tathāgata, the Arhant and most perfect Buddha, is the remedy. That I now declare [unto you]. By this speech the injury will be swiftly stayed and all the harvest be completely protected &c., &c."

Thereupon Vajrapāṇi, the great general of the Yakṣas spake thus: "The Blessed One is the healer of all living beings. We beseech him in kindness to utter the words of the *mantras* of this great *Dhāraṇī.* Then the Bhagvān in kindness said [the spell]: *Namo Bhagavte sarvā Buddhana namo Bhagavate Śākyarājava ! Oṁ jala hala giri giri bhavana, dipata vega mahāchaṇḍanata hridaya jalani. huru huru. hana hana. daha daha. patsa patsa. sarvasasana nāga-kula paśana, &c. &c. &c. Nāga dindhārini huṃ phaṭ-jalamaṇi phaṭ jalini phaṭ phaṭ phaṭ phaṭ svāhā !*"

(The subsequent pages go on to enumerate the various specific ills and diseases, demons, and animal pests against which the spell is efficacious, and also details the necessary offerings to be made. The only other reference to 'Beak', which I have observed is the following, "the owl and the rat and the various kinds of *long-beaks* and swarming pests shall not come forth on the muttering of this spell." It ends by restating the title correctly as *Vajra-tuṇḍa,* and adds that it is the thunderbolt-heart[36] for allaying the harm done by *Nāgas* to the harvest. In the colophon no name of author or translator is mentioned).

(*To be continued*)

References

1. *The "Dhāraṇī" Cult in Buddhism, its Origin, Deified literature and Images:Ostasiatischen Zeitschrift,* 1912, 155-195.
2. Of the Pāli *Parittā* several have been translated by Gogerly – "Collected Writings" edited by A.S. Bishop, Colombo, 1908. Of *Dhāraṇī* a few have been translated or summarised from the Sanskrit by R.L. Mitra (*"Nepalese Buddhist Literature"* 1882), by Max Müller (*Uṣṇīṣa-vijaya D*); by R. Hoernle (*"Mahā-mayūrī* in *Bower MS.* "). From the Chinese, a few by S. Beal (*Catena*); by H. Kern (*Sacred Books of the East.* XXI); and a list of others contained in the Chinese *Tripitaka* in given by B. Nanjio (*Catalogue*). Of the Tibetan collections, the titles of several are given by Csoma Körosi ("Analysis" in *Asiatic Researches* XX) and more fully by J.J. Schmidt (*Index,* St. Petersburg 1848), and for part of those in the Tan-gyur by F.W. Thomas (*Sādhanas* in "Museon," Louvain, 1903) and Dr. P. Cordier (in his *Catalogue of the Tan-gyur Collection,* Paris 1909). From the Uigur Dr. F.W.K. Müller has translated a few (*Uigurica,* II Berlin 1911).
3. *"Tibetan MSS. collected in the Lhasa Mission," Asiatic Quarterly Review* 1912, 80-113. The collection was dispersed between the libraries of the India Office, British Museum, Oxford and Cambridge Universities.
4. *Hiuen Tsiang's Records* (Beal) II. 165, Watters, *do.* II. 160; Kern's *Manual Indian Buddhism* 46.
5. A fragment of this *Dhāraṅī* from the Sanskrit has been published with translation by Dr. Hoernle from a Stein MS. in *J.R.A.S.* 1911, 461, etc, and a full translation of another Stein MS. is I understand to be published in the final Report on the Expedition Results. An Uigur version of the same is translated into German by F.W.K. Müller, *Uigurica* II. 1911, 50.
6. For further descriptions of this bird-god from Buddhist sources with illustrations, see my article on "the Dhāraṇī Cult" above cited, pp. 187-191.

7. "The Indian Buddhist Cult to Avalokita and Tara," *J.R.A.S.* 1894, 83, No. 4.
8. *Indra-saila-guhā* in the Rājgir Hills.
9. Or 'spirit,' 'heart,' or 'essence', Tib. *sñin-po*. Secondarily it means *vajra* or thunderbolt, also the blue jewel of Indra–*Indranīla*.
10. *Mt' u-po*.
11. Literally "the other side" [of life]–*pa-rol zib-gyis gnon-pai mt'u-po*. The word which I have translated 'compelling,' namely *gnon-pa*, literally means to suppress to 'overcome by force,' and is frequently used in magical operations (*cf.* Jaeschke, *Tib., Dic.*, 307).
12. *'Bar-ba*.
13. *Mt'u-ch'e-wa*.
14. Jam-buhd. =Skt. *nala*. There was a hermitage of this name on the Ganges near Vaiśāli.
15. Or coverlet: *sa-ke'bs*–Skt. *kumba* (?).
16. Literally 'possessed of the eight limbs or arms,' which the *Dictionaries* state is the Ganges.
17. *Mdsc-nad*. defined in the *Dictionaries* as 'disease caused by *Nāgas;'* also leprosy, *kuṣṭa*.
18. *gnad kr'o-bo*. literally 'furious spirit.'
19. *Ichags-kyi gzer*=Skt. *kila*, a form of Indra's bolt.
20. *t'ig*, also 'lines' or 'spots.'
21. In Jewish mythology Brass is symbolic of irresistible weapons Dan. 2, 39; Mic. 4, 13; Zech. 6, 1.
22. *Chu'-ser*, may also mean 'yellow water' or 'putrid water.'
23. *Bur-du*, which may also read 'by (his) bolts.'
24. The construction here is very involved and obscure; and Buddha is not mentioned, probably intentionally so, in order that the spell of so bloodthirsty a being should not be directly ascribed to the placid Buddha.
25. *Lha-ma-srin*, literally=god or spirit+mother (or not)+ fiend (*rākaṣa*), can read 'the fiends who are not gods *i.e.* (*Asurā*); but the eight *mothers rākṣini* form a well-known group.
26. This title suggests Kubêra, who was lord of the Vasu spirits, and the *rākṣasī* were latterly placed under him; but he is not usually described as a Nāga himself, yet in the Jatakas he is given control

over *nāgas*. In later Brahmanism the chief of all the Nāga kings is Vasuki.

27. *Bram-ze-rin-poche'.*
28. *Cha's-pa* literally 'implement,' or weapon.
29. The last-named, who is called in one copy of this text, Ka-ba, appears to me to be the same as the Ka-ba l'albotsegs (or Srī-Kūta), who was a pupil of Padma Sambhava, *circa* 748-802 A.D.; see my *Buddhism of Tibet* p. 31 fn. 3 No. 17; Also Gründwedel's *Mythologie* 49, 55. Several of his works are in the Great Commentary, *Tanggur, mdo Section,* Vols. 117-124.
30. This is obviously a corruption of the copyist–the *Dictionaries* give *tunda* as the Sanskrit equivalent of the Tibetan *mch'u,* a beak; and the correct form is given in the colophons.
31. Bhagavān.
32. Gyog.' dor, literally servant+thrown off or forsaken or striding; a possible restoration by the *Sanskrit-Tibetan* lexicons is *Urana+dāsa.*
33. Tib. *pur-bu*. This is the name of the large nail of wood or mental used to stab demons. My *Sanskrit-Tibetan Dictionary* gives its equivalent as *killi* and *'śaṁku'* and the former manifestly is intended for *kila* 'bolt, pin or lance,' from *kil* to bind (Wilson's *Skt. Dict.* 232); and the latter is obviously corrupt for *śaṁba*=the thunderbolt of Indra, Wilson *S.D.* 848.
34. Literally 'untamed.'
35. Or *nirvāṇa.*
36. Or 'essence *sñiṅ-po.*

30

"Dharani", or Indian Buddhist Protective Spells

L.A. Waddell, C.C., L.L. D.

Translated from the Tibetan

4. The Black Iron-Beak

Loha Kala-tuṇḍa.*[37] Tib. *1 Chags mch'u nag-po

[*Ka-gyur Gyud.* Calcutta (& I. O. ?) Hodgson Coll. Vol. M: I.O., *Tib. texts.* (Waddell Coll.) No. K. 17. Vol. Y. (21), No. 264 in my list: Csoma, *As. Res.* XX. 540 (8)].

This purports to have been recited by Ananda in order to procure rain, etc. It is to coerce a large number of 'great *Nāga*-kings,' who are specified by name.

5. The Thunderbolt-Claw

Vajra-Ratiru.* Tib. *rDorje sder-mo

[I.O., *Tib. Texts* (Waddell Coll.) No. K. 17 vol. Ji. (31), No. 260 in my list].

It is addressed to several 'Mothers,' and other she-devils who are specified by name. No translator is named.

6. The White Umbrella-one of Buddha's Diadem

Uṣṇīṣa Sitātapatra Aparajita

The great Turner-away (of Evil)

[Tibetan: *Ka-gyur rGyud, Calc.* (& I. O. ?) Hodgson Coll. Vol. P. (13) fol. 181-188, 224-229; Csoma *As. Res.* XX. 519 (18); St. Petersb. Vol. Ph. (14) fol. 212-224. *Dhāraṇī Sect.* W. 133-138: J. Schmidt *Cat.* 162; I. O.; *Tib. Texts* (Waddell Col.) *Kā-gyur* as above. Sanskrit :—Raj. L. Mitra, *Nep. Budd. Lit.* 227; Stein, *Turkestan MSS.,* Hoernle, *J.R.A.S.,* 1911, 461 ff:

R.A.S. Hodgs. Coll. No. 77–Uigur; F.W.K. Muller *Uigurica* II., 50 ff–Chinese; Bun. Nanjio, Cat. *Tripitaka,* No. 1016 (?)].

"In the Indian Speech [it is called] *Ārya tathāgatosṇiṣa sitālapatre aparājita*[38] *mahāpratyaṅgira paramsiddha nama dhāraṇī:*in the Tibetan *P'ag-s-pa-de-bz'in gśegs-paī gtsug-tor-nas byuṅ-baī gdugs-dkar-po-chan gz'an-gyis mi-t'ub-pa p'yir-zlog-pa che'n-po mch'og-tu grub-po zes-byas baī gzuṅs i.e., "The Dhāraṇī* called The Noble White Umbrella One, invincible against othes who sprang from the diadem of the Tathāgata to accomplish[39] perfectly the great turning away [of evil]".

Salutation to all the Buddhas and Bodhisattvas, and Noble Hearers and Pratyeka Buddhas! Salutation to the Blessed One, (Bhagavān),[40] the invincible queen of the diadem !

This word was thus heard by me. The Blessed One was seated in the storeyed temple of the gods of 'The Thirty Three' with a great congregation of monks, a great congregation of the Bodhisattvas together with Śakra, the ruler of the gods. At that time, the Blessed One seated himself on a low cushion, and at that low level entered into the deep meditation called 'the perfect Vision of the Diadem' (*Uṣṇīsa vidarśana*).[41]

Not long after he was seated in that meditation these words of an esoteric spell issued from the middle of the diadem of the Blessed One.[42]

'Salutation to the Buddha, the Law,[43] the Congregation ! Salutation to the series of the seven All-perfect Buddhas, the congregation of Bodhisattvas and the hearers (*srāvaka*), Salutation to the great embodied Bodhisattvas, Maitreya and the rest !

Salutation to the saints (*arhanta*) of world, to those who have 'entered the stream' (of saintship, *stautāpanna*), to the saints who will transmigrate only once (*sakṛidāgāmin*) !

Salutation to the perfectly enlightened ones of the present age !

Salutation to the saints of the gods (*Devarīṣi*) to the useful power of the saints who hold the spells (*vidyadhāra-ṛīṣi*), to the saints (*siddhi*) who hold the spells !

Salutation to Brahmā, to Indra, to the blessed Rudra,[44] the lord-of Umā (the turner away of, or from, difficulties), [45] also to herself !

Salutation to the blessed Nārāyaṇa in his forms doing great deeds !

Salutation to the blessed Mahākāla dwelling in the fearsome three-tiered city in the cemeteries and the troops of Mothers doing energetic deeds, the adored ones !

Salutation to the line of the blessed Tathāgata !

Salutation to the line of the blessed Thunderbolt, the blessed Jewel, the blessed Elephant[46] the blessed Virgins (*Kumārā*), the blessed Nāgas !

Salutation to the blessed king holding hero-destroying weapons, the completely perfect Saint the Tathāgata, Buddha !

Salutation to the blessed completely perfect saint Tathāgata Buddha Amitabha !

Salutation to the blessed completely perfect Saint, Tathāgata Buddha Akṣobhya !

Salutation to the blessed completely perfect Saint, Tathāgata Buddha of medicine Baiṣaj-ya Guru, the king of beryl[47] light !

Salutation to the blessed completely perfect Saint Tathāgata Buddha, the vast flowery lord of the *Sāl-tree*[-grove ?] !

Salutation to the blessed completely perfect Saint, Tathāgata Buddha the 'king of the top-most jewel' (*ratna-sambhava ?*) !

Salutation to the blessed completely perfect Saint, Tathāgata Buddha Sāmantabhadra !

Salutation to the blessed completely perfect Saint, Tathāgata Buddha Vairocana !

Salutation to the blessed completely perfect Saint, Tathāgata Buddha, the vast-eyed king of the scented top of the *utpal*-lotus flower !'

Having saluted all these, the Blessed Mother,[48] the Invincible White Umbrella-One, the Great Turner-aside of Evil, issued from the diadem of the Tathāgata, to cut as under completely all the malignant demons;[49]

To cut asunder all the [hostile] spells[50] of others;

To turn aside all ultimately[51] enviroments;[52]

To save[53] the animated beings from all fetters[54] and from accidental death;

To turn aside all hostilities[55] and evil dreams and evil spectres (*bhūṭa*);

To frighten away the injuries of *yaksas* and *rakṣas;*

To frighten away the hosts of 80,000 malignant demons;[56]

To cause happiness throughout the 28 lunar constellations;

To turn aside all enemies and dangers and hatred;

To frighten away all evil demons, all poisons and weapons;

To turn aside fire and flood.

She is the saviour (Tārā)[57] from all fear of harmful things !

The great terrible destroyer (Ugrā)[58] is she, invincible against others (aparājita) !

Very fierce (Chaṇḍā)[59] is she, with great might !

Very fiery, with great shining brightness (*Marīcī*) !

Of great whiteness, a white one is she, clad in a garland of flames ![60]

The noble Tārā, with the frowning brows (*Bhṛikuṭi* (?) !

The renowned one known as 'The garlanded with thunderbolts of victory.' !

Her outward mark of the lotus is the mark of the thunderbolt !

The garlanded one, invincible against others (Aparājitā) !

With thunderbolt-beak (*Vajra-tuṇḍī*) [yet] the shape of a beauteous damsel[61] is she !

Placid (*Sivā*) is she, adored by all the gods !

The placid one garlanded with gold !

The great White One in the white robe of fire !

Noble Tārā great in might, the thunder-bolt enchaining others.

The thunderbolt maid, the upholder of the race !

Be jewelled with the juice of the saffron flower !

The famous thunderbolt diadem of Vairoçana !

May all this troop of thy mystic forms, protect our own circle and the [Buddhist] doctrine and all living beings!

[Here follows the especial incantation or spell, the *Dhāraṇī* proper, in crude Sanskrit. It is a shorter form of the above prayer for protection with some additional cabalistic words].

Oṁ sarva tathāgatosnīsa sitatapatre hūṁ hruṁ hṛī stoṁ.

Jambhanakari hūṁ hrūṁ hṛī ṣṭoṁ.

Mohanakari hūṁ hrūṁ hṛī sṭoṁ.

Lambhanakari hūṁ hrūṁ hṛī ṣṭoṁ.

Bhanakari hūṁ hrūṁ hṛī ṣṭoṁ.

Para piṣabhakṣaṇakari &c.

Sarva duṣṭana pradustana, &c.

Sarva yakṣa rakṣa grahā nām vidhvaṁ, sanakari &c.

Sarva para vidya che' danakari, &c.

Chautura-śitīnāṁ graha sahasrā naṁ vidhvaṁ, &c.

Astavi-śitīnām nakṣatra naṁ prasādhanakari, &c.

Astavi ṇaṁ mahāgrahā nāṁ Vidhvaṁ, &c.

Rakṣa rakṣa nām sarva satvaṁśça.

O White umbrella-one who issued from the diadem of the Tathāgata, the Blessed One !

The greater averter [of harm] to diadem-thunderbolt,

The great mother possessing a thousand hands,

the great mother with a thousand heads, with millions of eyes of unchanging fire,

The great vast thunderbolt by whom, in the cycles of the three worlds, we ourselves and all living things will become blessed.

The thunderbolt always gaping, possessed of eyes like glittering gold.

The white one with the gait of the thunderbolt [and] eyes like the Buddha.

The thunderbolt like the light of the sun, holding a thunderbolt like the moon.

Learned in all these various [mystic] forms and spells !

We beseech thee to protect us and all living beings !

Oṁ riṣigaṇa praśāsta sarva lathā jatoṣnisa sitātapatre hūṁ druṁ, Stāṁbhanakari, &c. . . .rakṣa maṁ svāhā.

O great averter, the thunderbolt diadem, the White Umbrella-one who issued from the diadem of the blessed Tathāgata !

O great owner of the thousand heads and a hundred thousand eyes ! thy distinctive name of the 'Fiery-one' is never changed !

Thy great vast thunderbolt is the terror of the three retinues of kings, of ourselves and the [other] beings !

It is the terror of everyone, the terror of water, of poison, of destructive weapons, of the hosts of foreign armies outside the frontier, of the famine, enemies, descending tongues, of untimely death, earthquakes, meteors !

It is a terror more than the punishment of kings !

It is terror to the gods and *nāgas,* to lightning, to the Garuḍa of the skies, to ferocious beasts of prey, the harmful spirits of the gods, the devils of the *nāgas* and *asuras,* the wind-dust-devils, *gandharva* [. . &c. several other classes of spirits are named].

Instead of the pricks of these demons let us obtain happiness.

Feed [us] with wholesome fresh food, with plenteous food, with red *amalaka* fruit,[62] and meat and the fat of the land !

Feed us with harvests of lifeless animals ! . . [here various foods are specified].

Arrange for us the spells for doing all these things !

Bestow on us by the thunderbolt-dagger[63] [favourable conditions] for our grain ! Arrange we beseech thee for this on a vast scale !

Bestow on us by the thunderbolt-dagger the spells necessary for performing these works by the sky-going fairies [*dākini*], by Brāhma, Indra, Nārāyaṇ, the Garuḍa and its associates, Mahākāla, the troops of [divine], mothers, human skeletons [spectres ?] and vanquishers of dreams, [also] for performing the deeds of a naked ascetic,[64] [Jaina] the deeds of a Buddhist monk,[65] of an *arhanta* freed from sensuous desire, of the followers of 'the creator of living beings' [*i.e.* Brāhmans], of the following Vajrapāṇi, of the male and female angels, of all the Saints, of all the gods !

Bestow by the thunderbolt-dagger the power of the Gandharvas (?)[66]

Salutation to the White Umbrella-One who emerged from the diadem of the Tathāgata. The Blessed One [who is] the means of performing deeds like those of the Buddha and all the Bodhisattvas.

We beseech you to protect us and all living things . . [Here follows an invocation to the goddess as 'the terror of . . .'[67] 'To destroy (evil)'].

Oṁ a sitāna lārka prabhā sphuṭa-vika Sitātapatre ! Oṁ jvala jvala, khada khada, hanahana, daha daha, dhara dhara, vidhara vidhara, ts'inda ts'inda, bhindabhinda, huṁ huṁ, phaṭ phaṭ, svāhā ! He he phaṭ, Ho-ho phaṭ, Amoghāya phaṭ, Apratihatāya phaṭ . Varadāya[68] *varapradāya, pratyaṁgirā ya, asuravidrā-vaṇakarāya, Varavidra-vanakaraya, Sarva devibhayah Sarva nāge-bhayah.*[69]

[Here follows the series of Spirits good and evil to each of which *sarvas* is prefixed and *bhayah phaṭ* is affixed, namely rakṣe, bhute, prete, piśatse, kuṣmaṇḍe, pūtane, kaṭpūtane, skande, unmāde, c'ch'aye, apasmāre, ostarāke, dākinī, revatī, yamāya, śakuni, mātigane, skamby kāmmaṁ, apalaṁavake, kantrane, gandharve, asure, kinnara, garude, mahorage, yakṣ e, durlaṁghite, duṣprakṣite, jāre, bhaye, upadrave, upasarve, krityakarmaṇika-khorda, kiraṇa vetāde, cicchapreśaka-sarvadaścchardita, durbhugte, tirthike (naked Jains) Śrar'mane, patake].

Sarva Vidyādhara phaṭ ! Jiyakara madhukara sarva arthasādhaye bhyo vidyācarye bhyaḥ phaṭ ! Chaturbhyobhaginīye [The four fear-causing sisters ?] *phaṭ* !

Sarva Kaumārī vajra, Kulandhari, vidyacarye bhayah phaṭ !

Sarva Mahāpartyaṁgirā[70] *bhayah phaṭ, Vajra Śaṁkhala pratyaṁgirāyai phaṭ*[71] *! Mahākālāya mātri gaṇa namaskritāya, Prahmaṇaye, Viṣṇavaya, Maheśvaraye, Randarye, Mahākālyé,*

Cāmundyé[72] *Kumāryé, Vārāhyyé, Indraya, Agnaya, Yasmāya, Varuṇāya, Marutya, Saumāye, Iśanā, Kāladaṇḍya, Kālarātré, Yamadaṇḍê, Rātrê, Kāpālyêe, phaṭ* !

Adhimukti śmaśāna vasidyê !

Oṁ stoṁ, bandha bandha, rakṣa, rakṣa, māṁ svāhā !

We beseech you to protect us all, the sinful as well as the worthy . . . May we become the first born for a hundred years, may we see a hundred thousand lives free from trouble by *yakṣ as*[73] and other demons may we obtain wholesome food in plenty . . . .

If the White Umbrella-One [be invoked] then the Thunderbolt-Diadem, the great turner away [of Evil], will save from death, wild beasts, accident . . . . . .

O White Umbrella-One [the product] of all the Tathāgatas and Buddhas destroy [all evil] ! Cause all the kings of the Nāgas, Ananta and Saṅkapāla and the great Maḥākāla to shed seasonable rain, to yield seasonable masses of cloud, seasonable loud-voiced thunder ! Be near to us in all dangers. Help us to perform the duties of a follower of the Buddha during the ages !

May the contents of this [book] through [the grace of] Buddha and all the Bodhisattvas be of use of gods, men, titans, (*asuras*) and angels (*gāndharvas*), to ourselves and fellow beings !

Praised be the word of the Blessed One, and may its meaning become fully manifest !

The *Dhāraṇī* here contained is named The Noble Invincible White Umbrella-One, which issued from the diadem of the Tathāgata to accomplish perfectly the great turning-away "[of Evil]."

[End of the Dhāraṇī]

As a postscript there are five pages containing a further list of Indian demons and diseases and other evils for which the spell is efficacious, including the following :–

'Tongues of fire, itching and ulcers, emaciation, cough, difficulty of breathing, insanity, poisonous drugs, curses, fire-water, fever, death by enemies, untimely (accidental) death, 'unworthy' beggary, scorpions, worms, leopards, lions, tigers, the black bear (*dom*), the red bear (*dred*), wild *yak* [possibly buffalo], water-devil.' It concludes with this prayer :–

"Against all these evil swarms we beseech you to protect us"!

Against all these may you be pleased to perform the binding spells (*mantras*).

O brilliantly shining one be pleased to bind evil ! Be pleased to perform the *vidyāmantra* spells against all others [counter-spells ?] !

Be pleased to fix their bounds ! :–

Tadyathā oṁ anale khasame . . . vaire, Some śānti, dānte viṣ ade vīre, Devi-Vajradhari, Vandhani, Vajrapāṇi phaṭ . . . . .

May it protect us ! *Svāhā* !

Oṁ Vajrapāṇi bandha Vajrapāśenamama sarva dustam vināyakaṁ phaṭ svāhā !"

Keep it near your heart !

Whoever having written this overpowering queen of magic spells (*videya-mantra*) named 'The White Umbrella-One', the great averter [of Evil], which issued from the diadem of the Tathāgata,; on birch bark, or cloth, or on tree bark,[74] and fixes it on his body[75] or on his neck or causes it to be read [then] throughout his whole life he shall not be harmed by poisons, by fire, by water, poisonous drugs, curses . . . &c. &c.

(*To be continued*)

References

37. One version reads '*duṣta.*'
38. The masculine gender here, as well as in the Tibetan translation of the title, presumes, I think, a form antecedent to the deification of this spell as a female goddess.
39. *grub-pa,* the Tibetan equivalent of the Sanskrit *siddha* means to accomplish by *yoga*-methods.
40. This is masculine.

41. In the list of 'religious stages' (*dharmapayaraua*) enumerated in the *Mahāvyutpatti* (No. 244, 82, St. Petersb. edn. p. 81) is mentioned *Uṣṇīṣa-vivarmurdhnah samadhi praveça.*

42. The Stein MS. does not contain the foregoing important matter, which locates the origin of the spell and explains its name from its mode of origin. The Hodgson *Sanskrit MS.*, (No. 77) omits the last sentence from 'at' to 'diadem'.

43. To avoid needless reiteration I omit several of the phrases 'Salutation to'.

44. *Legs-ldan drag-po;* my *MSS. Dictionary* restores *Legs-ldan* to '*Bhāgavati.*'

45. *Dkā-t'ub-zlog.* This Tibetan etymology for Umā, differing from the current Brahmanical one namely 'light,' is in keeping with the Brahmanist legend of the prohibition addressed to Durgā by her mother, *Umā, i.e.,* 'practise not austerities.'

46. In the Stein MS., Dr. Hoernle reads here *rāja* (*J.R.A.S.*, 1911, 463) for which the Tibetan would suggest *gagu*.

47. *Vaīḍurya.*

48. *Bchom-ldan-'das-ma,* here the feminine form appears for the first time.

49. *Gdon.*

50. *Sṅags.*

51. *Dus-ma-yin-par.*

52. *Ch'ib.*

53. *'Grol-pa'.*

54. *Bchiṅs.*

55. *Sdaṅ.*

56. *Gdon.*

57. *Sgrol.*

58. *Drog śul,* restored by my *MS. Dictionary* to Ugrā. Ugrā Tārā is one of the Nepalese series of the 'Fine Tārās' (Hodgson's *Essays,* reprint 94). See my *Buddhism of Tibet,* p. 436 for several of these fierce forms of Tārā.

59. *Gtum-ch'en-mo.*

60. *Rnam sgeg-mo,* literary 'shape'+dancing damsel.

61. Most of these epithets in this hymn of praise have been found by Dr. Hoernle in a Sanskrit text of this *Dhāraṇī* in the Stein collection, though in a different order.

62. *Myrobalan emblica.*
63. *P'ur-bus gdab-po.*
64. *Dge-sbyoṅ gcar-bus.*
65. *Mgo-reg.*
66. Literally 'the eaters of human offerings.'
67. It appears to read *bhyib,* which is not intelligible; possibly it is intended for a derivative of the Sanskrit *bhaya* 'fear'.
68. After each of these titles comes *phaṭ,* which I omit for brevity.
69. This is *bhayah* and not *bhyah* and clearly shows the word='fear' and that the latter form, which occurs in several places, is presumably an error.
70. This implies that there are several forms of Mahāpratyaṁgīrā.
71. From the following titles I omit *phaṭ* for brevity.
72. It is interesting to find that Çāmundā is identified with Sitātapatra (*i.e.,* Tārā), for this avenging form of Durgā was, like Sitātapatra himself, sent forth as an emanation from the head.
73. This prominence given to *yakṣas* suggests an early date.
74. *Śiṅ-śun* or tree+bark. It is restored by the Tibetan lexicons to the Skt. *valkal,* which in Wilson's *Sanskt. Dict.* (p. 766) is defined as 'the bark of a tree, garment made from bark.' In the Sanskrit scripts in Stein and Hodgson collections, the word is *kalke,* which Dr. Hoernle translates as 'paste' (*loc. cit.* p. 476), though he suggests it may be in error for *valka,* which the Tibetan version I find shows (and as Dr. Hoernle admits) is the correct form. See text in following note.
75. *Lus-du.* The Sanskrit versions have *kāyagate,* which Dr. Hoernle has translated as 'paper', but the Tibetan text indicates clearly that this should be *kāya,* the body.

    The Sanskrit text as given by Dr. Hoernle is :–

    bhūja-patre vā vastra vā

    Kalke vā kāyagate vā kanthagata vā likhitvā dhārīyeṣyata.

    The Tibetan text with its literal translation is :–

    gro-ga sam, ras sam, śiṅ śuṅ la bris-te,

    i.e., birch-bark, or cloth, or tree *valka*-bark upon having written

    l'us sam mgul-du btags sam l: log-par-byed ta,

    body or neck on fixed or caused to be read it.

31
"Dharani", or Indian Buddhist Protective Spells

L.A. Waddell, C.B., L.L. D.

Translated from the Tibetan

7. The Flaming Diadem

Uṣṇīṣa-jvala

Oṁ ! In the Indian speech [this is called] *Āryoṣṇīṣa jvala nāma Dhāraṇī;* in the Tibetan speech *'P'ags-pa gtsng-tor' bar.-wa zes bya-baī gzuṅs.*

Salutation to The Three Holy Ones ! *Namas samanta* buddhanām, apratikataśasanāmāṁ.

Oṁ ! kha-kha, khāhi, khahi, hūṁ, jvala, prajvala prajvala, tiṣṭha tiṣṭhaśti sarvadurani mitidusa svavana śānti kurū svāhā.

This indeed is the spell of the thousand Buddhas, it is the famous 'flaming diadem'. This famous luck-bringer makes all one's deed to be blessed, whether they be of different kinds [good or bad ?], whether they be hundreds of thousands, 900, or five fold. Evil dreams and evil omens[76] are made harmeless. Whoever mutters[77] it merely once has [harm] cleared away. The hosts of obstructing demons[78] are rendered powerless and utterly destroyed. Life and future happiness become increased ! *Mangalaṁ* ! (O happiness !).

8. The All-Victorious Turner-aside (of Evil)

Vijayavati-pratyaṁgirā [Dhāraṇī]

[From *Kā-gyur rGyud,* Hodgson Colln. Calc. (also I. O. ?) Vol. P. (13) No. 51 fol. 389-392: Csoma *An.* p. 524-51, St. Petersb. Vol. Tsh. (18) No. 730 fol. 225-227: Schmidt's *Index* p. 101: I. O. (Waddell) Tibet Colln. No. K. 17. (34).]

Oṁ ! In the Indian speech [this] is called *Ārya vijayavavavatina*[79] *nāma pratyaṁgirā;* in the Tibetan speech *'Pa'gs-pa p'yir-zlog-pa rnampar rgyal-ba-chan:* [that is, The Noble All-Victorious Turner-Aside or Repeller].

Salutation to the Buddhas and Bodhisattvas, the guardians who strive after the welfare of all living beings ! Salutation to all the Sādhanas (rituals for compelling visions of spell-spirits) ! Salutation to all the holders of spells (*mantras*) ! Salutation to Buddha, The Law and The Order ! Salutation to the Bodhisattvas, Mahāsattva Mahākaruṇa[80] and the illustrious Ārya Avalokisteśvara. All these were saluted by Vijayāvatī Pratvaṁgirā, who throws off life-destroying agencies and curses, pacifies the ghosts of the dead and excessive misfortune, dissipates fear [at the hands] of kings, fear of robbers, fear of fire, fear of flood-water, fear of *dākinīp-reta, pisācha, kumbhāṇḍa āstāraka, apasmāra, putana,*[81] fear of losing the track, fear of the cremation-path fear of those beings who walk in the darkness of the night and in the daylight. She makes them harmless and of a good disposition or entirely disperses them, repels all enemies, pacifies all upsetting and obstructing demons. She cleanses completely from all sin, from sluggishness in speech, the stiff in speech become charming in address and expression[82]. Salutation to the Bodhisattvas, Mahāsattva Mahākaruṇa and the illustrious Ārya Avalokisteśvara.

The essential spells[83] which will accomplish these [objects] are as follows : – *Oṁ dhara* (repeat 7 times), *dhiri* (seven times), *dhuru* (eight times). Protect us against fear, harm, destruction of life, curses, protect us ! *Sara* (seven times) ! *Siri* (seven times) ! *Suru* (seven times) ! *Mara* (seven times) ! *Muru* (seven times) ! Protect us from all disease, protect us ! *Hili* (eight times) ![84] *hulu* (eight times) ! *kili* (nine times) ! *mili* (eight times) ! *tsi-li* (nine times) ! *tsulu* (9 times) ! Repel all demons ! *Oṁ visara visara kaṁpa kaṁpa naśana naśayanaśaya !*

Against wrathful and malignant enemies whom you desire may come no nearer, make burnt-offerings and employ the above spells and afterwards repeat them once more. *Svāhā !* This will close the eyes of foes, close the ears, nose, tongue, bind the body, mind, and all the members, large and small it will bind. *Sphuṭa, sphuṭa, sphuṭa sphoṭaya* (three times) !

To clear away all destructive influences and curses, suppress every evil under every circumstance. *Sarvatru ūma, tutu* (four times), *Svāhā !* Protect us against fear and all kinds of harm, destruction of life, curses, ghosts and *apasmāra.* Protect us ! *Svāhā.*

To cleanse from all one's sins—a prayer to cleanse: *Tsara Tsara svāhā ! mara mara svāhā, Siri siri svāhā, kuru kuru svāhā, dhuru dhuru svāhā !*

For men desirous that harm shall not increase or that they be not befogged or stranded in solitude, or enraged or deluded, that they may turn aside all demons (*bhūṭa*), and all 'seizing'-demons (*graha*) and all diseases so that they do not drive people insane, do not befog the mind, stiffen, frighten, at all frighten, dismember, overpower, *Svāhā ! Nīle* (three times) ! *Keśe svāhā pīti* (three times)! *Keśe svāhā lohite* (three times) ! *Keśe svāhā mavadāte avadāte avabhata ! Keśe svāhā śveto śveto vastudhāraṇiye svāhā !* Turn aside the power of all demons ! Cleanse us from all sin, *Svāhā* ! Increase [good] deeds (two times), increase our good-luck and prosperity, increase our [good] deeds ! *Svāhā* ! Protect us against fear, harm, onset of sickness, all [evil ?] births and destruction of life, and all curses, and all disease-demons and all sin, and all evil planets and vast evils and all visible and invisible harm ! Protect us, *Svāhā* !

"This [spell] named The All-Victorious Turner-aside (*Vijaya Pratyamgirā*) produces victory.[85] Whosoever on their neck [hangs] this [spell] enfetters [evil] and thus becomes certainly the victor. The unblessed path of troublous dreams, sin, enemies of all kinds, robbers, fire and kings all these cannot harm. Whoever on their neck [hands] this [spell] enfetters [evil]; then the water-floods cannot carry him off. Sins become cleansed, every virtue becomes swiftly increased, illness is banished by profitable gain. the [book on the] noble *Vijaya pratyaṁgirā,* so named, is finished. *Mangalaṁ !*"

References

76. *mt'san. ṅan.*
77. *bzlas.*
78. *bgeg-s*=Skt. *gaṇa.*
79. This is obviously corrupt for *vijayāvatī,* the form in the St. Petersburgh text, and Schmidt p. 101, which is also the form given in the Sanskrit Tibetan Dictionaries.
80. This is an epithet of Avalokita, although here differentiated from that divinity by 'and'.
81. Classes of evil spirits.
82. Implies the attributes of the Vedic Vāch, the goddess of speech, the prototype of Sarasvatī.
83. *Mūla-mantra.*
84. This spell with *'Hili kili mili'* is evidently part of the great peafowl charm against snakes ascribed in simpler forms to Buddha. See my art. *Dhāraṇī Cult., loc., cit.*
85. Literally 'causes victory to arise.'

32

Vaishṇava Worship and Buddhism

K.P. Jayaswal

The date assigned by Sir R.G. Bhandarkar and other scholars to the rise of the Vaishṇava cult is too well known to be quoted here. I want to draw attention to a piece of evidence which carries one aspect of Vaishṇava cult to a period not later than 700-600 B.C. This was the worship of Trivikrama Vishṇu, curiously enough the form of worship was the worship of foot-prints.

The worship was current even before Yāska and was alluded to by a predecessor of his. That predecessor was Aurṇavābha, who was probably identical with the Teacher of that name in the *Bṛihadāraṇyaka Upanishad.* Aurṇavābha is cited in several places by Yāska who gives his *aitihāsika* or legendary and historical interpretations of the *Ṛigveda* hymns.

Commenting on the well-known Ṛichā इद॒ं विष्णुर्विचक्रमे त्रेधा निदधे प॒दम्, Yāska in his *Nirukta* (Daivata, 6.3.19) quotes Śākapūṇi first, who explains that Vishṇu crosses 'all this' with three steps placing them on the earth, on the *antariksha* (horizon) and on the sky. (यदिदं किं च तद्विक्रमते विष्णुस्त्रिधा निधत्ते पदं त्रेधाभावाय पृथिव्यामन्तरिक्षे दिवीति शाकपूणिः।) Then he cites Aurṇavābha who takes the verse in the sense that Vishṇu literally and physically crossed in the past (चक्रमे) in the manner described by Śākapūṇi, stepping over the earth, horizon and sky, and he says "in ascending (he stepped) at the *Vishṇu-pada* on the Gaya Peak"[1] –

समारोहणे विष्णुपदे गयशिरसीत्यौर्णवाभः।

Aurṇavābha is referring to the first step *pṛithivyāṃ* and is giving the Aitihasikas' view current in his time by referring to the "Vishṇu-pada" at Gayā-Hill from which place, they believed, Vishṇu actually went up. The "Vishṇu-pada" at Gayā-Hill is still worshipped and was being worshipped in the days of and before the *Vāyu-Purāṇa* (600 A.D.).

The passage is not only important for the history of the Vaishṇava cult, but throws light also on the religious history of early Buddhism. The custom of worshipping foot-prints, it shows, had been already an old institution before the time of the Buddha. It probably originated in this Vedic legend of Vishṇu's stepping over the earth.[2] His supposed foot-prints (Vishṇu-pada) were worshipped by the Aitihāsikas and those who believed with them.

The passage also shows that Gayā had long become a sacred place before the Buddha went there to do his meditation.[3] And it was a sacred place of the orthodox people who derived their cult from the *Ṛigveda*.

I take this opportunity of pointing out that the identification of the Trivikrama-Vāmana Vishṇu with Vāsudeva was complete before the *Baudhāyana-dharma-Sūtras* (see, II. 5. 9. 10). Also before the *Baudhāyana-dharma-Sūtras* child-Kṛishṇa (Dāmodara) and the cowherd-Kṛishṇa (Govinda) were known deities (*ibid.*)[4] This disposes off the view held by Indian and European scholars that the Kṛishṇa worship in the child-form is post-Christ. The accepted date of the *Baudhāyana-dharma-Sūtras* is "before 400 B.C." (Macdonell, *Sanskrit Literature,* p. 259).

My own view which will appear in my *Tagore Lectures* is that the date is over-estimated by two centuries. In any case the cowherd and the child-god Krishṇa was worshipped here before Christ was born.

References

1. For *Gayā-Peak* in the Jatakas, see J. I. 142.
2. The orthodox worship of foot-prints to-day is confined to Vishṇu-pada (Vishṇu's foot-prints) only.
3. Apparently he went there because it was a sacred place.

4. In the *Ānandāśrama* edition the twelve named Keśava, etc., are given separately. But see Bühler, *S.B.E.* XIV. The identity is established by the *Vaikhānasa-dharma-Sūtra* (lately published) which gives the *pratika* "Keśava" of the Baudhayana *mantra* and calls the 'the twelve names'. (The date of the *Vaikhānasa* in the present form is *cir.* 200 B.C. Its earlier shape which can be easily detected goes back before the Buddha's time and Pāṇini. It is quoted by Gautama and Baudhāyana and the quoted *sūtras* are to be found in the present *Vaikhānasa,* I discuss its date and importance in my *Tagore Lectures.* The MS. known to European scholars was a later book than the present one.

33

A Buddhist Parallel to the Avimāraka Story

A. Venkatasubbiah

No. 536 of the Buddhist Jātaka stories (Kuṇāla-jātaka; V, 412 ff. of Fausböll's edition) has for its theme the natural wickedness of women. The bird-king Kuṇāla delivers in it a long address on this subject to the cuckoo-king Puṇṇamukha and others, and in the course of it, mentions among the wicked women known to him, the princess Kuruṅgavī who, though in love with Eḷakamāraka, sinned with Chaḷaṅga-kumāra and his disciple Dhanantevāsī. the story referred to by him is related in full by the author of the *Jātakatthavaṇṇanā* (p. 428 ff.) and is as follows: –

King Brahmadatta once fought with and killed in battle the king of Kosala. He then took his kingdom and also his chief queen, and made her his chief queen, although she was pregnant at that time. Some time later, this queen gave birth to a handsome boy-child, and thinking that, if the boy grew up there, king Brahmadatta might at some time have him killed because he was the son of his enemy, she bade the nurse cover the child with a piece of cloth, and to carry it to the burial-ground and abandon it there. This was done; but the child's dead father constituted himself its guardian deity and impelled one of the goats grazing there to take compassion on the child and to go and suckle it frequently. The goatherd, seeing the goat going and coming frequently, followed it and found the child; and being childless, he took it home and gave it to his wife. She began to love it and to bring it up on goat's milk; but fro that day onwards, the goats of the goatherd began to die by tows and threes every day; and he, apprehending that, if he kept the child, the whole herd would die, abandoned it in his turn by placing it in an earthen vessel and casting it adrift in a river. This vessel was found and the child rescued by a Caṇḍāla, who, being childless, adopted it and brought it up.

The child grew up into a handsome boy, and after he was sixteen years old, he used to go with his father every day to the king's place and work there. He was there seen by princess Kuruṅgavī, the handsome daughter of king Brahmadatta; and the two fell in love with each other and carried on an intrigue unsuspected by others.

In course of time, this became known, and the king, becoming exceedingly wroth, was deliberating about the punishment to be inflicted on the daring Caṇḍāla youth. The king of Kosala, the guardian deity of the boy, then possessed the boy's mother and made her say that the boy was not a Caṇḍāla but her own son born to the king of Kosala, that she caused him to be abandoned in the burial-ground soon after birth, etc. Brahmadatta, on hearing this, questioned the nurse and others, and being convinced that the boy was in truth not a Caṇḍāla but the son of the Kosala king, gave his daughter to him in marriage. He was also named Eḷakamāraka because the goats had been killed by him.[1]

Brahmadatta then sent Eḷakamāraka with an army to Kosala to rule there; and because he was uneducated, a teacher named Chalaṅga-kumāra was also sent with him to instruct him in the arts and sciences. Eḷakamāraka made him his *senāpati;* and Kuruṅgavī committed adultery with him and also with his servant Dhanantevāsī, by whose hands Chalaṅgakumāra used to send her presents of clothes, jewels and other things.

Leaving out of consideration the last paragraph, it will be seen that the story related in the Jātaka[0] is essentially the same as that described in the *Avimāraka-nāṭaka. Avimāraka* and *eḷakamāraka* both mean 'goat-killer'; and in the play, as in the story, Goatkiller, who passes for a Caṇḍāla youth, sees and falls in love with princess Kuraṅgī or Kuruṅgavī (her name is given as Kuruṅga-devī in two of the MSS. used by Fausböll), who too falls in love with him and is given in marriage to him by her father after it becomes clear that the youth is not a Caṇḍāla, but is in reality the son of high-caste parents.

There is thus no doubt that both the play and the story are concerned with the same persons and incidents, as likewise are *Kathāsaritsāgara,* 112, vv. 89-108, and the Jayamaṅgalā commentary on Vātsyāyana's *Kāmasūtra,* 5.4.14. There are, however, differences in detail between all these versions of the story, and I shall point out some of them here:

1. The hero is called Eḷakamāraka in the Jātaka° because goats were killed by him, and Avimāraka in the Nāṭaka (because he killed a demon named Avi) and the Jaya° (because he was so strong even as a child that goats and sheep died when grasped by him).

The Katha° does not give his name, but merely calls him Mātaṅgakumāra or Caṇḍāla's son.

2. The heroine is called Kuraṅgī in the Nāṭaka and Kathā°; her name is not given in the Jaya,° while in the Jātaka° she is called Kuruṅgavī or Kuruṅgasundarī.

3. There is nothing said in the Jātaka° about Goatkiller's saving the life of the princess. The other versions, however, make out that he saved her from an elephant. This incident took place in a park in the city according to the Jaya° and the Nāṭaka, and in a forest according to the Kāthā°.

4. The Nāṭaka and Jātaka° make out that Goatkiller married the princess according to the Gāndharva form; the Jaya° too seems to suggest the same, while the Katha°, on the other hand, makes out that the marriage took place regularly.

5. Goatkiller's real father was the king of Kosala according to the Jātaka°; according to the other three versions, it was Agni, the god of fire.

6. Goatkiller's mother was a Brāhmaṇa maiden according to the Katha° and a Brāhmaṇa's young wife according to the Jaya°. According to the Jātaka°, she was the chief queen of the king of Kosala (and of king Brahmadatta), and according to the Nāṭaka, the queen of Kāśirāja.

7. Goatkiller's foster-father was a *Śabara* according to the Jaya°, while, according to the Katha° and Jātaka°, he was a Caṇḍāla.

According to the Nāṭaka, he was a Kṣattriya, who temporarily, for the period of a year, was a Caṇḍāla.

Of these four versions of the story, that of the Jaya° is most free from supernatural elements; it is more natural than the other three versions, and seems to be nearest to the original form of the story. The versions of the Nāṭaka and Jātaka°, on the other hand, seem to diverge widely from the original story. That of the Nāṭ aka has in it a great number of supernatural elements; and there can be no doubt that they are, mostly, due to the author of the play, and have been introduced in order to embellish the plot. The divergences in the Jātaka°, on the other hand, seem to be due to what may be called the habit of caricaturing, which the Buddhist writers indulged in when rewriting Brāhmanical stories[2]; compare, for instance, the story of Kṛṣṇā and the five Pāṇḍavas related by the author of the Jātaka° on V. 426-7 of Fausböll's edition and the story of the Andhaka-Vṛṣṇis related in the Ghata-jātaka (no. 454; IV, p. 79 ff.).

Regarding the name Avimāraka or Eḷakamāraka, the explanations given of it in the above-cited versions are hardly satisfactory. It is difficult to believe that there was a demon who was named Avi; and it is equally difficult to believe the far-fetched explanation given in the Jātaka° that Eḷakamāraka was so called because two or three goats belonging to the goathered used to die every day after he took home the abandoned child. Similarly, the explanation given in the Jaya°, too, is not very credible.

The reading *Eḷakakumāra,* therefore, that is found instead of *Eḷakamāraka* in two of the MSS. used by Fausböll (the same two MSS. as contain the reading *Kuruṅgasundarī* instead of *Kuruṅgavī*) is of interest in this connection. *Eḷakakumāra* means 'son of goats'; and not only is it very common for infants separated from mothers (or of mothers who have no breast milk) to be brought up on goat's milk, but we find it explicitly said in Kathā°, 112, 105: *tatas taṃ prāpya caṇḍālair ajākṣāreṇa vardhitaḥ,* that the abandoned child was brought up on goat's milk. It seems to me, therefore, under the circumstances, that it is not too farfetched to conjecture that the name of the hero of the story was originally Avikumāra and that this was in course of time corrupted into Avimāraka and explanations then invented in support of the corrupted name.

References

1. This is somewhat obscure; for the author of the Jātaka[0] has not on any occasion said that the boy had killed goats. The reference perhaps is to the circumstance of the goats of the goatherd dying after he took home the abandoned child.
2. Compare in the connection Albrecht Weber's observation,*Die Jaina haben die brahmanischen Sagen durchweg nach freier Willkür umgewandelt und ihren eighnen Phantasieen angepasst* made on a similar occasion on p. 474 of his *Verzeichnis der Sanskrit und Prakrit Handschriften in der Königlichen Bibliothek zu Berlin,* vol. II.